Jean Calder was born in Mackay, Queensland, and educated in Queensland and the United States. She was awarded her PhD from Penn State University, USA. In 1981 she became a volunteer with the Palestine Red Crescent Society, the Palestinian equivalent to the Australian Red Cross. She went on to become the Director of the Children's Unit at Haifa Rehabilitation Centre in Lebanon, the Director of the Ain Shams Rehabilitation Centre in Cairo, and the Director of the Rehabilitation Department of Al-Amal City in the Gaza Strip. She is the 'adopted mother' of three and currently lives with her adult children in the Gaza Strip. In 2005 she was awarded Australia's greatest civic honour, the Companion of the Order of Australia, for her inspirational work.

WHERE THE
ROAD LEADS

AN AUSTRALIAN WOMAN'S JOURNEY
OF LOVE AND DETERMINATION

JEAN E CALDER

HACHETTE AUSTRALIA

HACHETTE AUSTRALIA

Published in Australia and New Zealand in 2007
by Hachette Australia
(An imprint of Hachette Livre Australia Pty Limited)
Level 17, 207 Kent Street, Sydney NSW 2000
Website: www.hachette.com.au

National Library of Australia
Cataloguing-in-Publication data

Calder, Jean E.
  Where the road leads : an Australian woman's journey of
  love and determination.

  ISBN 978 0 7336 2037 9 (pbk.).

  1. Calder, Jean E. 2. Women pediatricians - Australia -
  Biography. 3. Children with disabilities - Rehabilitation -
  Gaza Strip. 4. Children - Hospitals - Gaza Strip. 5.
  Humanitarian assistance, Australian - Middle East. 6.
  Refugee children - Medical care - Middle East. 7. Refugee
  camps - Palestine. I. Title.

362.120956

Cover design by Christabella Designs
Maps by Ian Faulkner
Text design by Bookhouse, Sydney
Typeset in 12.4/15.81 pt Abode Garamond
Printed in Australia by Griffin Press, Adelaide

Hachette Livre Australia's policy is to use papers that are natural, renewable
and recyclable products and made from wood grown in sustainable forests.
The logging and manufacturing processes are expected to conform to the
environmental regulations of the country of origin.

For Hamoudi, Dalal, Badr, and
all children growing up in a conflict area.

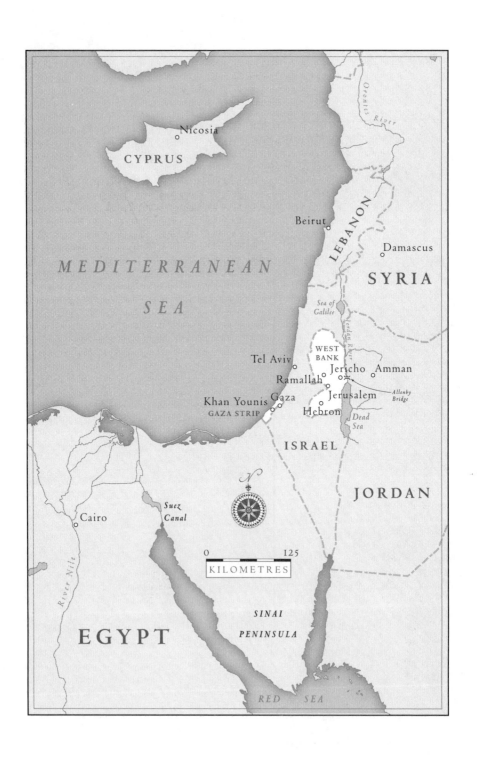

CYPRUS

Nicosia

MEDITERRANEAN

SEA

Beirut

LEBANON

Damascus

SYRIA

Sea of
Galilee

Orontes River

Jordan River

Tel Aviv

WEST
BANK

Jericho

Amman

Ramallah

Jerusalem

Allenby
Bridge

Khan Younis

Gaza

GAZA STRIP

Hebron

Dead
Sea

ISRAEL

JORDAN

Cairo

Suez
Canal

N

0   125

KILOMETRES

River Nile

SINAI

PENINSULA

EGYPT

RED   SEA

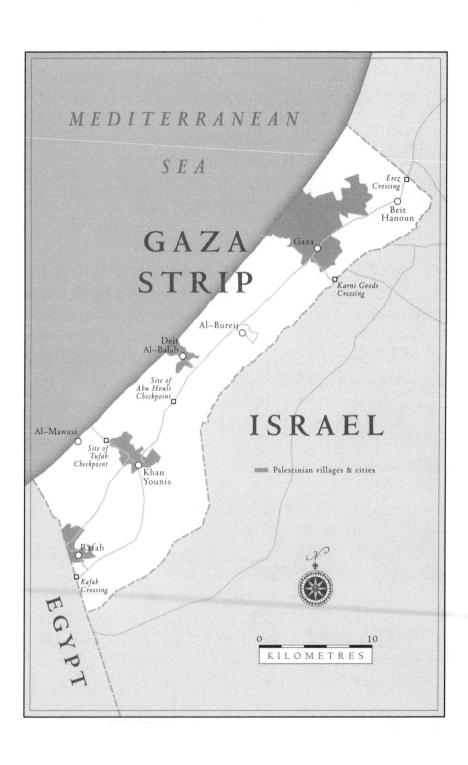

MEDITERRANEAN

SEA

GAZA
STRIP

ISRAEL

Erez
Crossing

Beit
Hanoun

Gaza

Karni Goods
Crossing

Al–Bureij

Deir
Al–Balah

Site of
Abu Houli
Checkpoint

Al–Mawasi

Site of
Tufah
Checkpoint

Khan
Younis

Palestinian villages & cities

Rafah

Rafah
Crossing

EGYPT

N

0   10

KILOMETRES

PROLOGUE

Zanana

AS I SIT WRITING THIS MORNING I am bothered by the noise of the *zanana*. It has been a constant, intrusive noise for several days now. There have been times when it has been non-stop over several weeks – day and night.

Zanana is an Arabic word which means 'the buzz or drone of an insect'. It is also the local name given to the pilotless spy planes of the Israeli army, which hover over us in the Gaza Strip. I have a headache from the noise and am bothered by it – in the same way the constant buzz of a mosquito is irritating. The name *zanana* is most appropriate.

The planes are very small and I find it difficult to locate their presence in the sky during daylight. At night, if I look at the stars, it is sometimes possible to spot a 'star' bigger and brighter than the others. A 'star' that moves its position, or which moves out of vision. A *zanana*.

It is impossible to watch television when the *zanana* is present – both the picture and sound break up. Sometimes its presence also interferes with the reception on the mobile phones. Most of all, it makes us feel unnerved – like all our activities are being viewed by others. And there is fear. The *zanana* is also used as a weapon – rockets have been fired from it causing destruction and death. Will the zanana up there now make a strike? When? Where? Why?

I have been working at my desk in in the Gaza Strip town of Khan Younis. A volunteer with the Palestine Red Crescent Society, my work involves the development of programs and services for children and adults who are disabled. The annoyance of the *zanana* is but one of the many difficulties that I share with the Palestinian people, both in the Gaza Strip and the West Bank, as they deal with life under occupation.

WHY?

My humanity is bound up in yours,
for we can only be human together
ARCHBISHOP DESMOND TUTU

AS FAR BACK AS I CAN REMEMBER, I have been interested in the diversity of the global community and the richness of this diversity. As a child in Sunday school I loved the picture of Jesus surrounded by children from many different ethnic backgrounds with different colours of skin; to me it represented the concept of the love of God encompassing all peoples. As I grew older I became aware of and concerned about the inequalities and intolerance that exist in the world. I was attracted to stories about the endeavours of people working in developing or conflict areas. I was also significantly influenced by my childhood in a loving, hard-working family with high moral principles, a firm belief in God and a commitment to helping others. However, as I pursued my studies, entered the working world and took time out to travel beyond Australia, my desire to work with people in a developing area remained dormant.

What was clear to me was that I had many opportunities in life and was living in a secure and peaceful country. My life was one of privilege while millions of people throughout the world were denied even the most basic human needs and opportunities in life. It seemed that there must be more equality; that there should be more sharing.

It was only when I became aware of the complexity of the problems of the Israeli–Palestinian conflict that my thoughts translated into action. I became friends with some Palestinian students, which gave me the opportunity to ask many questions about the conflict. They gave me answers, but also encouraged me to do some reading on the subject, and to read across the different opinions about the conflict. I did so, and soon realised just how complex the conflict was. There seemed to be an endless stream of fact, myth and propaganda that was difficult to sift into reality, plus a confusing mix of religion and politics. There was also an underlying pattern of international intrigue. As I read further, I noticed something very curious. Many people who were concerned about human rights issues, and were active in promoting the causes of oppressed peoples throughout the world, seemed afraid to identify with the Palestinian people and their struggle, even though they acknowledged the existence of an injustice against them.

Why this ambivalence, I wondered. Granted, the complexity of the subject created difficulties in understanding; however, it seemed that the standard reaction to anyone showing concern or support for the Palestinian people was one of suspicion. The dominant image of the Palestinians was as a negative, aggressive people; a view that, in my opinion, clouds the reality of the people and their situation. I read pieces that claimed the Palestinians do not exist at all; and read about those who attempted to address such matters and as a result suffered threats, lost their jobs and had a range of false accusations made against them.

I also heard individual stories of dispossession and dispersion. 'I was born in Jaffa, and was going to school in Jerusalem when my family fled in 1948,' one friend told me.

'My family fled Palestine before I was born,' another friend said, 'but I cannot return to their village to visit my relatives who stayed.'

'My mother has a photograph of herself dressed in the Red Cross uniform – she was a volunteer in the Red Cross in Jerusalem during the troubles in Palestine in the 1930s,' another friend told me. Then added, 'But there is no way I can get a permit to visit there.'

When I met some of the older generation of Palestinians, it was common to be told details of the history of events in the early twentieth century, and to be shown the key to the door of the home they had left behind. For these people, the hope of return was ever present.

I had found the path that I should follow, and many of my earlier experiences in life had led me to this point, without my being aware of it. I rejected the negative stereotype so often attributed to the Palestinian people and reacted instead to the situation of a people unfairly maligned. This was an issue of humanitarianism and justice. I knew that was the way for me to go, but how? What could I do?

I found the answer in a film called *The Palestinians*, about the siege on Tal Al-Za'tar in Lebanon during the 1970s. The camera closed in on a tiny child in a cot in a temporary hospital set up by the Palestine Red Crescent Society (PRCS). A tiny child with cerebral palsy. With my background working with children and adults with disability, I felt this was an area in which I could help. From that point, the road in front of me led, eventually, to my joining the work of the PRCS in Lebanon.

The PRCS is a Palestinian national society associated with the International Federation of Red Cross and Red Crescent Societies (IFRC), of which it became a full member in 2006. Through the PRCS I was able to fulfil my desire to work directly with people in need, on the ground and on their terms. I chose to work with a local organisation rather than an international one as I wanted to experience the situation alongside the people whose lives it was affecting so deeply. I realised it would be difficult, but it was something I had to do.

When I arrived in Beirut and began my work with the PRCS, I was amazed to realise that one of the children in my care was that tiny boy with cerebral palsy who I had seen in the film; the child who had convinced me to take the road that had led me to the Middle East. He and two other disabled children were soon to become central to my life.

ONE

IT IS OFTEN SAID THAT 'LIFE IS A JOURNEY'. As I look back on my own life, I realise just how much my early years both prepared me for and influenced me in selecting the road I followed. I cannot but wonder at my great fortune in being born into a united and caring family; a family that was special in every way.

My father, Tom Calder, immigrated to Australia from Scotland as a young man of eighteen. We children were always fascinated by his stories of growing up in Scotland and his early days in Australia. He told us that he and his friend couldn't decide between Australia and Canada, so they tossed a coin. Australia was the winner and so the men arrived in Sydney in 1908. Dad was a tall man with a quiet and kind nature, and popular with everyone around him. He had been severely wounded twice in World War I, and some shrapnel remained in his body throughout the rest of his life. It caused him pain at times, but he made light of it. Mum told us that he had been offered a war pension when he returned, but he had refused, saying that he could work.

My mother, Winifred McDonald, was born in 1897 in a farming area near Mackay; her forebears were all Scottish. Mum was more outgoing and talkative than Dad. She was very friendly and loved by many. Like Dad, she was very hardworking and even when she was in her eighties she would say, 'I'd rather wear out than rust out.' She was also deeply religious.

I was the first child, born in 1936. Apparently, I was an adventurous child, curious about everything around me and always on the move. My family often recalled the day I discovered a hole in the chicken wire under the house and ventured onto the road. Fortunately, our faithful family dog, Digger, ran in front of me, pushing me out of the path of an oncoming car.

My sister, Clarice, was born in 1939, and three years later Alexander Thomas was born. Sadly, Alex died of pneumonia as an infant.

When I was about two, my parents opened a general store in Evans Street, South Mackay, and we moved into the house at the back of the store. Dad built a wire fence over six feet high to stop me from wandering from the yard. It seems I often managed to climb over the top, usually to be caught in the act by Dad, or rescued by a customer going into the shop.

The shop was a small post office store when my parents moved in, but with hard work and customer care the business expanded until it was almost a small department store, selling groceries, drapery, confectionery and hardware, and containing a bakery, the post office and a newsagency. There was also a petrol pump and telephone booth out the front. My mother ran the post office and kept meticulous accounts. There was nothing she enjoyed more than adding up pages of numbers and ensuring the books balanced. Many years later I bought her a calculator but she took days before even trying it out. When she did, she said, 'I added the numbers in my head to check if the calculator was correct.'

As children, Clarice and I helped with various shop chores. Clarice enjoyed serving customers and chatting to everyone. I preferred to work in the quiet of the office assisting with the book-keeping. One day when I was serving, I was caught placing very generous scoops of ice-cream on cones for a few of my friends. When Dad appeared, my friends scattered quickly, all clutching huge ice-creams.

At primary school I was very impressed when some of the children talked about receiving pocket money. This seemed like a great idea, so I suggested to my parents that perhaps I could receive pocket money for the tasks I carried out in the shop and at home. My parents weren't impressed with the idea. 'Why?' they said. 'We're family and we help one another in many different ways. Why should you receive payment for that? If you need money for any reason, you can get it from us.' I realised that what they said made sense and it's an attitude that has remained with me, so much so that receiving payment for work that I think is important always seems somewhat strange, even when the money is very much needed.

Our parents were loving but strict. I was encouraged to bear any childhood troubles with courage. Mum would say, 'You must be brave, you're a soldier's daughter.' Each week we attended Sunday school and church at St Paul's Presbyterian Church. This involved wearing our best clothes, socks and shoes, and a hat, all of which felt very formal and serious.

For several years during my childhood we had a woman 'living in', who helped with the housework. Emma was an orphan and had been brought up in a convent. She was alone in life and I think, in retrospect, she was possibly mildly intellectually disabled. She was included as another family member, and Clarice and I were expected to help her in chores such as washing dishes and setting the table. Emma kept us well up to the mark with her characteristic call of 'Quick smart!' For some years, Mum's elderly aunt lived with us too. 'Patch', as we called her, was blind and I often sat with her for chats and stories. She also taught me how to knit.

Clarice and I both attended the Victoria Park State School in South Mackay. I enjoyed my primary school days – the lessons, the play and sport, the teachers and my friends, some of whom I remain in contact with. Life was carefree, there was no school uniform and we were all bare-footed. I especially enjoyed sports days and was keen to be involved in any event available, although running, jumping, gymnastics and tennis were the activities I liked most. I remember being very distressed by one of the stories in one of our lesson books: 'The Little Match Girl'. I didn't want to read the story again and just thinking about it made me cry. I thought it was so cruel that a child could suffer so.

There were a number of children in our neighbourhood and we spent hours together playing in the open paddocks or climbing trees. We often made a cubbyhouse in our backyard out of empty boxes from the shop. Family and relatives considered me to be a tomboy, and Dad sometimes called me 'Johnny'. Clarice was less adventurous when it came to physical activity but kept up as best she could. Once, I nailed steps into the sloping trunk of the poinciana tree in our backyard so she could climb up to join us in its branches.

Our early school days were during the period of World War II. Although I was too young to fully understand what was happening, I was aware of the tension in the adult world – in part related to the commonly held fear that the Japanese army would invade Australia from the north. The government-proposed defence line was to be at the southern end of Queensland, which meant people in central and northern Queensland felt very exposed. Dad was a volunteer air warden, so needed to hurry to his post whenever there was a practice air-raid drill. We had a dug-out stocked with supplies in the backyard, but never used it. Nevertheless, Mum kept us on the ready so we'd be able to move quickly if the practice became a reality. At school there were trenches along the side fence and we carried out air-raid drills there wearing special sugar-bag capes over our heads. We also wore identity discs around our necks and, for some reason, were given small rubber blocks for teeth- and earplugs.

Toys and clothes were handmade and many items were in short supply. I became very attached to a home-made rag doll – more so than to sophisticated toys that became available later. People came to our shop with ration coupons for essentials such as tea, sugar and butter; and some people brought food parcels to the post office to be sent abroad to families or the Red Cross. Many women knitted socks and scarves to send to the troops.

At the height of the conflict in the Pacific region, a large community of Javanese was evacuated to the South Mackay area. The Javanese children in our class struggled to learn English, but our teacher supported them and also learned some Javanese words. We all enjoyed the marvellous rice cakes the children shared with us. Once the United States joined the war, there were many American troops in Mackay. We were fascinated by these men and their accents, and through them discovered chewing gum.

Having completed grade five at the Victoria Park School, I transferred to the Intermediate School in the centre of the town. This was a new adventure: the school was farther from home and I was in class with children who had come from different schools, studying new subjects and with a different pattern to the school day. I also had to wear a uniform and socks and shoes. My parents laughed at how, when I arrived home from school, the hat and shoes were always first through the door, followed by me. Again, I found school enjoyable. I was introduced to team sports and a range of athletic events. Outside of school, I became involved in activities such as Girl Guides and the YWCA. My bicycle was important to me throughout my childhood. As well as a means of transport to and from school, as I got older it took me everywhere. One trip was to a friend's beach house at Slade Point, where I rather foolishly joined the good swimmers to swim out to an old jetty. Somehow I made the distance, feeling scared but not admitting my struggle.

Thinking back on family times I realise just how special they were. At the end of the day, when the shop closed, Mum and Dad would go over the books, then we'd all sit together around our radio to listen to our favourite serials. When news broadcasts came through we had to be very quiet while our parents followed the reports. They would explain main events to us and I often wondered about the children in the troubled places they talked about. I was always interested in information about different cultures.

Living in South Mackay, we were very close to Far Beach and had a small one-room shack there. Often at weekends we would bundle into Dad's utility and go to the beach. There were a few other shacks, but mostly the area was covered with lovely spreading gum trees and wild plants that grew in the sand. At low tide, the sea drew back for what seemed miles, leaving a wide expanse of uncovered sand and a myriad of water puddles. Playing there was a delight: small sand crabs scuttled here and there, and armies of soldier crabs moved their units across the sand in formation. On summer evenings, we often drove to the north side of the Pioneer River, to the harbour, where we sat or walked on the breakwater wall. We wondered at the endless horizon in the distance and enjoyed the splash of the waves on the rocks below.

The time came to move on to secondary school, which was a big and exciting step for me. There was a tradition in our family to go to a boarding school in Warwick, a town on the southern Queensland tablelands. Boarding school was like stepping into a different world. The days were very ordered, but full of activities; it was like living out the stories I'd enjoyed reading in books. Midnight feasts and their preparation were always exciting. Looking for a novel place 'to study' seemed to take more time than the study itself; on one occasion a teacher caught me and a friend climbing down from the roof of the school building.

For music lessons the whole of the senior school was gathered in the large all-purpose hall. The teacher seemed to concentrate on the children at the front, who were in the choir, so some of us started to skip this class. One day, the headmistress became aware of the situation and all the missing children were rounded up. Following the evening meal that day, she spoke to the whole school about the problem, saying that she had gone into the music lesson and 'missed seeing the smiling face of Jean Calder'. I was mortified, suddenly feeling responsible for the trouble now being faced by all the others who had been absent too.

Unfortunately, my various escapades resulted in examination grades below what they should have been. During the holiday between first and second year, my parents received a letter from the Education Department warning me to take my studies more seriously or my scholarship would be cancelled. This made me feel very ashamed, and my parents were cross with me. It was a lesson to me to be more responsible about the opportunity I had. I knew I was keen to learn, to discover more about myself and the world around me. I didn't stop enjoying life, but I did pay much more attention to my studies.

At that point I didn't have any expectation of continuing to further studies. That seemed to be the realm of children who were exceptionally bright or came from families that were very wealthy. Although I dreamed about becoming an architect or a police-woman, the general expectation for a girl from my background seemed to be to get a good job, preferably in a bank or a company. My mother had been managing the office at Lamberts Department Store and an opportunity came for me to work there. I also enrolled at night school to learn to type – a skill that has since assisted me in so many ways. Working at Lamberts was pleasant, but I knew working in an office wasn't me, even though I had no idea what I really wanted to do.

In early 1952, I became aware of a teacher-training program that involved attending a local school as a student teacher while completing the university entrance exam by correspondence. I applied, and was appointed as a student teacher at Victoria Park School, my old primary school. Some of the teachers I'd known were still there and I learned a great deal about teaching during this period in a very friendly and enthusiastic environment.

This was an important period for me. I was excited about the opportunity to study and to learn new things, and pushed myself to my limits. I enjoyed teaching and developing lessons and teaching aids. It was fun to see the children learning, and responding to their many questions was always a challenge.

At the end of that year, the Queensland government – which was facing a severe teacher shortage – gave student teachers currently placed in schools the option of attending teachers college in Brisbane. This seemed a wonderful opportunity. As always, my parents were supportive and so preparations were soon under way for me to travel to Brisbane at the beginning of the following year.

The Queensland Teachers College was a grand old building over-looking the city of Brisbane. It was all very impressive and I felt somewhat in awe on my first day there as a student. I soon settled into college life, however. The other students were from different parts of Queensland and different backgrounds, but they were all very friendly and we soon formed a cohesive group. Much to my delight, one of my friends from boarding school was there too, and together we enrolled in some senior subjects at the night school. I found the expressive, creative subjects especially enjoyable – physical education, art, music, needlework. I also played in the college field hockey team – a sport I had newly learned and enjoyed very much.

Living in a city was in itself an experience for me. At first I missed my bicycle and the independence it gave me, but soon I found my way around the transport system of trams and trolley buses – and walked when I had no money. The first time I saw a ballet I was enthralled, and this was followed by other firsts – opera, theatre, orches-tral concerts. It was a world of magic as far as I was concerned. Initially, I lived in a student hostel, but when my parents moved to Brisbane not long after my arrival there, I was pleased to live with my family again.

Early during my second year at college, the principal came into the classroom one day. He asked for any student who was attending night classes to stand. In our group, there were just two of us – my old schoolfriend and myself. He demanded that we cease the night classes, as the workload was too much and it was likely we'd fail the college exams, fail the senior exams and experience a breakdown in health. For me, however, it wasn't possible to stop. I had to complete my senior studies. From August until exam time I pushed myself to my limits to cover the study needed. The principal's predictions were partially accurate when it came to exam time. I topped my college group, but I failed some of my senior subjects, and I was exhausted. I had by this time decided that I wanted to enrol in the Diploma in Physical Education at Queensland University. During the summer holidays I attended some coaching classes for the supplementary examinations. I passed well and now had the requirements to enter university. I was very relieved and realised that the struggle had been worth it. I could hardly wait for the term to begin.

This was the beginning of my teaching career, and at the same time I would be a student at university. It was a new era for me. My first teaching responsibility was for children in grade three at Newmarket Primary School. I was just settling in when I was transferred to Mitchelton Infant School, to teach children in grade one. Although at first I was a little apprehensive about my ability to teach a grade one class, I discovered this was a very interesting and challenging age group. I acquired a greater understanding of child development and of the patterns and importance of play. The skills I learned during this period proved to be of great value later in both physical education and special education.

One day, an unfortunate reaction of the headmistress to a child raised my awareness of the sensitivities of very young children and how easily an adult can trample on them. Leslie, one of the little girls in my class who was repeating grade one and came from a very poor family, walked into the classroom crying. She had proudly presented a bunch of 'flowers' to the headmistress – actually flowering weeds that she had picked on her way to school. The headmistress, always neat and with only the best of ornaments and flowers in her office, rejected the offer with the brush of her hand as she walked past Leslie. I tried to console the crying child, who still clutched her treasure in her hand. Listening to her story through her sobs, I took the bunch of flowers, and together we found a vase and gave them pride of place on my desk. The other children joined me in thanking Leslie for her thoughtfulness in bringing flowers to the classroom. It was wonderful to see this little girl regain her pride in herself.

During my second year I was transferred to the Physical Education Branch of the Education Department, as the government needed to increase the number of physical education teachers in its schools. This was a major change – from teaching in a classroom to teaching outdoors – but I was happy to be able to work full-time as a physical education teacher. This involved weekly classes in two high schools, giving monthly demonstration lessons for teachers in several primary schools, and teaching swimming in the summer.

I found myself attracted to working with children who had difficulty in physical activity situations. One little boy, John, who was about eight years old, had once experienced a bad fright when swimming and had developed a great fear of the water. On the first day, John didn't enter the pool. We chatted and played together at the side of the pool, and occasionally he let me splash some water on him. On subsequent days, we progressed to sitting on the edge of the pool, splashing our feet in the water, and again splashing water on his body. We eventually reached a point where I was able to encourage him to get into the shallow water with me, even though he was afraid and clutched at me for support. It took time, but by the end of the summer, it was a very different little boy who came to swimming lessons. He looked happy and eager to get into the pool, and quickly became one of the best swimmers in the group.

This was surely a success story for John, and for me it was very valuable training in how to read the various stages of readiness of a child learning a new skill, and how to establish an environment for the child to feel confident to begin a learning process.

Around this time, I became increasingly fascinated by the study of human movement. I was particularly interested in developmental aspects of movement and the importance of both functional and expressive movement to our lives. Although physical education is often equated with coaching and playing sport, I was always more interested in the broader dimensions of the profession. Working with children, and later with students, I gravitated towards those who either didn't like physical education classes or tended to be inept in physical activities. I gained a great deal of pleasure from seeing their joy when they were given an opportunity to participate in an activity that interested them and at a level where they could succeed and have their success recognised.

The following year I was surprised, and a little apprehensive, to be seconded as a junior lecturer in the Physical Education Department of the Queensland Teachers College. It was an honour, but teaching students was completely different from the work that I had been doing in schools. Also, although I had completed my Diploma in Physical Education I was still attending university as I had commenced a Bachelor of Arts as an evening student. I spent a couple of years at the Queensland Teachers College before yet another move, this time to the new Teachers College at Kedron Park. It was a wonderful opportunity to be involved in the development of a physical education program in a new college. There were various difficulties to overcome initially but the first intake of students was small, just two or three hundred, and a very special atmosphere developed: the shared feeling of taking part in a new venture. I realised that I particularly liked being involved in starting something from the beginning, more so than working in an established environment. The challenges of responding to a need situation suited me.

Although I was absorbed in the life I was leading – college, university studies, spending time with family and friends – at times I felt that I needed something different. During the 1950s it had become very popular for young Australians to travel to Europe on a 'working holiday'. I had a strong connection to Scotland through my family ties, as had my cousins in Mackay. Together we suddenly decided: 'Let's go!' My family, although somewhat apprehensive, shared in my excitement as I prepared for the trip. Clarice organised the most marvellous bon voyage party at our home. In her usual artistic manner, and with the assistance of her friends from the Brisbane Arts Theatre, she planned it around the theme of travel by ship: the master of ceremonies was dressed as a ship's captain, and King Neptune himself was present.

In early 1960, my cousins Elspeth and Isla and I stood on the deck of the P&O *Oriana*, throwing streamers and waving farewell to our families, who looked up at us from the wharf of Circular Quay at Sydney Harbour. The whole atmosphere was charged with excitement and anticipation, with the noise of the crowds, broadcast music and endless streamers coming from every direction. It was hard to believe that we were really on the way.

The voyage took about four weeks. Life aboard ship was entertaining, but for me the ports of call en route were the highlights: Ceylon, Aden, Cairo, Naples, and an offshore stop at Gibraltar. When we went ashore I longed to be able to stay longer, to mingle with local people, to meld in with the life of the place.

We chose to go ashore in Egypt as the ship negotiated the Suez Canal. There was still a strong military presence there after President Nasser's nationalisation of the Suez Canal and the subsequent war, and the buses carrying us drove in convoy with a police escort. I was fascinated by Cairo – the beauty of the Nile, the old markets of Khan Al-Khalili, the mysteries of the artifacts in the museum, the grandeur of the Pyramids and the sheer fun of riding a camel. The contrasts and complexity of the city were evident, and they made a strong impression on me. I remember saying to my cousins, 'Cairo is so fascinating. I really would love to come back for some weeks so I could look around in a more leisurely way.' I wasn't to know then that I would return to Cairo and live and work there for more than ten years.

When we finally arrived in Southampton and caught the train up to London, we encountered another new experience: snow. We opened the carriage windows, in spite of the cold, and tried to catch the snowflakes as they fell.

It was so very special to be in Scotland and to meet with relatives known to us through letters and photographs all of our lives. I stayed with my cousin George Moir and his wife, Jessie, who were both deaf. Their children, although hearing, did have some problems and attended speech therapy sessions. Living with George and his family I soon learned sign language and we all chatted together for hours. When my skill was inadequate, we wrote notes. I was amused when after one of my visits Jessie wrote to me and said the house was so quiet when I left.

Back in London, my cousins and I bought a small Austin, a tent and some maps and set off to travel around Europe. Driving north along a mountain pass in Italy, with snow piled on both sides of the road and the most magnificent views all around, I felt on top of the world. I was meeting people and experiencing the atmosphere of different places. Although we were travelling on a budget, sometimes sleeping in the tent and sometimes in the car, we felt privileged to be able to see so much. Yet, after some weeks, although enjoying every minute of our adventure, I began to have the strong feeling that I wanted to do something worthwhile with my life. It was exciting, educational and fun to travel in such a carefree way, but I needed something more.

Back in London I found a job as a physical education teacher at Frien Secondary Modern School – a girls school where the majority of students, both black and white, were from disadvantaged backgrounds. Student behaviour was something of a problem, and at times I struggled to cope with some of the situations I faced. The students tried every trick they could think of to test the teachers, and I met some of them with more success than others.

During the summer I attended a creative dance course at Loughborough University, conducted by teachers of the Laban Institute, which was informative and stimulating. This was a methodology with emphasis on the child, leading the child to discover the range and quality of his or her own body movement both in creative expression and in the function of daily activities. This approach was in sharp contrast to more traditional methods of presenting children with simplified adult skills for them to copy and learn. Combined with my interest in a developmental approach to working with children, the knowledge that I gained from this course and others like it was to have a great influence on my approach to teaching physical education in the years to follow.

By the end of my year working at Frien I was wishing that I could stay longer.

The period abroad had been a wonderful experience; a time that gave me a greater understanding of the diversity of people's living situations in different countries. I was fascinated by the richness of this diversity and wondered again how I could become involved in working with people living in disadvantaged conditions. It was a matter that pressed on my mind, but one to which I did not, as yet, have an answer.

TWO

ON RETURNING TO AUSTRALIA I was immediately aware of the colours, the smells, the feeling of space – the uniqueness of the country. For the first time I realised the extent of adjustment that people immigrating from Europe must experience in dealing with the sense of endless space. I missed many aspects of living abroad, but at the same time I appreciated that each place has its special features. It was good to be back.

While I'd been away Clarice had become engaged to Alan Barker, a chief officer in the British Merchant Navy. I was pleased that I was back in time to participate in their wedding. The wedding day was perfect. Clarice looked radiant, Alan very handsome, and Mum and Dad were so obviously happy and proud.

Soon after the wedding, Clarice and Alan set off to live in England, but it was a very difficult time for them to leave as Dad was suffering health problems and was hospitalised because of a thrombosis in his leg. The situation became very serious and he was scheduled to have a leg amputation. Dad was amazing in how he coped with his new situation; although he was often in pain he was always cheerful. I remember the Red Cross lady who used to visit telling me, 'I enjoy my visits with Mr Calder, he always cheers me up. It is so good to work with someone so enthusiastic.'

Once Mum and Dad no longer needed my support, I returned to work – at the University of Queensland, where I had been offered a position in the Department of Human Movement Studies. Professionally, this was a very interesting period for me. I was working with students who would be physical education teachers and had the opportunity to share with them the Laban principles of movement and the discovery approach to physical education that schools in the UK were following. In addition, I was given the responsibility of conducting courses in recreation and group work for students from the university's Physiotherapy and Occupational Therapy departments. My experience with these students opened up a whole new field for me as I researched the links between my profession and issues related to people with disabilities. In many respects, this was a turning point in my professional development. I wanted to be more directly involved in getting to know and work with people with disabilities. My work at the university began to feel too remote: I wanted to be 'on the ground', working with people.

When I read an advertisement in the local newspaper for APEX scholarships for students wishing to study for the one-year university certificate to 'teach and train subnormal children', I could hardly believe what I was seeing. I applied and was overjoyed to gain one of the scholarships. Most of my friends were surprised by the change in direction, and some told me I was crazy. My colleagues at the university didn't understand either and tried to persuade me not to resign. Despite such reactions, I was convinced that what I was doing was right for me and I set out eagerly on my new venture.

I hadn't had any contact with children with intellectual disabilities and that first day, as I sat in a classroom observing one of the teachers at the Queensland Sub Normal Children's Welfare Association (QSNCWA) school at Bowen Hills, I wondered what I was doing there. I soon discovered that I was indeed in the right place and learned a great deal during that course, as well as gaining many friends.

At the end of the year I was very willing to accept the QSNCWA appointment of supervisor of physical education and recreation. This was a new position and one that I felt I could develop. As a member of the medical and educational panel, I had the opportunity to increase my understanding of people with intellectual disabilities and the situation of their families. In addition to the physical education programs with children, I was keen to introduce a range of recreation and fitness programs for the adults attending the sheltered workshop. In doing this, I felt it important to work on two levels: enabling the young adults to develop specific skills while preparing them to participate in community activities.

Two incidents convinced me of the importance of my approach. The first involved a group of young men who became very proficient at tenpin bowling. They began to regularly attend the local bowling centre, where one of them won a special medallion for qualifying for the high-scoring level (something I could never manage to achieve). The bowling centre management became interested in the young men's team and was keen to assist in any way. They agreed to buy a special frame that could be placed at the end of a lane to enable a person with severe limitation in the use of their hands and arms to direct the ball down a chute and towards the pins. This meant people with such a disability could participate rather than just observe.

Another time, I was able to arrange for a group of young men with intellectual disabilities to participate in a game of volleyball with students at the Kelvin Grove Teachers College. Instead of my team playing against the students, I organised a mix of the two groups. The students had greater opportunity to interact with their visitors; and although the intellectually disabled players were equally skilled physically, the mix reduced the pressure on them in dealing with scoring and complex rules. It was an event enjoyed by both groups.

Another program I introduced into the sheltered workshop was pause gymnastics, a concept that was receiving great international interest at that time. This involved workers, in their workplace, spending five or ten minutes following the directions of a leader to perform a series of exercises to music. The director of the workshop was somewhat sceptical about the idea but agreed to give it a try. The workers, however, were very enthusiastic. To everyone's surprise, one of the most eager participants was a young man who was renowned for being 'lazy' and refusing to take part in activities. The workshop director became much more supportive of the program, noting that 'anything that can motivate Barry to become so involved is certainly worth doing'.

My work with the QSNCWA was being met with enthusiasm and I was keen to encourage further developments in the physical education and recreation programs. I was convinced they would help to enhance the lives of people with intellectual disability. At the same time I became increasingly involved with professional associations that addressed issues concerning people with disabilities in general and approaches being followed in both physical education and recreation. Through these connections I also got to know more people with different types and degrees of disability.

At a meeting of the Australian Association of Health, Physical Education and Recreation I had a lengthy conversation with one of my friends about my concerns about the imbalance of opportunity that exists in the world. I expressed my desire to go 'somewhere' to help in 'some way'. His view – which seemed to be that of many of my friends at that time – was that while acknowledging there should be more international involvement in assisting people in disadvantaged areas of the world, our focus should be on contributing to developments in our own country. I also was concerned to contribute to developments within Australia, but I suggested that different people obviously had different roles to play. We agreed to disagree on how we saw our future directions in our profession.

Again, I was persuaded to return to teaching at the university. I agreed on the condition that my teaching duties would be in the areas of physical education and recreation for 'special populations'. I was convinced that with the upsurge of interest in the field I would be able to bring a greater focus into the department.

I was drawn to the situation of children with severe and multiple disabilities, and through my network of valued friends and contacts I was able to visit centres that offered such care and discuss the range of approaches being used in working with these children. I was interested in learning more about cerebral palsy and about children with both intellectual disability and cerebral palsy. With these children, the challenge seemed to be, in part, to reach in and find their individual personalities, to respect and tune into their level and timing when working with them.

The more involved I became in the field, the more obvious it was that I had so much more to learn. The 1960s had seen considerable advances in the approach to working with children and adults with intellectual disability, and their families. The Kennedy family in the United States had spearheaded much of this advancement with their announcement that they had a family member who was intellectually disabled. They set up a foundation through which they introduced the Special Olympics and other programs. It was also during this period that the concept of 'normalisation', with its emphasis on including people with intellectual disabilities in normal community life activities, was being promoted in relation to approaching work with intellectually disabled people. It was a concept that, although misunderstood at times, made a significant contribution to advancing the acceptance that intellectually disabled children and adults also had rights, and to the movement of deinstitutionalisation.

Much of the literature I was reading was focused on developments taking place in the US, so I began to search for scholarships that would enable me to undertake graduate study there. I was very fortunate to be accepted into the Masters program at the University of Connecticut at Storrs under Professor Hollis Fait. Professor Fait had written one of the first books on special physical education, which included a section on physical education for the intellectually disabled – the only material I'd found on the subject. Professor Fait was friendly and encouraging, but also demanding of his students. There was course work to follow before moving into the development of my thesis, all of which I found interesting and stimulating. An added bonus of my time there was living in the graduate dorm, where I met students from many different countries.

I had been given contact details for Dr Rosemary Dybwad and her husband, Professor Gunnar Dybwad, who were known internationally for their work in the field of intellectual disability. I had been disappointed some years before to miss them when they visited Brisbane, as I was ill. I'd listened with interest to reports of their visit, and was especially impressed by their response to the work being carried out at a special centre for children with severe and profound intellectual disability. The staff were very nervous about a visit from such eminent professionals and when the Dybwads entered the centre, they said, with some embarrassment, 'We don't have a wide range of programs like at the school. The children with us aren't able to do anything so we try to give them some activities.' Professor Gunner's response was: 'What do you mean they cannot do anything? Look! They are walking, are they not? This is a major achievement!' The message was to place value on the positive; to acknowledge the importance of even the smallest of achievements; to recognise the uniqueness of each individual. It was a morale booster for all those working in such programs.

I felt a little shy at approaching the Dybwads while I was in the US, but I needn't have been. They made me so very welcome, and I had the pleasure of spending some days at their home in Boston, accompanying them on visits to centres, and having the opportunity to discuss many issues with them.

Professor Fait was keen for me to include in my thesis a topic of particular interest to me: working on a motor age for severe and profoundly intellectually disabled children. I began testing children in the Mansfield Training Centre to collect data, and was fascinated by the range of personalities of these children and what they could do. I thought a great deal about how to begin to understand them and try to find ways towards enhancing their development. Two children made a special impression on me for different reasons. One was a small boy with the most wonderful smile; he was profoundly intellectually disabled with very limited motor abilities. The other child, also a boy, had been brain damaged due to a hunting accident. One of the items on my test was related to balance and required the child to stand on one foot. It was necessary for me to do the action and encourage them to copy me. The latter boy seemed to think I was somewhat strange to be standing on one leg and instead of copying my action, he moved towards me and placed my foot back on the ground.

With my Masters thesis completed and accepted, I returned to my position in the Department of Human Movement Studies at the University of Queensland. As much as I enjoyed working with students there, I was becoming increasingly involved in the situation of people with disabilities at the community level. I realised I was a 'grass roots' worker and needed to build up my knowledge of needs and approaches from the ground. I established myself as a freelance consultant in physical education and recreation for the handicapped, under the name: 'Learn to Play – Play to Learn'. I set up some playground equipment in the backyard and gathered a range of other equipment that I could use outside, in the garage or in my study. I mainly worked with children referred to me with perceptual motor problems or who were otherwise in need of a physical activity program. There were so many children, and families, from whom I learnt a great deal, but one child gave me a special lesson.

Christine was fourteen years old at the time I was working with her. A pretty girl, and big for her age, she was severely intellectually disabled. She was able to walk, but became afraid when she needed to change position, such as from standing to sitting, or step over an object on the ground. Her parents were keen to include Christine in family outings, but were concerned by her difficulty in managing to step up onto a tram or from the platform onto a train. I developed a program for her that focused on both body and spatial awareness and built up her confidence in her movements. The program encouraged her to practise a wide range of basic movement patterns in a fun way, and her effort and her success were enthusiastically praised. Christine's parents commented on the simple equipment I was using and how much Christine enjoyed the program. I knew she enjoyed coming as I could hear her excited voice as she walked from the family car to the activity area.

In such work with children with severe problems, I coined the phrase 'the complexity of simplicity'. Often we fail to observe simple cues these children make, which may be so important in understanding possible openings for progress. The timing and the levels selected need to be those that suit the child, not those of the time-oriented adult used to placing value on advanced levels of skilled performance.

During this period, I was also working part-time with the Australian Council of Rehabilitation of Disabled (ACROD) as a consultant on recreation and physical education. This provided me with the opportunity to work with many different people, all involved in some way with improving the quality of life of people with disabilities. One of the committees I was involved with was related to a study of access. I was delighted by a remark by the architect on the committee: 'The built environment is only suitable for fit, twenty-five-year-old males. It presents problems for everyone else.'

Although a great deal of my time was spent in my various professional activities, I treasured my time with my family. Dad, in spite of his health problems, was always cheerful and enthusiastically participated in family life. Mum kept her constant caring vigil over him, although Dad tried to encourage her to continue with her previous community activities.

In January 1971, Dad became seriously ill and was transferred to hospital. It was a worrying time for Mum and me, and we spent as much time as possible with him at the hospital. Dad died a short time later.

THREE

AS I PREPARED TO TRAVEL to the US to take up a scholarship for graduate study in recreation at Pennsylvania State University, I was vaguely aware of news coverage of events in the Middle East. I knew of the histories of discrimination against and oppression of Jewish people, especially in Europe, and I was also aware of the rich cultural heritage of the Arab people and the diversity of cultures within the Arab world. However, I didn't really grasp why there was such conflict between these two interesting and historically important peoples.

Later, I would learn much more about the history of the conflict. For example, the recognition of the Palestinian people in the 1970s with the right to an independent Palestinian State; and the recognition in October 1974 by the UN General Assembly of the Palestine Liberation Organisation as the representative of the Palestinian people. In the same period the Arab League Council accepted Palestine, represented by the PLO, as a full member of the Arab League. On 13 November 1974 the PLO leader, Yasser Arafat, addressed the United Nations in New York, making his famous plea to follow the path of the olive branch rather than that of the gun. This was followed by the reaffirmation of the UN General Assembly of 'the inalienable rights of the Palestinian people'. In 1975 there was the beginning of the civil war in Lebanon, a very complex situation. In August 1976, the siege on the Palestinian refugee camp of Tal Al-Za'tar took place, followed by a massacre.

Although none of these events was known to me as I prepared for another period of study overseas, during my flight across the Pacific Ocean I had a very strong feeling that my life was about to change.

Soon after arriving at Penn State I was invited to a function where I met a number of students, foreign and local. I was particularly thrilled to meet Hideko, a Japanese student, because I had studied Japanese for my BA degree and was fascinated by the culture. Hideko and I were soon chatting away, and our discussion led to recent news coverage of the Middle East. I expressed my interest in the area, and also my lack of understanding of the conflict. She confessed that she was also very puzzled about the situation, and mentioned that there was a Palestinian girl living in the dorm near her and perhaps I would like to meet her.

Naheel was working towards a doctorate in psychology. I had many questions I wanted to ask her, especially in relation to recent news coverage. Why was there such a problem in the Middle East? What was the background to the current situation? Why was there a refugee population in Lebanon and why was it a problem? What exactly was the PLO? Why were those associated with Palestinians labelled as 'terrorist' and 'anti-Semitic'?

Naheel said she was very willing to talk to me about the problem, but suggested I should also read writings by Palestinians and other Arabs, Zionist Jews and Israelis, anti-Zionist Jews, and a cross-section of European and American authors. One of the references she gave me was *The Decadence of Judaism in Our Time* by Moshe Menuhin. This book made a special impact on me because it presented an approach to the issue I had not previously been aware of: a devout Jew questioning political Zionism and its relationship to Judaism.

Naheel, and other Palestinians I met, were very clear in their distinction between the Jewish people and their religion and political

Zionism. She described how her Muslim family had lived peacefully in Palestine before 1948 (when the state of Israel was created) alongside Jews and Christians, with people from these three faiths often sharing with one another the celebrations of their different feasts. The horror of the Holocaust during World War II was carried out by Europeans against Jews and other minorities. Why were Palestinians required to pay for such crimes?

The Palestinian issue was becoming one that I couldn't ignore – neither personally nor intellectually. The more reading I did, the more I became aware of the gross injustice that had been done to the Palestinian people, and which was ongoing. Many people, on becoming aware of the situation, often ask, 'But how can Jewish people, who have themselves suffered so much oppression and discrimination, do the same to another people?' Obviously the situation is far more complex than that, and I soon realised that it was important to consider the many different aspects of the problem and the way these are inter-related. Political, nationalistic and religious issues were evident. What was not so obvious, initially, was the importance of the area of Palestine – geographically and socio-economically – to other nations, which has resulted in conflict between countries seeking power and influence in the region. This conflict involves the actions of political Zionism and in no way compromises the religious faith of Judaism, except, as Menuhin and other anti-Zionist Jews would claim, when the faith is abused for political purposes.

The Zionism movement began in the late nineteenth century, in reaction to the pogroms against Jews in Russia and Poland and general discrimination in Europe. Its objective was to establish a homeland for the Jewish people in Palestine. I was interested to read that this initial approach came from a secular political perspective. A wave of immigration of European Jews to Palestine followed, to which the colonising power of Turkey objected, as did the indigenous population.

The Ottoman Empire had controlled the area known as Palestine since 1516. With the outbreak of World War I, Britain promised the

Arabs independence if they helped overthrow the Ottoman Empire. The Arab revolt – which aimed to create a unified Arab state from Syria to Yemen – began in June 1916. Unknown to the Arab leaders, however, Britain and France had signed the Sykes–Picot Agreement in May 1916, which would divide Syria, Iraq and Lebanon into British- and French-administered areas. Palestine, because of its holy places, was to be an international protectorate. When this situation became known there was great anger throughout the Arab world, which intensified in December 1917 with the announcement of the Balfour Declaration. The Balfour Declaration stated its support for the establishment of a national home for the Jewish people in Palestine. It also stated that the rights of non-Jewish inhabitants should be protected, as well as the rights of Jews living in other countries. I was interested to note that influential Jews in Britain strongly opposed the Balfour Declaration; there was fear that such a development would greatly endanger the situation of people of Jewish faith in other countries and could lead to the emergence of religious fundamentalism. My Palestinian friends pointed out to me that this declaration had amounted to one nation promising another nation – which at the time was being occupied by yet another nation – to another people.

At the end of World War I in 1918, Britain assumed military responsibility for Palestine, its mandate being approved by the newly formed League of Nations in 1922. Later that year, the Churchill White Paper confirmed the Balfour Declaration. At no time during this process were the wishes of the Palestinians, the indigenous population, considered. The British census of Palestine in October 1922 showed a total population of 757 182 people, only 11 per cent of which were Jews.

The situation became increasingly unstable, with the flow of Jewish immigrants being challenged by Palestinian Arabs in the form of revolts, the most significant taking place in 1929 and 1936–1939. Several Zionist resistance organisations supported the increased immigration and settlement of Jews from Europe. The Haganah was an underground organisation that initially confronted the Arab population, but following a British white paper in 1939 that restricted Jewish immigration to Palestine, it turned its attacks against the British. Other resistance groups, most notably the Irgun and Stern, were led by men later to become prime ministers of Israel: Menachem Begin and Yitzhak Shamir. These organisations carried out a wide range of actions against the Arabs and the British.

The problems in Palestine increased during World War II, and following the end of the war in 1945 the British declared military rule in Palestine. In 1947 the problem was submitted to the United Nations. The UN solution was Resolution 181 recommending partition, which was a contradiction to the earlier promise of independence. The conflict escalated rapidly with the Arab population strongly rejecting the partition plan. In April 1948, Zionist militants massacred Palestinians in the village of Deir Yassin, a western suburb of Jerusalem. The UN appointed Count Folke Bernadotte as a mediator to resolve the conflict in Palestine on 13 May 1948; the State of Israel was proclaimed on 14 May; and the British Mandate ended on 15 May. Arab states joined together to confront the Israeli army, the core of which was made up from the Haganah. During 15–17 May both the US and the USSR recognised the State of Israel. By mid-1948, Bernadotte had submitted his peace plan, with its recommendation that Jerusalem remain Arab. In September 1948 he was assassinated in Jerusalem.

During the conflict, hundreds of villages were destroyed and thousands of Palestinians fled. The UN General Assembly Resolution 194 of December 1948 stated the right of displaced Palestinians to return to their homes. This resolution was never implemented and has remained one of the key issues in perpetuating the conflict. The situation of the Palestinians was disregarded, and in May 1949 Israel was conditionally admitted to the UN. The UN General Assembly Resolution 303 of December 1949 called for the internationalisation of Jerusalem which eight months earlier had divided into an eastern half controlled by Jordan and a western half under Israeli rule.

My Palestinian friends shared with me their feelings of encouragement in May 1977 when it was reported that the US State Department had released their Human Rights Report charging Israel with crimes against the Palestinians, including illegal expulsion from their homes and property, detention without charge, destruction of properties, and no provision of judicial remedy for detainees. At last they felt the US was acknowledging and acting on some of the oppression the Palestinian people had suffered.

In May 1978 my friends invited me to join them and some other Arab students to drive to New York to take part in a counter-demonstration to the Zionist parade that was marking the 'independence' of Israel. They said that extra attention was being given to the parade this year as the Prime Minister of Israel, Menachem Begin, was expected to be participating. I had never taken part in this type of activity before and, although I felt a little apprehensive, I was interested in supporting the event. In my search to understand the Palestinian–Israeli conflict, I'd frequently come across discussion of the celebration of Israeli 'independence' day and the meaning of the event to the Palestinians. May 1948 is described by Palestinians as the *Naqba* (the catastrophe). As we drove to New York, my friends said to me, 'Why independence? Independence from what? The leaders of the Zionist movement were European, and the whole movement viewed from our perspective is colonisation which has brought great suffering to our people.' I could understand why the Israeli celebration was a day of sadness for the Palestinian people, based on a feeling of injustice and loss that remains at the core of the conflict to this day.

I was very impressed by the way the counter-demonstration had been organised. There was a large crowd: Americans of different ethnic backgrounds, Arabs and various other nationals – all ages and styles of people. The organisers stressed that this was a peaceful demonstration of solidarity with the Palestinian people and in no way should people be provoked into violence – and we were warned that there would be provocation. As we moved off, an African–American man played his guitar and sang popular freedom songs and those around him joined in. This created a special atmosphere of sharing: a feeling of peace and hope. At various locations, we stopped and listened to speakers. The last stop was outside the World Zionist Organization office, where a representative of the Palestinian Women's Union spoke of conditions in occupied Palestinian territories. 'There is a very brave woman!' commented one of my friends, thinking of the possible ramifications of speaking publicly in such a place; the woman could be denied entry when she tried to return home, or be imprisoned.

At Penn State, I had been focusing on how to ensure that people with disability were included in community activities; and how to structure recreation opportunities so as to make a direct contribution to their quality of life. So many questions, so many ideas. I was aware of international trends and felt the need to gather data for my study in both the US and the UK. During June and July of 1978, I carried out field work in Mississippi and Texas, then travelled to the UK in early August. I was able to spend some time with Clarice and Alan and their children, Geoffrey and Wibby, before beginning my work.

It was an especially interesting time to be visiting large institutions. In the 1960s there had been calls to deinstitutionalise people with intellectual disabilities and to include them in community life. This had created changes to the operational patterns of institutions, the effects of which were still being dealt with by both management and professional staff alike. Significant also was the clear distinction now made between the diagnosis of intellectual disability and mental illness. Along with this came the awareness of the very different needs of these two groups of people, and also of the individual needs of any one person regardless of any classification label given them.

I felt quite distressed when I met a group of middle-aged residents in a cottage in the grounds of one of the large institutions. They had been classified as intellectually disabled because of their failure to respond to people speaking to them, and had been institutionalised as small children, losing contact with their families. The tragedy for these people was that it was not until many years later that it was realised they were deaf, not intellectually disabled. After living for so long in the confines of an institution, without appropriate stimulation and education opportunities, they were afraid to move into the community when given the opportunity to do so. The authorities, realising their particular situation, had established their current residential arrangement and were working at developing a more appropriate quality of life for them.

Whilst in the UK, I travelled to Scotland to visit my relatives. At Penn State I had enrolled in a class in sign language for the deaf, and thinking to show off my newly refreshed skills I began using some of the American signs in conversation with my cousins. Instead of impressing everyone, I created some confusion and hilarity; I hadn't realised that sign language, like any language, has different dialects. The sign I used for 'world' so delighted one of Jessie's friends that each time she saw me she made the sign and collapsed into laughter.

On 17 September 1978, back at Penn State, I sat in the common room of the graduate dorm, together with my Palestinian friends and many other students, to view on the large television there the signing of the Camp David Accords by US President Jimmy Carter, Israeli Prime Minister Menachem Begin and Egyptian President Anwar Sadat. For many students present it was just an interesting international event, but for the Palestinians it was an emotionally charged occasion. Sitting near us was a Jewish friend and her boyfriend, both of whom felt very positive about what they saw as the friendly action of Sadat and the promise of steps towards peace. Apart from cordial greetings, however, there wasn't enough familiarity or trust between these two groups of my friends to enable any discussion about the event.

The accords proposed a settlement of the Middle East conflict that bypassed the Palestinian people and their sole representative, the PLO, which meant neither the Palestinian people nor the Arab world in general could accept them. 'How can such a unilateral decision that ignores the main issues of the conflict contribute to justice and lasting peace?' was the common concern. 'How could Sadat do this?' my Palestinian friends asked in disbelief. 'Look at the situation now. It completely ignores the situation of the Palestinian people and the fact that UN resolutions such as 194 relevant to refugees and 242 concerning borders have not been honoured. Further, there will be no need now for Israel to use its army to guard its southern borders with Egypt, which means it can deploy all of these troops to other areas. For sure, soon there will be a full-scale invasion into Lebanon.' In fact, the Israeli army did invade southern Lebanon before the end of that year.

My friends also recalled the controversial statement attributed to Golda Meir, the Prime Minister of Israel between 1969 and 1974, who claimed 'there is no such thing as a Palestinian'. In light of this statement and the events taking place now, with the peace treaty between Israel and Egypt, they pointed out that Israel could continue its aggression against the Palestinian people unabated. To them, the international advances that had stirred their hopes were being revealed as no more than words on paper.

In mid-1978, my Palestinian friends told me about a conference organised by the Arab American University Graduates Association (AAUG) in Minnesota. This seemed an opportunity for me to gain greater knowledge and understanding of the Arab world and the situation of the Palestinian people. I was realising just how little I had been taught at school or university about the Arab world – the culture, the contribution towards early advances in modern civilisation, and its situation during the height of the period of western colonisation. There were two aspects of the conference that became highly significant for me, both providing direction for future decisions I would make.

The first was a screening of the film *The Palestinians*, produced by Vanessa Redgrave in 1977. Redgrave, moved by the plight of the Palestinian people and the particular tragedy of the siege on the Palestinian refugee camp Tal Al-Za'tar in Lebanon in 1976, was determined to make a film with an underlying plea for peace in the region. The siege on Tal Al-Za'tar led to the massacre of over 3000 people by right-wing Falange militants with links to Israel. The Jewish lobby in the US branded Redgrave as a terrorist and anti-Semitic. Her effigy was burned, shots were fired at her office, death threats were made, and many acting roles were denied her. Initially, the film was banned in the US. It wasn't until the 1990s that the harassment against her diminished.

Why is a person who questions the actions of the government of Israel accused of being anti-Semitic? This puzzled me a great deal and I did a lot of reading on the subject. The term Semitic, according to the *Concise Oxford Dictionary*, includes members 'of any of the races supposed to be descended from Shem, son of Noah (Gen. 10:21ff.), including especially the Jews, Phoenicians, Arabs and Assyrians: so Semitic . . . languages of family including Hebrew and Arabic . . .' This explained to me why my Palestinian friends often referred to Israelis as their 'cousins', but only added to my confusion in trying to understand the meaning of the term anti-Semitic and its use. The term is commonly used to indicate discrimination against Jews, which would seem to be a misnomer as it should logically imply discrimination against all Semitics rather than targeting a subgroup. It would seem especially inappropriate to label Arabs or other Semitics as anti-Semitic. It seemed the term came into use during the nineteenth century to describe actions against European Jews, and emerged in its most extreme form in Nazi Germany in the early twentieth century. However, my question remained: why is such a term used against a person who questions the political actions of the Israeli government?

For me, *The Palestinians* also brought the complexity of life in the area into some focus; for the first time I became aware of the work of the Palestine Red Crescent Society (PRCS) under the energetic and inspiring leadership of Dr Fathi Arafat. The other people watching the film with me reacted excitedly when Dr Fathi appeared on screen to talk about the conditions the Palestinian people had faced. 'Look,' the person beside me said, 'he is the brother of Abu Amar [Yasser Arafat]. He is a medical doctor and president of PRCS.' And it was in this film that I saw the child with cerebral palsy who was to influence my decision to seek work in Palestine. Still today I can remember the commentary that accompanied this scene: 'Even in this very difficult situation, the Palestinian people take care of those who are disabled.' This tiny child in a cot in the temporary hospital looked up at the camera with the widest smile one could imagine. To me, this was like finding the missing piece of a puzzle. *Cerebral palsy*, I noted to myself. *Yes, I am sure that I would be able to work in some way with the Palestinian people in the Middle East.* The questions of *how*, *where*, *when* were still to be answered, but the *why* and *what* were taking shape.

Also at the conference was a campaign called 'Palestinians Have Human Rights Too'. It had attractive posters with the phrase written in English, Arabic and Hebrew, and the drawing of a hand in the 'stop' position but also looking like a dove. It was a very simple, inclusive message with a focus on peace. Some time later I was walking through one of the university buildings at Penn State and passed a noticeboard where my friends had pinned one of these posters. A small group of young men were approaching from the opposite direction. One of them saw the poster and ripped it down with such vigour that he almost dislodged the whole board. I had never before seen such blind hate. I moved quickly away, feeling a little scared by what I had seen. I wondered how young people could reach such a level of irrational hate.

In 1978 I returned to Brisbane to the University of Queensland, as a lecturer in the Department of Human Movement Studies and as a research assistant at the Schonell Educational Research Centre. In many respects this was an ideal situation for me. The work in the Department of Human Movement Studies was involved with people with disability, while my research at the Schonell Centre enabled me to look more closely at programs for young children with disability, the role of play, and the manner in which parents approached the management of a disabled child. Further, I was back in an environment with friends and colleagues I had worked with over a number of years.

During this period I made contact with some Palestinian families in Sydney and Brisbane, and gained more first-hand knowledge of their situations. By now I was convinced that I should go to the Middle East to work with the Palestinian people, even if just for a few years. I decided to take advantage of the long university summer vacation, withdraw my savings from the bank and go around the world to knock on doors and search for the best way to do this.

One thing led to another, as if pieces of a puzzle were just waiting to be put in place. In the UK, at the Council for the Advancement of Arab–British Understanding (CAABU), I found a very helpful person in John Reddaway. He explained that it would be unwise to go to Lebanon because of the degree of instability in the country, and that Jordan would be a safer choice. He made arrangements for me to meet people there and to visit some of the Palestinian refugee camps. He also put me in contact with the PLO representative in London and the European Committee on Palestinian Human Rights in Paris.

I knew that the PLO was somewhat equivalent to a government in exile, overseeing the needs of the diaspora of the Palestinian people. However, the actions of the military wing of the PLO had resulted in it being branded as a terrorist organisation – leading to a stereotype portrayal of Palestinians in general that still persists in some places. Founded in 1964, the PLO is actually an umbrella organisation of several different groups. Fatah, a secular organisation established in 1959, became the dominant organisation within the PLO, with Yasser Arafat as leader of both. The organisational structure of the PLO includes the Palestine National Council (PNC), the Palestine Central Council, the PLO Executive Committee, the PLO Army, and subsidiary organisations, one of which is the Palestine Red Crescent Society (PRCS).

By chance, there was a PRCS employee in London at that time, seeking specialists to work in Lebanon. Samir told me that the PRCS had been established in 1968 and was equivalent to both a Ministry of Health and a Red Crescent Society for the Palestinian people in the diaspora. As such it had observer member status in both the World Health Organization and the International Federation of Red Cross and Red Crescent Societies. 'It is a humanitarian organisation with a mission to provide health and social services for the Palestinian people,' he said. 'In addition to emergency services, it has hospitals, clinics and educational institutions. In the field of rehabilitation there are physiotherapy centres, a workshop for making artificial limbs and aids for people with disability. A small rehabilitation hospital is in the process of being upgraded. The organisation is looking for international volunteers who may be interested in being involved in these developments.' I decided to make a visit to Lebanon, in spite of the reservations that John Reddaway had expressed.

While in the CAABU building, I spent some time in the library. I wanted to read more about the period between the two World Wars and the leadup to the creation of the State of Israel and the dispersion of the Palestinian people. It seemed that the events of that time set the pattern of the conflict as seen at the end of the 1970s. Terror was something that was ever present, at both State and individual level. What caused people to carry out terror acts didn't seem to be given adequate attention; surely causes had to be looked at if solutions were to be found? I wondered why some terror acts were justified and others condemned. Given how frequently Palestinians are branded as terrorists, I was especially interested to read that following the July 1946 bombing of the King David Hotel in Jerusalem, where the British Mandate administration offices were located, which killed more than ninety people, the British government issued a special white paper on terrorism in Palestine. It was stated in this document that the Jewish Agency was involved in acts of terrorism through the activities of the Irgun and Stern.

I made my first visit to Lebanon in January 1980. Flying into Beirut is a very special experience. The mountains rise up immediately from the very narrow coastal area and the view is so majestic it is breathtaking. Beirut, the capital of Lebanon and its largest port, was also the leading financial capital of the Middle East before the civil war, which began in 1975. By the mid-1980s the population for the whole of Lebanon was estimated at over 2.5 million, with 1.5 million living in Beirut.

The government structure in Lebanon was complex, based on proportional power-sharing of the different religious groups. The ruling power during the 1980s and '90s was the Christian Maronites, even though at that time Christians (Maronite, Greek Orthodox, Armenian and Protestant) made up only around 25 per cent of the population. The majority was Muslim, with the biggest sub-group being Shiite. Although the Shiite were the biggest single group in the country, they experienced the most poverty and held the least power.

The complexities of the mix of religious and political factors had caused instability in Lebanon, and in 1975 confrontations between

Christians and Muslims had led to the beginning of the civil war. Other countries and groups, such as France, Syria, Israel, Iran and the PLO, had also contributed to the conflict. In 1976, Syrian forces entered Lebanon to confront the PLO, which had its own forces within the refugee camps, having built up a presence there since its expulsion from Jordan in 1970. Later in 1976 the Arab League imposed a truce. In 1978, Israel entered southern Lebanon and attacked PLO positions, which was followed by the entry of a UN monitoring force. Israel continued to support the Maronite Christians. Apart from European interest and involvement in the area, the continued Israeli occupation of Palestinian and other Arab lands was an ever-present 'powder keg' in the region. A powder keg ready to explode at any time.

My plane came into land at Beirut airport, and I was soon swept up in the bustle and confusion in the arrivals area. Eventually I found people from the Palestine Red Crescent Society waiting to take me to a hotel in West Beirut

Not being used to guns, or anything military, I was a little apprehensive about being in Beirut. During that visit in 1980, I heard shooting at night and had no idea whether I should hide or whether it was just routine exercises that I could ignore. I dealt with the situation by pretending to myself that I wasn't worried and there was no problem; in fact, this seemed to be the case. Another new experience was having to pass through checkpoints along the road to the south. I didn't really know if the soldiers were Lebanese, Syrian or PLO, but there was a frightening array of armoury. It also struck me how young were these soldiers manning the checkpoints.

My visit to the PRCS in Beirut focused on the rehabilitation facilities. There were hospitals, clinics, a nursing school, a kindergarten, a physiotherapy centre and an associated workshop that made artificial limbs and walking aids. There were also the beginnings of the development of a rehabilitation hospital in the Burj Al-Barajneh refugee camp. In the south were other clinics.

Having seen something of the work of PRCS in Beirut and in the south, I was then taken to meet the President of PRCS, Dr Fathi Arafat. This was conducted with a certain amount of theatre, and I felt somewhat overwhelmed in the presence of this charismatic leader. Accompanying me was Hadla Ayoubi, the vivacious and very efficient director of public relations for PRCS, who acted as translator.

Dr Fathi made me feel very welcome and asked about my visits to the various programs. 'Do you think you could help us?' he asked.

'I think I could,' I answered.

'Good,' was his reply, 'Hadla will follow up the details with you.'

I explained that it would take me a while to organise both my personal and professional life, but that I would be available to return in one year's time. Dr Fathi said that he understood and that he would write to me in about three months to formally invite me to Lebanon in order to be a volunteer with the PRCS. I was told that volunteers received a basic living allowance, which reassured me as I wasn't in a position economically to be a volunteer in the sense of working without any financial support.

I was offered several excellent positions in Australia, but none of these deterred me from my desire to travel to the Middle East and begin work with the PRCS. My family reminded me that there were disadvantaged groups in the Australian population and perhaps I could follow my interests nearer to home, but once they realised I'd made up my mind, they were completely supportive. Still, it wasn't easy to make such a big move.

My decision had a major impact on other family members too. Clarice and Alan were still living in England with their two young children – Mum's only grandchildren. Mum decided that if I was going to the Middle East, then it would be best for her to go to England to live near Clarice and her family, even if that meant leaving her sister, Rene, and her many friends. Many people warned Mum against the idea, with stories of older women moving to be near their daughters only to find that it was too difficult to adjust to a new place, but Mum was as convinced about her decision as I was about mine.

At the end of 1980 my mother and I flew to the UK. We spent a few weeks with Clarice, Alan and their family, and I was able to see Mum settle into her new life in the village of Newton Ferrers. In mid-January 1981 I left them to go to Beirut. I was both excited and a little apprehensive as I entered this new and unknown situation.

FOUR

THE HEADQUARTERS OF THE PALESTINE RED CRESCENT SOCIETY was
located in Ghobeiry, a southern suburb of the district of Mount
Lebanon, within the governorate of Beirut. The complex of buildings,
in addition to the administration and information offices, included
Akka Hospital, Naserah Children's Hospital, an emergency centre,
clinics, a physiotherapy centre and orthopaedic aids workshop, a
kindergarten and nursery, and a small market. There was also a small
'hotel', which provided accommodation for foreign volunteers. The
complex was near the main road to the airport, and the Chatila and
Sabra Palestinian refugee camps. Most of the people living in the
camps were Palestinian families who in 1948 or 1967 had fled towns
and villages in the northern coastal areas of what is now Israel. Across
the road from the PRCS, a few yards to the east, was the Shiijah
camp, housing Lebanese people who had fled the constant Israeli
shelling in the southern areas of Lebanon. About a ten-minute drive
along the airport road was the entrance to another Palestinian refugee
camp, Burj Al-Barajneh.

I received a warm welcome on my arrival at the PRCS complex.
Once my accommodation had been organised, Hadla Ayoubi, the
director of public relations, took me to meet with Dr Fathi Arafat
to discuss the pattern of my work. Dr Fathi suggested that I work
mainly with the physiotherapy department in the Akka Hospital

complex and the Haifa Rehabilitation Hospital in the Burj Al-Barajneh refugee camp. He gave me the freedom to decide where and how I could best use my skills. My particular interests and skills were in working with children using discovery and play-oriented approaches. I was also introduced to one of the social workers, Namiti Odeh, who had been assigned to assist me. Often worried and upset about situations around her, Namiti never hesitated to become involved in helping others. I owe a great deal to her for her assistance during my settling-in period.

The staff in the physiotherapy centre at Akka Hospital had difficulty in dealing with children who were afraid and cried throughout therapy sessions. They didn't have an understanding of the special therapy techniques that were currently being used for children with cerebral palsy. Instead, they were carrying out general exercise patterns, which weren't very relevant to a child with cerebral palsy as their movement problems are brain-related and not to do with the muscles themselves. Although I was aware of my own limitations in not being a physiotherapist, I was able to help by using my experience as a physical educator specialising in working with disabled children. My approach was to establish contact with the child in a play situation before commencing any activities, to get to know the child and gain their trust. I then gradually incorporated activities I wished the child to perform within this play atmosphere. Very soon, the staff were passing children to me.

I enjoyed the work and was keen for the staff to learn some of my techniques, which I felt would help them. I wasn't in a position to suggest this, however, and realised that seeming to impose my ideas could have the reverse effect. So I did the work I could when asked without any further involvement. To my joy, one of the physiotherapy assistants soon asked me to teach her what I was doing.

Not long after I had commenced my work with the PRCS, one of the foreign volunteer nurses told me about two children with disabilities in the Naserah Children's Hospital who weren't receiving any stimulation. She thought I might be interested to see them. My request to the medical director to work with the two children wasn't received with any enthusiasm, however. 'What is the point?' he said. 'What can you do? You will come for some weeks and then leave. This is not helpful.' Once I was able to convince him that I had no intention of leaving and that I really thought I could be helpful, he became much more friendly towards me and called on a nurse to take me through to where the children were.

Hamoudi, severely disabled with cerebral palsy, was in one of two cots in a room. He was about seven or eight years old (his actual age was unknown) and had lost his family during the siege of Tal Al-Za'tar in 1976. He was brought to the PRCS temporary hospital at that time and had remained with PRCS ever since. Cerebral palsied quadriplegia from birth, Hamoudi had spent most of his life lying on his back in a cot, being fed from a baby's bottle or with spoonfuls of soup. He relied entirely on others to change and bathe him. It was not lack of compassion that resulted in him being left devoid of stimulation, but rather a lack of understanding of how to work with such children.

The nurse told me that the other bed was usually occupied by Dalal, a girl of about five years old who was totally blind. At this point, Dalal was in an adjacent room as she had measles, so we went to meet her. Dalal had been found after a bombing raid in a camp in the south of Lebanon when she was about two or three years old. No one knew who she was. And, like Hamoudi, no one knew how old she was. She was taken to a PRCS clinic and then to the children's hospital in Beirut, where she too became a 'child of PRCS'. As I spent more time with Dalal, I noticed that she often sat on the ground with her head down and her fingers in her eyes. People fed her by placing food into her mouth which she swallowed. She was not toilet-trained.

Once Dalal recovered from the measles I only saw her at weekends because she attended an international evangelical school for blind children in West Beirut. The school was some distance away, so during the week she stayed in the home of the family responsible for the school, the De Smidts, a South African missionary family. I made contact with the De Smidts to discuss Dalal's situation so we could work together to enable her to catch up on her development. Each Friday I drove to the school to bring Dalal 'home' for the weekend, and returned her on the Monday morning.

It was obvious that both Hamoudi and Dalal were in need of a wide range of stimulating activities and the opportunity to learn basic skills. Hamoudi was severely disabled and needed movement activities to change his position and the opportunity to experience life outside of his room. His diet and the method of feeding him also needed to be looked at. Dalal seemed to be a very bright child, and I was impressed by her knowledge of English language, which she had picked up from visitors to the hospital. I felt her lack of basic daily living skills came from her circumstances, not from an inability to learn.

My mind was spinning with enthusiasm as I considered how best to structure my time with the two children, and what activities and experiences to introduce. It wasn't difficult to develop a strong bond with them. They were both delighful people and I enjoyed being with them; and they were overjoyed to see me, as usually they were left in their cots without attention. One day during a play activity, I realised I had seen Hamoudi before. He was the child I'd seen in the film that had inspired me to seek for a way to work with the Palestinian people in the Middle East. It was with a very strange feeling of surprise and amazement that I exclaimed, 'You are part of the reason I am here!'

In my first week of working with Hamoudi, I took him out to the balcony near his room. At one end was a cluster of plants, mostly vines and the tops of shrubs growing below. It was obvious that he was attracted to this greenery and enjoyed being out of his room. A week later, I decided to take him out of the hospital. As we approached the exit I was stopped by a nurse.

'Where are you going?' she said.

I told her I was taking Hamoudi to see outside.

'Impossible,' she said. 'It was too much to take him onto the balcony. But outside, no!'

As I argued with the nurse, one of the doctors came by. 'What is the problem?' he asked.

When I explained, the doctor took one look at Hamoudi, who was laughing and clearly delighted by his new adventure. 'Look at the boy – he is happy! *Yalla*, off you go!'

It is impossible to describe Hamoudi's reaction. We stepped out into the bright daylight, with many people walking about and cars coming and going. Hamoudi's little eyes opened wide and his mouth was agape in wonder. He was clearly amazed at what he saw, and I am sure he wondered what all of this activity was about.

The extent of the impact on him was obvious. Each day we would do some activities on the mat, going through movement patterns with Hamoudi lying on his front, propped with pillows under his chest, while I encouraged him to use his arms to reach towards toys. Then we'd leave his room. If we turned right, he knew we were going to the balcony; if we turned left, he knew we were going outside. A turn right resulted in objection now; it was the turn left that brought the reaction of absolute joy.

It was an interesting experience working with two such different children: Hamoudi, severely and multiply disabled; Dalal, although blind, curious and bright. Dalal was dependent on sounds, but Hamoudi startled at any sudden noise. Dalal needed guidance when moving around; Hamoudi needed to be carried. On our excursions outside the hospital I tied a scarf around my waist for Dalal to hold so that I had my hands free to carry Hamoudi. It was only later that I was able to purchase and adapt a stroller for Hamoudi. At a much later stage I was given a backpack baby-carrier, which I sometimes used when taking him to the camps. Often, the only way to move around with him, though, was to carry him.

We often walked around the block, passing a lovely avenue of trees that threw shade across the footpath. Again, Hamoudi's attraction to nature and greenery was evident – he just loved passing under these trees. The other fun thing about these outings was our naming of the streets. We walked along *sharaa* (street) Hamoudi and *sharaa* Dalal and into *sharaa* Jean.

After some weeks of working with Hamoudi and Dalal like this, Dalal said to me, 'You can be my mother.' This statement bothered me. I tried to explain to Dalal that she'd once had a mother, who had loved her very much, so I couldn't be her mother. What I could be was her Australian mother. As my relationship with both children deepened it was clear that whatever we were called, we were becoming a family.

A short time after I began working with Hamoudi and Dalal, the director of the PRCS kindergarten came to ask me to see one of the babies attending the nursery linked to the kindergarten. Badr was about eight months old and lived in a special residence with about ten orphan babies and toddlers who were also 'children of PRCS'. The nursery staff were puzzled that he wasn't moving and doing things the others were doing – his skills were well below his chronological age. When I met him I could see his obvious left hemiplegia (paralysis of the left side of the body), which would certainly interfere with his movement. So began my involvement with Badr, a delightful, happy little child.

The kindergarten was a couple of floors below the children's hospital. During school holidays Dalal was sometimes taken to the kindergarten and when I started to work with Badr, I involved her in some of the activities. She would bring his chair for me, and be delighted to feel how small his little hands and feet were. I also took

Hamoudi into the kindergarten on one occasion to see if it would be a suitable place to do some activities with him. He wasn't impressed – these were small children. From then on whenever I took Hamoudi out and we passed the door to the kindergarten, he stiffened in my arms and began to object by making noises and moving up and down. I got the message! He was saying, I am older than these children and don't want to be treated like a baby.

My program also involved working at the Haifa Rehabilitation Hospital in Burj Al-Barajneh refugee camp. Haifa Rehabilitation Hospital was in the process of being upgraded at that time. I remember Dr Fathi proclaiming that it would one day be 'the best rehabilitation hospital in the Middle East'. At first, I worked with mainly adult patients there, but there were also a few children. Most of the resident patients were physically disabled, but those who were just attending day programs included people who were visually disabled. By far the majority of the patients had acquired their disability as a result of the conflict. I introduced some activities that could be done while in bed, in addition to other group activities. The women wheelchair users particularly enjoyed the movement-to-music sessions I conducted with them.

Haifa Rehabilitation Hospital was a few hundred yards from the entrance to the camp. Life in the camps was difficult. People lived in small basic cement dwellings, crowded together with narrow laneways between. Frequently open drains ran down the middle of these laneways. Windows were mostly small so the houses were dark inside. Floors were cement, but covered with mats. Mattresses were arranged along the wall for sitting, or stacked in a corner to be brought out at night. I was always amazed by how clean and neat people kept these dwellings, and how some even managed to make them attractive inside.

The camp environment was friendly and hospitality ever present, with coffee, tea or a cold drink being served as soon as anyone entered a house. In spite of the very difficult living conditions, people greeted me as I passed, usually with Hamoudi in my arms.

One particular family in Burj Al-Barajneh camp I remember very well. One of the family members, Hanan, was about eighteen years old and severely disabled with cerebral palsy – athetoid quadriplegia. She was obviously an intelligent young woman, very aware of her surroundings and keen to participate in any activities offered. She did not have speech, and I began to introduce her to an alternative method of communication, using a combined picture–word conversation board. Hanan had a very loving family who cared for her needs in every way they could, and were keen to follow any suggestions that might increase her abilities. They also enjoyed meeting Hamoudi, and some of the family members would play with him when I was working with Hanan. I had only been working with Hanan for a few months before the Israeli invasion of 1982. As with so many people I knew, I never saw Hanan or her family after the invasion. I don't know what happened to them.

I lived in the PRCS 'hotel', with a number of other volunteers. Meals were provided, so I had no need to shop for groceries or take time to prepare meals. I wasn't really involved in activities other than my work; I was completely engrossed in what I was doing. It had become a way of life, not a job. I received many invitations to go out – for a meal, to the mountains to take a break – but I was enjoying my work too much. Also, to go out on the Sunday (my day off) when I knew that Hamoudi and Dalal would be left in the hospital, with very few staff on duty and no attention, became impossible for me. They were my family now, and Sunday was time for fun in our own way. I was also struggling to learn the Arabic language – I found it very interesting, but difficult. I would have liked to be able to go to classes, but those available were in the downtown area and it was impossible to structure time to attend. Instead, I bought some books and asked questions of people around me.

One of the features of life with the PRCS was the many visitors who came to see the range of activities they offered, to understand the problems being faced and often to arrange for assistance in the form of financial support for specific projects and/or professional volunteers to work with the local staff. Therefore, I had the opportunity to meet people from many different countries and from many different walks of life. Of particular interest to me was the visit of the Australian senator George Georges. I had heard a great deal about Senator Georges, and it was encouraging to meet someone from the Australian government who was interested in the work of the PRCS. He was surprised to find an Australian working with the PRCS and asked many questions about my work and the difficulties we faced. He was very impressed with the range of PRCS facilities and services. One of the features of the work of the PRCS, which was pointed out to Senator Georges and other visitors, was the extent to which the services – structured to meet the health and social needs of the Palestinian people – were also available to and widely used by others in the community. In Lebanon, approximately 60 per cent of the clients were Lebanese, the majority being people from the lower socio-economic scale who were unable to afford other, more expensive, services available.

Dr Fathi often introduced me to visitors by saying, 'I had placed Hamoudi in a prison, thinking that I had provided him with the care that he needed, but she came and released him from this prison and gave him a life.' Unfortunately, so often throughout the world, severely and multi-disabled children, whose need for recognition is so great, are so little understood.

It was only many years later that I realised just how disadvantaged Dalal had been when I heard her say to a foreign visitor, 'When I was a small child, I never knew that I had a visual problem. I always thought we are all the same. When going out with my mum, I used to always ask myself, "Why is she telling me what is in the street? To step up or step down? Why is no one telling her? What does she know different from me?"' When I heard Dalal say this it really made me stop in my tracks and think. It hadn't occurred to me that Dalal was not aware of her situation.

When I asked her about this she said, 'All of these questions grew in myself.' She told me about a time when she was taken to the kindergarten and the children seemed to be playing a game that involved holding up their fingers. 'I remember feeling upset as I did not know why I did not know how many fingers they would show, but I just pretended.'

Dalal explained that she later learned that each person is different, and that she had a problem that needed people to tell her more information than normal. She said to me, 'We really were lacking in stimulation. Can you imagine at five years old I did not even know that I was blind? This demonstrates just how vital it is that a child, from a very young age, always needs lots of stimulation.'

I recalled something I heard an internationally renowned speaker say at a conference on intellectual disability: 'It is not the disability that is the problem. It is our lack of creativity, our lack of ability, to find ways and means to reach the child with multiple disabilities and to draw out his/her potential.' That statement has stayed with me, and I continue to wonder about children like Hamoudi. I continue to marvel at how much they can develop, and to puzzle as to how we can reach these children, how can we really find out what they understand, in order to help them develop even further. And to recognise what they contribute to the lives of people around them, in spite of the severity of their disabilities.

Hamoudi, for example, has the most interesting personality, with the biggest and brightest laugh that brings joy to all who know him. He contributes a great deal to the knowledge of anyone working with him about how to work with children who are severely and multi-disabled and how to enable them to experience something of community life. My staff soon realised just how valuable this work was to them as people, and how it helped them to work with other severely disabled children and their families. Very soon Hamoudi was being referred to as 'our professor'. I have certainly learnt a great deal from him; not only about working with severely disabled children, but also about myself.

I started to notice that he was experiencing absences (petit mal seizures) that indicated he could be epileptic. I took him to hospital to have an EEG test. The technician was very friendly and agreed to carry out the procedures with Hamoudi sitting on my lap. Hamoudi seemed to be fascinated by her attaching the electrodes to his head with a glue-like substance, and especially enjoyed her using a hairdryer to dry the glue. The technician was surprised, saying that often children were frightened of the hairdryer. I explained that Hamoudi was used to the hairdryer as I used one after washing his hair. He then sat very still on my knees as the test was conducted. The technician was amazed. 'This is the first time I have carried out an EEG on a child with this severity of disability without having to sedate them in order to proceed,' she said. The test results confirmed his epilepsy.

There was always an element of uncertainty to life in Lebanon. The Israelis carried out frequent bombing raids in the south, and there were ongoing conflicts between the many diverse groups within the country. One of the things that surprised me when I first arrived was the frequency of Israeli fighter jets flying over Beirut – we regularly heard the boom of the planes breaking the sound barrier. How can this be? I thought. When I asked the people around me they just shrugged and said, 'Oh, this is normal.' One Sunday, when I was returning to Beirut from the south, war planes suddenly appeared, flying low over the crowded highway. There was panic, and like the other people, we left our car and ran to what we hoped to be a place of shelter at the side of the road. On this occasion, there was no bombing. After some time, as the planes did not return, we went back to the car and continued on our journey.

In late 1981 there was a buildup of tension in Beirut and people seemed to be expecting some form of outbreak of conflict. One evening I was sitting in a room with a group of about twelve foreign nationals – all PRCS volunteers – discussing whether to 'stay or go'. The instability in Lebanon seemed to be increasing, and a full-scale invasion by the Israeli army was predicted. Those working in the south had already been evacuated to Beirut. We were told that if we stayed, it might be difficult to leave later if the situation worsened.

'I would really like to stay on, but the situation seems to be deteriorating rapidly. I have my family back home and I really can't take the risk associated with staying,' someone said – a sentiment shared by many.

'My time here is limited to three months and this is almost at an end,' another person said. 'For such a short period left, I think that the risk makes staying out of the question.'

'I feel guilty to talk about leaving the people, but I am afraid to stay on in such a dangerous development,' another volunteer confessed.

Talk of this nature went back and forth for hours, together with endless cups of coffee or tea. I felt obliged to be with the group, but I was feeling increasingly apart from the discussion taking place. Eventually one of the volunteers said, 'You're being very quiet tonight, Jean. What's your opinion? What are you going to do?'

I didn't really know how to respond. What was the relevance of my position? How would others react to what I had to say? All I could offer was my own decision, while trying to remain sensitive to the real difficulties many of the others were suffering.

'Actually, I think that decisions at times like this are very personal. We all have our own reasons for being here, and our own commitment in terms of time available to support the work of PRCS. I can appreciate why people feel extra worried at this time, and why the situation may be such that some people do need to leave. For me personally, I do not have any questions or uncertainty. I knew before I came that Lebanon was unstable and that the situation could become dangerous. I will stay, whatever happens.'

For some, my statement wasn't at all helpful as they grappled with the pros and cons of staying or leaving. I eventually excused myself. Leaving Lebanon at this time was not an option for me. I was completely involved with my work and it was a very interesting and challenging period. So often I thought about my friends from different professions back in Brisbane and wished they were there with me. The experiences I had shared with them gave me the base from which to cope now. Working with families in their homes gave me the opportunity to interact with the local people and gain a greater understanding of the situation they faced and how they managed. In spite of difficulties and, in many cases, poverty, I was always greeted warmly and given a cold drink or tea or coffee. I felt I was accepted, that I belonged.

Towards the end of 1981, the upgraded Haifa Rehabilitation Hospital was to be officially opened by Yasser Arafat, leader of the Palestinian people. This was a highly anticipated event and the general excitement throughout the PRCS increased as the day approached. In all of the excitement Dr Fathi forgot to make arrangements for me to bring Hamoudi and Dalal to the ceremony, but at the last moment he sent a driver for us. Hamoudi was still in his pyjamas and there was no time to change him, so off we went. It was an exciting day for all, and Yasser Arafat (also known to Palestinians as Abu Amar) stopped to greet Hamoudi, Dalal and myself during his tour of the hospital. In his characteristic manner, he kissed each one of us and said how pleased he was to see us.

A little time after the official opening of the hospital Dr Fathi called me to his office and asked me to take responsibility for the development of a children's section. I was surprised but very excited.

The whole of the second floor was organised as a children's section, with two wards (separate for boys and girls) who had suffered injury from shelling or shooting, and a large all-purpose area. I had a small room adjacent to the wards so I was available twenty-four hours.

Both Dalal and Hamoudi were transferred from the Naserah Children's Hospital to live in this new department. I was delighted that they would be in an environment that wasn't a hospital. The day I moved Hamoudi to his new home, the car to take us was late coming so I decided to walk with Hamoudi in his wheelchair. He had very few possessions so it wasn't difficult to manage. It was a wonderful journey – I was singing and Hamoudi was laughing as we walked along.

Setting up the program at the children's department wasn't easy. The children had previously been mixed in with the adult patients and had no specific routine. I required them to wake up at a certain time, dress, and come to the dining area for breakfast. During the day, we scheduled pottery and music activities, and I was able to link with personnel from the United Nations Relief and Works Agency (UNRWA) for assistance with education material. It didn't take long for the children to begin to feel the benefits of such a routine and programming and they soon became a happy, active group. It was small initially: just three girls – Abir and Ream, both wheelchair-users, and Dalal – and three boys – Ahmed and Nour, also both wheelchair-users, and Hamoudi. In addition to the work with these children, I was able to begin a day program for about eight children from the camp with different developmental disabilities – most being intellectually disabled or cerebral palsied. Hamoudi joined this program too, and later Badr came on a daily basis from the centre where he was living.

Life in the rehabilitation centre was great for Hamoudi, sleeping in the dorm with the other boys and following the day program with the children in the group. He was able to learn new skills while enjoying the company of those around him. Many people in the hospital and in the community were getting to know him, capti-vated by his happy personality. He was making friends all around.

The new environment also contributed a great deal to Dalal's development and she soon fitted into a pattern of being a 'little sister' to the older children, with a special relationship with Abir and Ream. Nour, a very caring boy, enjoyed giving Dalal rides on the footrest of his wheelchair, much to her delight.

Whenever I took Hamoudi with me on a home visit, or took him and Dalal on an outing, we attracted a lot of interest. It was surprising for people to see a child as disabled as Hamoudi enjoying a normal pattern of life. On several occasions people came and spoke to me, saying, 'We have a child like him at home' or 'My sister has a child like him.' On one occasion when I was getting out of a share taxi (*servees*) with Hamoudi and trying to manage his stroller, a man selling fruit left his barrow and came running to assist me. Again that phrase: 'We have a child like him at home.' Often these children were just lying on a bed in a back room at home; people cared, but they didn't know what to do. I would invite them to bring the child to the PRCS, and many parents did just that. They were so pleased to feel that their child was valued, and they were keen to participate in activities to enhance their child's development. I often referred to Hamoudi as 'my public relations boy'.

FIVE

IT WAS ON A FRIDAY AFTERNOON IN JUNE 1982, when I was driving to Dalal's school to bring her home for the weekend, that everything seemed to fall apart. I was crossing the bridge in Khola, near the stadium, when, without any warning, Israeli war planes roared in and bombed the area. The sound of bombs and planes was terrifying. The tall buildings at the side of the road were shaking. I was on a highway bridge with no walkways and had no idea what to do. Some drivers sped up. Others abandoned their cars. On the down slope of the bridge I decided to leave my car too. I jumped down to the road below and ran into a pharmacy. People were gathered there, afraid and listening intently to the radio. My Arabic was weak so I was unable to understand the information being given. Often it was drowned out by more planes and bombing.

After some time, things became quieter and it seemed that the bombing had stopped. I decided to return to the car and drive on. When I arrived at Dalal's school, I found that all was well. The school was in an area far from the focus of bombing and would, most likely, remain a safe area. I discussed the situation with the De Smidt family and the local staff and we decided it would be best to leave Dalal there for the time being as it was much safer than in the camp. Also, we had no idea how safe the route home would be. I explained the situation to Dalal and she was quite happy to stay where she was.

By the time I left, it was night. I couldn't return on the main road as it had been severely damaged by the bombing, so I had to take a road nearer to the coast. It was probably the most difficult drive I have ever experienced. Cars were everywhere, and all drivers seemed to be in a state of panic. Sometimes there was shooting ahead and cars would suddenly turn back. I was scared, but there was nothing I could do except keep driving and try to get home. There was no way of making contact with the staff and children back at the camp and I was worried about them.

When I eventually reached the Haifa Rehabilitation Hospital in Burj Al-Barajneh camp, it was to find everyone gathered in a room on the ground floor. We were all relieved to see eath other. Bombs had been dropped near the hospital in the first wave of attacks.

'I was so scared I didn't know what to do,' one of the nurses told me. 'The glass of the windows was breaking. I fell down onto the floor, and I stood up again, and then I fell down again. The children in wheelchairs were crying and some crawled along the floor to the steps. We did eventually get organised and got everyone down to the ground floor.'

The hospital staff had been very worried about Hamoudi. One of the staff had been out walking him in his wheelchair. They were some distance from the hospital when the first bombs fell. The girl panicked and didn't know what to do, so she ran with Hamoudi in his chair to her own house. Once there, it was too dangerous to try to move, and there was no way to make contact with the hospital. There were several hours of anxiety at the hospital as people wondered what had become of her and Hamoudi. When the situation quietened, she cautiously walked back with Hamoudi and it was a great relief to all to see them both safe. When I arrived safely some time later, it was like a major homecoming following a long absence. There were kisses and hugs all around.

With continuing overflights of war planes and some bombing nearby in the camp, the ground floor was the safest place available in the hospital. The children and I spent some days there, sleeping on mats in one of the rooms. We were joined by a young girl, Amira, who hadn't been with us long, and her mother. There were usually one or two nurses with the children too, depending on their shifts and their other duties. During the day, if there was respite from the planes, we would go out into the alley beside the hospital for a change and some fresh air, but speedily returned inside at the sound of planes.

After a few days, the children and I were transferred to the Akka Hospital complex. This was considered to be safer than the camp, and had the additional safety of rooms underground. We were moved in a PRCS car during no more than a fifteen-minute drive, but the driver was clearly nervous and keen to complete our transfer as soon as possible. We were taken to the underground area in the physio-therapy gym. One of the doorways from the gym led directly to the entrance to the emergency section. This was unfortunate as there was a constant stream of injured people being rushed through with their distressed relatives and friends.

We spent some days there on mats on the floor, together with other people who were sheltering from the bombs. Eventually, most of the children were taken home, leaving just Nour and Hamoudi with me. Dalal was still at her school in a safe area of West Beirut. During the night, I positioned Hamoudi on his side and slept with him in the crook of my arm. This new sleeping arrangement, combined with the exercises I had been giving him, actually brought about an exciting result. For the first time in his life, Hamoudi rolled from his back onto his side independently. In spite of the stress and tragedy all around, I felt great joy at this accomplishment, and Hamoudi looked so proud of himself as I praised him.

The attacks increased in intensity. There was constant bombing and an ongoing flow of injured people being rushed to the emergency centre. People were obviously worried. Because of my language limitations, I often couldn't understand all of the details. I just kept on the alert, tried to make the children as relaxed as possible, and followed any directions given me. On one occasion there was shelling from land, sea and sky simultaneously – the noise was intense. The mirrors on the wall of the physiotherapy gym cracked with a swishing noise. More injured people were being rushed past the doorway. The atmosphere was extremely tense. People were tired and afraid. For some reason, Hamoudi began to laugh. He has a very infectious laugh, and the most amazing event occurred – gradually people in the room began to react to Hamoudi, and very soon everybody was laughing with him. Just a few minutes before it had seemed these people would never laugh again, but Hamoudi had helped them to relax for an instant.

During one of the breaks in the bombing I decided to go up to the top floor of the building to assess the situation. I'd been so occupied with the children that I hadn't moved away from them at all. I asked a nurse to stay with Hamoudi and to keep an eye on Nour. I crossed to the adjacent building, walked up to the fifth floor and surveyed the city of Beirut. Grey smoke was wafting up into the sky. The whole place was damaged and burning. Suddenly I heard the noise of war planes returning. I moved so quickly back down the stairs I think I slipped through four or five steps at a time. I can't describe my relief at arriving at the bottom step and getting back underground. However, when I returned to the children I was confronted with a worrying situation. While I was gone, Nour had had a fit – nobody knew why or how. He had no history of epilepsy. It turned out to be an isolated mysterious occurrence and he soon recovered again. But it left me feeling that I never wanted to leave the children again, not even for a few minutes.

The intensity of the bombardment continued and the PRCS considered it necessary to move us again. They had been converting the Triumph Hotel in West Beirut into a temporary hospital and decided to take us there. We were moved during the night in a PRCS ambulance, together with an elderly man who had been wounded and his wife. The experience was like being in a movie. We travelled quickly through the night with the headlights off – except when the driver flashed them quickly to check the road ahead, which was badly damaged from bombing. It was obviously risky to be on the road, but we arrived safely at the hotel and Nour, Hamoudi and I were allocated a large bed. The PRCS group of eight orphan toddlers, including Badr, had also been evacuated to the hotel and were in a room near us. It was a relief to see them and know they were safe.

The next day we were moved again, to the converted premises of College Protestant on Ras Beirut. The college was being shared by the Lebanese Red Cross and the PRCS as temporary hospital accommodation. The area was spacious and we were allocated sleeping mats on the floor of a classroom. There was also an open playground for the children. By this time, Ahmed and Abir had returned to my care as their families were living in less safe areas. I brought Dalal back from her school as we were now in a safer situation; and, in any case, I thought it was time she was back with her family. Two boys who had not been able to return south because of the invasion also joined us, as did the orphan toddlers, including Badr. A number of the disabled men from Haifa Rehabilitation Hospital were also brought to College Protestant and were allocated to rooms that were set up as a temporary hospital. I didn't always understand what was happening, but felt confident that arrangements made for the group of children with me would be the best available in such difficult circumstances. I concentrated on dealing with whatever situation we were in, and structuring our days so the children had the care they needed and an opportunity to be involved in as many activities as possible.

Badr was using a baby-walker at this time and was very active, pushing with his good (right) foot and moving in every direction. We placed chairs across the doorways to prevent the children going out into the playground after fears there were some live bombs there following a recent attack. Badr delighted in pushing himself to the chairs to try to remove them. When someone chased after him to bring him back, he would chuckle with glee and push himself back into the room away from his 'rescuer'.

It was a very demanding time for me as I was responsible for supervising the preparation of breakfast for everyone. This meant getting up at 5 am, organising Dalal and Hamoudi to come with me, and getting the nurse to check that the three wheelchair-users and the other two boys were okay. Water was a problem, especially as I needed to wash the children's clothing frequently; one had a non-disposable colostomy bag that needed to be emptied and cleaned, and often leaked onto clothing, which then needed special cleaning. Life was very basic and very tough, but we managed like this for many weeks.

The children had lovely singing voices and liked to sing as a group with one of the men, who played a lute. When visitors came, the group loved to perform for them.

Abir, who was about fourteen and spoke very good English, translated for me when needed. One day Dalal said to me, 'What would you do if Abir was not here to translate?' I knew very well that she wanted me to suggest she could translate, as her English was quite good even then. Her whole little body was poised with anticipation for my answer.

I decided to tease a little and said, 'Oh, that would certainly be a problem. I can't imagine what I would do. Who could possibly help me?'

After a brief pause, Dalal could no longer contain herself. 'What about me!'

'Oh,' I said, 'what a good idea. I didn't even think about that.' And then I gave her a hug.

Dr Fathi, Hadla and other PRCS officials came regularly to check that we were all right. Hadla even organised to send some sheets to use on the mats that Dalal, Hamoudi and I slept on. These visits were so important during such a difficult time and contributed to everyone's morale. I greatly appreciated this care, realising the extent of work and stress these people were experiencing themselves. In addition to checking on us, they were working with the main PRCS temporary hospital in an underground location in the centre of the city, the emergency services and following up on people's needs.

The children were very good and helped where they could and kept busy together. Sometimes we had upsets and disagreements as is to be expected in such conditions. I used to tease them sometimes when they complained about the monotony of the food, how little there was to eat, or asked for food or other items it was impossible to obtain. They wanted more water; and when we were able to get more, they thought we should have a refrigerator, and so on. I tried to help them understand that we had to be realistic about our situation and that we were far better off than many other people. I even suggested they should go out and join some of the queues of people trying to find food and other essential items for their families. These little upsets were few and far between, however, and the strong bonds between all in the group overrode any problems.

As we had been moved in such a hurry I had no change of clothing, and no way of having a shower. At one stage, a friend lent me a pair of jeans and a top for a couple of days so that I could wash my clothes. I looked funny in the clothes as she was bigger than me, but I found a piece of rope to tie around the waist to keep the jeans up. Later, another friend brought me a long skirt and top and a *hatta* (the black and white checked scarf identified as a Palestinian symbol), which proved to be very helpful indeed.

Some volunteer helpers at College Protestant invited me to visit them for a meal and to have a shower. I refused, as the situation was too insecure and I didn't want to leave the children. After some weeks though, things became quieter and I decided it would be possible. As I stepped out of the elevator into their apartment, I just froze. I felt completely out of place – I had an image of myself as Eliza

66

Doolittle in the musical *My Fair Lady*. I had got used to not washing, and wearing the same clothes for some weeks, but suddenly I was in a normal situation again and it felt like luxury plus. The joy of a hot shower followed by a wonderful home-cooked meal was out of this world. Great as it was to have this break, however, part of me was nervous at being away from the children, although it was only an hour or two at the most. I soon returned and all was well.

During the period at College Protestant, Nour became very ill with a urinary tract infection and needed to be transferred to a local hospital. I went in the ambulance with him and saw him settled in. I was told the hospital was an even safer place and he would be okay.

That night there was a very heavy bombardment on Beirut and great panic. We had evacuated the classroom some days earlier – I had run through the night with Hamoudi under one arm and Dalal under the other, calling a nurse to assist with the children in wheelchairs. We had settled into a space under the stairs, away from the general traffic of staff and others through the college. The corridor was full of patients on mattresses – it was safer there than in the rooms above ground. During the strong bombardment, the building's high windows smashed and glass rained down. There was absolute panic as people tried to break down the door of the storeroom at the end of the passageway, thinking it would be a safer area. The children under the stairs with me were crying. I held Hamoudi and Dalal, trying to comfort them. Ahmed crawled over to be closer to me. Abir was sitting on her mattress at the edge of our area. I was worried about her in all of this panic, but couldn't move towards her because of the other children. I called out to a nurse to comfort her and to check on her. Abir heard me and called out, 'Don't worry about me, Jean. I am all right.' The strength and courage in that statement amazed me.

I felt glad that Nour was in a safer place and not having to deal with the bombardment. He was always especially frightened when there was bombing. The next day I was horrified when I heard that the hospital where he was had actually been hit by a bomb and all of the patients had been evacuated. Was Nour okay? Where was he now? I had to search for him, but I didn't like leaving the other children alone. The PRCS arranged a ride for me in one of the ambulances that was taking staff to check on other patients. Eventually I discovered that Nour had been taken to a French hospital in the centre of the city. It was overcrowded and understaffed so I decided it would be best to take him back with me to the PRCS temporary hospital.

It was great to have Nour with us again, and fortunately he made progress with his treatment. We remained living under the staircase, with his infusion hooked up to the stair rail, for more than a week. There was just enough space to fit in five mats for the children to lie on (I slept on the join of Hamoudi's and Dalal's mats), and we stacked some cartons against the inner wall to hold our few possessions. Fortunately, the toddlers – Badr with them – had been moved some days previously to the International College of the American University of Beirut, which was in a safer area.

Whenever a child was brought to the PRCS temporary hospital, they were placed under my care. Ali was one such child who joined us at College Protestant. He wasn't disabled but had been wounded from Israeli shelling. He had been in Gaza Hospital in Sabra refugee camp at the time of the invasion and had been ready to return home, but as his home was in the south, he was completely cut off by the invading army. He had recovered from his wounds and was restless, so sometimes he was naughty and a bit tricky to handle. Generally, though, he was a really nice kid and helpful with the children in wheelchairs.

When there was a lull in the bombing, the PRCS advised me that they were taking a car into Burj Al-Barajneh camp, to Haifa Rehabilitation Hospital, in order to get some important equipment and supplies. They asked if I needed anything for the children. I did need more of their clothes, disposable nappies and sundry other items, so decided to go along. It was a weird feeling travelling between the large dirt embankments beyond the frontline of the battle. Everything was eerily quiet – the strange atmosphere of a war taking a rest.

Once we arrived at the hospital we hurried to gather as many things as quickly as possible so we wouldn't get caught in any renewed fighting. One of the men helped me carry items I needed for the children. I went into my room to see if there was anything I should take for myself and he noticed photographs on the shelf. 'Take those with you,' he said.

'But I have nowhere to put them,' I replied.

He didn't argue further, just picked up the photos, and so I took some others, too, which were collected in an album. I will be forever grateful to that man. When I returned to my room after the war, all that was left was a black shell – it had been gutted by a fire bomb and all my possessions destroyed.

The situation worsened, and it was decided to move us to the International College in a room adjacent to where Badr and the other toddlers were living. The electricity was cut off, water was in short supply, and the siege on Beirut was at a very serious stage. These factors, combined with the heat of summer, resulted in dangerous situations for older people and babies in particular. A women's march was organised to protest the siege and to call on the international community to put pressure on Israel to recognise the inhumanity of the situation and stop this treatment of innocent people.

The women planned to march to the 'green line' – an area of the city that had been designated as the line of separation between East and West Beirut during the Lebanese civil war. The Christian militia, the Falange, were in control of East Beirut, and they had some links with Israel. West Beirut had a largely Muslim population, but there were also many Christians of different denominations living there. The Palestinian refugee camps were all located in West Beirut. The Israeli invasion had increased the underlying sectarian divisions between the people of Beirut and strengthened the role of the 'green line'.

Lebanese, Palestinian and foreign women took part in the march. Because of the serious situation faced by the people, I thought I should join this strong humanitarian action too and so I organised carers for the children. I made a point of being near the front of the march as I thought there might be photos in the international press; perhaps my family and friends would see me in the photos and know that I was still alive. There had been no way for me to make contact with anyone outside Beirut throughout the invasion.

We were still at the International College on 30 August 1982 when the PLO left Beirut according to the agreements made in relation to a ceasefire. This evacuation took place by sea and land. Ships would take the men to either Athens or Cyprus from where they would be transferred to countries such as Sudan, Yemen, Egypt and Tunisia. Trucks carried other groups of men to Syria, from where they would be transferred.

We didn't see the emotional scenes of the departure, but we heard people talking about the occasion. Abir's entire family were leaving Lebanon, which was very unsettling for her. Her father was travelling by ship, while her mother had to travel overland with Abir's siblings to Syria. Before leaving, her mother came to see me and asked me to take care of Abir. This was a very emotional moment for me, and I cannot imagine how Abir must have felt. She had no idea where her family might end up, or what kind of future she would have without them.

We watched the ships move out to sea from our vantage point at the International College. Abir knew her father was aboard one of those vessels. Then, before our eyes, the Israeli navy confronted the departing ships. All around us, people feared the worst possible fate for the men on board, who had departed trusting both in their own safety and the safety of their families and others whom they had left behind. Abir became very distressed as she watched the tense scene and thought of her father. I did my best to comfort her. After some hours the problem – whatever it was – was resolved and the ships continued their journey without further interference.

Eventually, we were moved back to the Akka Hospital complex. We were housed in what had been the kindergarten and given mats for sleeping on the floor. At this stage, in addition to Hamoudi and Dalal, our group comprised Abir, Ahmed, Nour and Ali. Once the local people realised we had returned, they brought children to me, asking me to work with them. I remember one little boy in particular: his name was Mohammed and he had a similar type and level of disability to Hamoudi. The two boys seemed to understand they had something in common and obviously enjoyed one another's company. Soon after we returned to the Akka Hospital complex, Ali's family found out where he was and came to take him home. I was grateful, because with the events that followed and Ali's restless and sometimes cheeky ways, I fear he would not have survived.

Things were beginning to feel more secure and I ventured into the town to follow up on some information about Arabic language classes. I was planning another trip into town when suddenly we heard loud explosions that seemed to be very near the hospital. There was an overwhelming sensation of fear that a new invasion was about to take place. Eventually we heard that the Israeli army was working with the Lebanese army to clear the mines that the Israelis had laid on the main north–south road. In spite of this partial reassurance, we were still worried, wondering what the whole action really meant.

On Wednesday 15 September 1982, just one week after the mine-clearing exercise, the President of Lebanon, Bashir Gemayel, was assassinated. Initial news broadcasts indicated that he was injured but alive; about 5 am the next day it was announced that he was dead. Immediately, Israeli war planes came over Beirut, flying low in a frightening and threatening manner. The children panicked. They had experienced too much of war. Ahmed dragged himself across the floor to the steps, trying to get downstairs to a safer place. He was too scared to wait for assistance.

I persuaded them to stay where we were for the moment, and looked out the windows at the line of Israeli tanks and soldiers as they entered the area. I thought the Israeli army must have maintained a military base nearby to have appeared so suddenly. Throughout the earlier invasion, the Palestinian refugee camps had been one of the Israelis' main targets. Now they entered the Chatila and Sabra camps again. People from the camps – mainly women and children and some older men – stood on the roadside gazing at this spectacle. There was an eerie quiet, shattered only by the metallic clanging of the tanks. What was happening? the people must have wondered. What does this mean? Later in the day, the Israeli army withdrew and was replaced by Lebanese soldiers. We heard that the high building on the hill at the end of the road that overlooked the Sabra and Chatila camps was occupied by the Israeli army. Another across the street was occupied by Lebanese soldiers. Tension was rising, creating an atmosphere of uncertainty and danger.

Once again the whole area became very unsafe, with shelling, shooting and fires everywhere. I thought the area was being burnt out. We moved the children down to the underground section of the hospital again, and set up in one room. In the room next to us were babies and toddlers who had been brought down from the Naserah Children's Hospital. There were some nurses with them – including an Australian nurse, Mary Bowring. There were still some patients above ground, in the hospital, with both local and foreign staff looking after them. We all wondered what was happening. When the PLO departed, they were promised that the people left behind – mostly women, children and the elderly – would be protected and kept safe.

The Egyptian husband of a Finnish nurse went out of the building to see what was going on. He was killed by sniper fire and there was great difficulty in recovering his body.

At one point during a lull in the shelling, I crossed the compound to the kindergarten to get some of the children's things. Suddenly, intense shelling and shooting broke out again. I had no option but to crouch in the farthest corner of the room away from the windows until it stopped. I have no idea how long I was there; all I remember is the noise all around me and my fear. When it went quiet, I picked up the things I had collected and ran at great speed down the steps, across the compound and back to the children. 'No one,' I told them, 'is to go back up to the kindergarten again.' I don't know who I was talking to, as I was the only person physically capable of moving around freely.

We began to hear terrible stories about what was happening in the camps across the street. In the dark, we could see flares lighting up the sky above the camps. A group of women with a white flag walked up the hill to plead with the Israeli army to stop the killing in the camps. That same night, many people came into the underground area of the hospital. There was a continuous flow of frightened people with terrifying tales. The atmosphere was extremely tense and heavy with fear. Stuck as I was in the confines of the hospital, it was difficult to comprehend the magnitude of the horrors they were talking about.

With us that evening was Um Samir, a woman who had worked at Haifa Rehabilitation Hospital, assisting with the children, prior to the invasion. Now we were back in the area, she and a couple of others had come to assist again. Because of the deterioration of the situation she hadn't been able to get back to her home in Burj Al-Barajneh camp that day. Very early in the morning of Friday 17 September, there was a great deal of movement: the people who had come into the hospital during the night were leaving. Um Samir told me she had to leave too, and that I should also go. I explained there was no way that I could leave the children. I tried to assure her that the children and I would be okay, but that she must go. I don't know on what basis I was claiming that all would be fine; everything around us looked impossible. I can still see Um Samir as she left that morning. She was a stout middle-aged woman and she had her few belongings tied into a small scarf, which she held at her side as she walked away. She was with the last people to leave, and she kept turning to look back at us. I never saw Um Samir again, but hoped and prayed that she was safe.

Representatives of the International Committee of the Red Cross (ICRC) came to us that Friday morning. They said that the Israeli army wouldn't permit them to take us out, but they had been given permission to ask who we were and whether we had food, medicines, etc. They said they had been trying to get in to us for a couple of days but were prevented by the Israeli soldiers.

Soon after, the two Palestinian doctors on duty in the hospital came to me and explained that they were trying to organise for the children to be evacuated. I found it difficult to believe such an idea could be possible; all I could see outside were burning buildings.

Not long after this discussion, I heard footsteps and the voices of many people. I looked towards the window that opened onto the passageway and saw the two doctors walk past. They had their hands above their heads and a soldier walked behind each of them, pressing a gun into their backs. These two doctors were not seen alive again. Two Palestinian nurses were taken at the same time; one was raped and killed.

There was a mass of people and shouting. Soldiers came into our room and, with a wave of their guns, demanded that we go up to the ground floor. I helped the three children in wheelchairs to organise themselves, and attended to Hamoudi and Dalal. I placed Hamoudi in his stroller and Dalal walked behind the stroller in front of me. We moved out as demanded, but when we arrived at the foot of the steps I gestured to the soldiers, saying 'Keif?' (how?) After going through this performance – a gun gesture to get up the steps and my gesture asking how – a few times, the soldiers left us at the bottom of the steps. 'What are they doing here?' they asked me, indicating the children. I reminded them that we were in a hospital.

The soldiers covered us with their guns at all times, even doing a dramatic turn to maintain cover as they ascended or descended the stairs. It was just like watching an old, very bad film. Hamoudi, who always enjoys a situation that is unusual or seems silly, began to laugh. I was afraid this would make the soldiers angry and perhaps they would attack us. Fortunately, this didn't happen.

Dalal, who loves to sing, was reminded by the other children that she must not sing any of their nationalistic songs. If she must sing, she was to sing a song she'd learnt at the Christian school for blind children. True to form, Dalal began to sing one of her school songs: 'This is the day that the Lord hath made'.

'Where are the soldiers? Where are the guns?' the soldiers kept demanding. We answered that this was a hospital and there were no soldiers or guns. We were then told there would be explosions as they intended to blast open locked doors on the ground floor – doors that led to the hospital pantry and storerooms. As we knew, there were no soldiers hiding in those rooms. There were no guns.

During this situation – which went on for an hour or so – a group from the Norwegian Embassy was allowed into the hospital to take out any Norwegian volunteers. They were also able to take with them the small children and babies who had been patients in the Naserah Children's Hospital. However, there was one small child who was very ill and on infusion, whom they couldn't take because of lack of space. Mary, the Australian nurse who had been working in the children's hospital, stayed with the child and they became part of our group.

Eventually, the soldiers carried the children and their wheelchairs up to the ground floor. We gathered there in a small cluster, wondering what was going on, what would happen to us. Some men arrived and told us they belonged to the Lebanese political organisation Amal, and that they had an ambulance to take us to safety. I was very wary of them, fearing it was some kind of trap. Abir seemed to think the offer was genuine, and said that people from that organisation had lived near her family and it would be all right. However, they returned and told us their ambulance had been stolen by the soldiers so they couldn't take us away after all. They promised to try to get back for us.

We needed some of the children's belongings. Mary volunteered to go down to the room to get them, with permission from the soldiers guarding us. She returned quickly saying that everything was in darkness downstairs and the soldiers were troublesome. We decided that no one should go down again. Some of the soldiers near us were beginning to show an interest in fourteen-year-old Abir. I was feeling very nervous about the situation as the day drew on and nightfall approached.

Fortunately, before darkness fell, an ICRC convoy managed to get through to us. They had already evacuated patients and staff from the PRCS Gaza Hospital in Sabra camp, and now collected us, along with the few patients left in the hospital and some foreign volunteer nursing staff. The long convoy weaved its way out of the burning area. When we arrived at the Israeli checkpoint into the main part of Beirut we were forced to turn back. We eventually managed to enter the city at a different checkpoint and were taken to a building with garage space underground that had been converted into a temporary hospital. Preparation was made to take in the patients, but all foreigners were told to go to ICRC headquarters. I refused, explaining that I was responsible for the children and they could not be left alone. Mary said she would stay with me too, as the baby needed special nursing care. Eventually it was agreed that we could stay and that ICRC staff would come the next day to obtain details about us.

We were given a small area for the five children with me, plus the baby with Mary, and two injured boys who were patients from Gaza Hospital. Mary and I set up the space in the best way for us.

We agreed that we would take shifts to cover supervision of the children and their needs, and organised our schedule so that Mary would be on at the times when the baby required nursing treatment. Once all that was organised, Mary slept and I took the first shift. Some hours later, I woke Mary as it was time for the baby to receive his treatment. I started to settle to sleep, but the baby was crying and Mary couldn't manage alone. I cradled the baby, singing to him to soothe him, and together we tried to quiet him. This all took some time and soon it was morning and time to organise food for the children. It wasn't until later in the morning that I could catch some sleep, and I just crashed.

The De Smidt family from Dalal's school came to check she was safe, and although I sat up to greet them, I was so exhausted that it was only later that I realised they had been there at all. Many people streamed through this temporary PRCS hospital, some with photographs asking if we had seen the people in them. They were seeking family and friends who had disappeared during the attacks on Chatila and Sabra in which hundreds of Palestinian refugees were killed. We had heard various accounts of the horrors of the massacre carried out in the refugee camps, and the looks on the faces of those seeking to find relatives reflected the trauma they had faced.

Life in the temporary hospital was very basic, but at least we were safe. Nour became very distressed when nurses from the main section wanted to borrow his wheelchair to transport an older patient to the toilet area. The boys' wheelchairs often got damaged when they were borrowed, and the loss of a chair meant being confined to bed until it was repaired. There were so many needs and so many problems, but usually a solution of sorts was found.

The situation became extremely tense again when the Israeli army entered Beirut. We had to make sure that the children who could move independently didn't wander up to the footpath. We had all enjoyed the respite of being able to go into the sunlight for a period each day, but now it was too dangerous. The drabness of our surroundings and these restrictions made it very difficult to create positive experiences for the children.

Several people came to see me, concerned about my safety. All other foreign volunteers who were working with the Palestinians during this time were associated with a particular international or national organisation. I was linked to the Palestine Red Crescent Society only, and it was in a very difficult situation. There had been pressure for some time to force the closure of its programs and facilities, and some local staff had disappeared. Others were known to have been in prison since the invasion. People from Oxfam UK, Mid-East Council of Churches, and Save the Children UK all suggested that I be listed as part of their organisation. I was deeply moved by these suggestions and appreciated the concern they showed, but I intended to remain an independent volunteer with the PRCS as long as was possible. If, however, the situation became such that I needed an alliance with an international organisation, I would be grateful to accept such offers – on one condition. I could only accept such protection if it included Hamoudi and Dalal. My visitors thought this could be arranged. Fortunately, the situation never reached that stage.

During this very dangerous period we also had a visit from Hadla Ayoubi, Um Walid and others from the PRCS. They, as leaders of the PRCS, were in a very vulnerable position and were living under the protection of the ICRC at the ICRC headquarters. I was both surprised and grateful for the visit. They were very distressed at having to hide in such a way, but it was evident that they were also concerned about us and the patients from the hospitals – so much so that they were visiting us at great risk to themselves. Hadla explained that the PRCS could not overtly assist in any way. She gave me some money to cover Hamoudi's and Dalal's needs and advised me to take them with me to the Mayflower Hotel in West Beirut when it became possible. By this stage, families of the other children had come looking for the other children and had taken them home. The sick baby was moved to another temporary hospital and Mary went with him.

The situation for the PRCS continued to be difficult for some time. In spite of the promises made to the PLO before their soldiers were evacuated from Lebanon, the tragedy of the Chatila and Sabra massacres followed their departure, and there seemed to be an ongoing campaign against any existing infrastructure related to the PLO. The earlier incursion of Israeli soldiers had created a great deal of damage to some of the PLO offices, such as information and cultural affairs. The PRCS was a division of the PLO and its mission was humanitarian, providing health and social services for Palestinians and many poor Lebanese people. However, it was still a Palestinian organisation, and Lebanon at the time seemed to be under the control of the Maronite Christian Party (Falange) together with the Israelis and a southern Christian militia which worked directly with the Israeli army, all of whom were against any Palestinian presence in Lebanon.

When we did move to the Mayflower Hotel, it was as if we had stepped into another world. We were very comfortable and felt safe. It was a strange feeling.

The hotel was below the Beirut International Airport flight path, and the airport had just been reopened, so there was often the roar of planes overhead. Hamoudi and Dalal were both now afraid of the sound, and Hamoudi would immediately cry when he heard it. I managed to reduce their fear by playing a game with them. I talked about the planes coming from other countries, and when the noise came Dalal would join me in singing about a country or city the plane was going to or coming from, and Hamoudi would stop crying and join in with his laughter.

I was very anxious to make contact with Clarice and Mum, and asked where I could find a phone with an international line. I was directed to a hotel within walking distance and went to make my call. What a wonderful relief for me and for them to be able to talk and exchange views. They were just so happy that I was safe and told me to take care.

SIX

WHILE WE WERE AT THE MAYFLOWER HOTEL, I received a phone call from the Australian Embassy requesting me to go there to meet with Mr Perry Nolan, the chargé d'affaires. It seemed the embassy had traced me through the ICRC as the result of a query as to my where-abouts by Senator Georges during question time in the Australian Senate. From what I have been told, there was a report in a newspaper that I had been killed during the massacre in the refugee camps. I had no one to stay with Hamoudi and Dalal while I reported to the embassy so I took them with me. I was a little apprehensive about the visit, but I need not have been. Everyone was very friendly, and Perry was keen to know about my situation as well as that of the children and the people around me in general.

Not long afterwards, I received an invitation to attend a luncheon at the Australian Embassy to meet the ambassador to Syria and Lebanon, Mr David Wilson. Luckily, Mary, the Australian nurse, was still in Beirut and I was able to arrange for her to stay with Hamoudi and Dalal while I went to the luncheon. Dressed in some 'new' clothes given to me by a friend (who had apologised for them being second-hand) and clutching my old handbag that had served me so well during the war and the time of the massacre, I headed off to the embassy. There were at least twenty guests, and I soon felt uncom-fortable in my plain clothes alongside the sophisticated women with their smart leather handbags. I consoled myself with the thought that, in the scheme of things, such matters were surely irrelevant. My next hurdle was the luncheon itself. I was seated next to Mr Wilson on one side and the Lebanese Druse leader, Walid Jumblat, on the other. Ambassadors from Canada and Japan were across the table from me. It was so long since I had sat down at a formal meal and I felt somewhat overcome. The next shock was that the waiter came to me first; for some seconds I really had no idea how to respond. However, all turned out well. People around me were keen to make me feel at ease and very interested to know more about the events I had experienced and the situation as I was aware of it at present.

The situation gradually became more stable and we were able to move back to the PRCS complex. Dalal, Hamoudi and I moved into a small apartment in one of the buildings there. Some of the staff I had been training came back to assist me, although it wasn't safe for them to stay late. I became very involved in trying to get the range of rehabilitation services back into working order; this included the main physiotherapy unit at Akka Hospital; the physiotherapy department at Gaza Hospital in Sabra refugee camp; and the activity programs and house visits from Haifa Rehabilitation Hospital in Burj Al-Barajneh refugee camp.

When I first went back into Chatila and Sabra camps, I was almost overcome by the strange quietness in the area. Thoughts of what had taken place there were uppermost in my mind; there was a heavy, eerie atmosphere. Despite all that had happened, the people showed amazing resilience; I was astonished by their friendly openness to me and others as we passed by.

I was at the Akka complex one day when I saw a fleet of ICRC cars preparing to evacuate the PRCS group of toddlers to Syria. Badr was with them, and although I was glad that he and the others were being taken to a safer place, I was sorry that he would be far away from us. I wondered if I would ever see him again.

Even though times were tense, we also had some fun. I often spent time at the damaged Haifa Rehabilitation Hospital, where I was re-establishing day programs and home visits in the refugee camp, and sometimes took Hamoudi with me. On this particular day, I was walking back to the Akka complex with Hamoudi straddled across my hip. As we reached the main road, an Italian ambulance working with the UN came around the corner. Hamoudi was delighted as he loves cars, and he began to laugh and move up and down in my arms. The ambulance screeched to a stop and a couple of medics jumped out saying they could take me to the American University Hospital. It seemed they thought Hamoudi was having a seizure and they were keen to assist. As I didn't speak Italian and the medics didn't speak English or Arabic it took some time for the actual situation to be understood. Once they realised that there was no problem, that Hamoudi was just a severely disabled boy who loved cars, the whole atmosphere changed from one of concern and confusion to one of play. They urged Hamoudi and me into the ambulance and, to the accompaniment of sirens, flashing lights and much laughter, we raced along the main road to Akka Hospital.

The arrival of the Italian ambulance at the hospital caused some concern for the people at the entrance, but their worries quickly dissolved when the doors opened and I descended with Hamoudi in my arms, clearly overjoyed by the experience. I thanked the medics and they drove off with a big wave for Hamoudi.

I was in the PRCS physiotherapy department in Akka Hospital, involved in a program with a small cerebral-palsied child, when suddenly a group of people ran into the centre amid much confusion and noise carrying a young woman who was obviously in distress.

The girl, Khadija, and her family had been relaxing on the beach some weeks earlier during a lull in the frequent shooting associated with the Lebanese civil war. Unexpectedly, militia opened fire on the people on the beach. Khadija was shot in the head and was now hemiplegic, unable to walk, unable to speak, and disoriented and confused. She was about sixteen years old.

It was obvious that it was a major family project to bring Khadija to the centre. Her mother and sister were with her, and her brother had taken the day off work and arranged for a friend with a car to drive them all. On questioning the family I found that they lived in the Lebanese refugee camp, Shiijah, just across the road from the Akka Hospital. I made a general assessment of Khadija's needs and advised that I could come to their home the next day, instead of them bringing her to the centre again.

Khadija needed a wide range of treatment, from physiotherapy to occupational therapy, speech therapy and psychological help. These were skills way beyond the capacity of the small group of assistant physiotherapists with whom I worked, young people who had received only very basic training.

I was very conscious of my own limits too, but as there was nobody with the skills Khadija and her family needed, I felt I should do my best to help. I spent that evening searching through the few books and papers I had with me, and thought a great deal about my professional colleagues and friends in Australia who could have helped.

I began visiting Khadija each day. The family was from the south of Lebanon, but had been forced to leave because of the dangers associated with the frequent Israeli air raids there. Their house in the refugee camp was extremely basic, with a dirt floor and a tin roof. Khadija's old father was blind and her mother had sight in one eye only. One of her sisters and her family lived close by and she obviously took care of her parents and wounded sister. They were a delightful family and I enjoyed spending time with them. It was sad to see the problems they were experiencing and I felt very inadequate about the limited support I could offer.

Khadija obviously enjoyed my visits, however, and she soon made progress. I used what was available in terms of the sparse furniture, window bars, etc, as equipment for exercises; and once I took along a bag of bean seeds and asked the family to place them into a bowl for Khadija to move around with her fingers. Some days later I asked for the beans as I wanted to see how Khadija was managing. There was silence. The family had cooked and eaten them.

As Khadija was able to move around more, I encouraged her to take care of her personal appearance and to assist her mother in small ways. She was severely affected by her injury and needed so much help in so very many dimensions that it was a huge achievement for her to do anything for herself or for others. I had been able to get a wheelchair for her and felt that the time had come for me to reduce the number of days I went to the house and to have her come to the centre some days. It was important that she didn't become too dependent on me. I spoke to the staff in the physiotherapy department about Khadija, but was taken aback by their lack of enthusiasm in becoming involved. I felt a little angry and thought that they were being lazy. Fortunately, I soon became aware that the situation was much more complicated. The staff weren't qualified to deal with a disabled person – they had undertaken various short training courses for specific routine-type work – and they were afraid. This was an important lesson for me. I took the time to explain that only very simple activities were needed, all within their capabilities, and that the most important thing was to give Khadija and her family moral support and to encourage Khadija to be more active and aware.

There were other lessons I learned while working with Khadija. One day when I was in their home, Israeli war planes flew low overhead. When they'd passed, we went outside to see what was happening. Suddenly the planes returned with a threatening roar and we ran back into the house. I couldn't help but laugh at myself as I ran. What protection would this little shack give if the plane dropped a bomb?

On another occasion, Khadija, her sister and her mother were at the centre for Khadija's program when there was a roar of war planes coming in low and the accompanying loud explosions of bombs falling. There was absolute panic as people ran from the centre to find safer underground areas. My instinct was to run too, and I indicated to Khadija's sister that we needed to get to a safer place. She and her mother just looked at me and shrugged their shoulders. Obviously it would be difficult to move Khadija, but their lack of interest seemed more a matter of tiredness from the constant fleeing to survive. 'How can we manage to go anywhere?' they said. 'If we get hit, we get hit. God willing (*Inshallah*) we will be okay.' They were perfectly calm and resigned, whereas I was afraid and wanted to go to a safer place. There was no way I could leave these people though; I had been working with them and felt responsible for them. So we waited it out. And although I felt scared, I gradually experienced a strange calm in spite of the commotion all around. I gained a new strength from these people and their state of mind in the face of danger.

By April 1983 the situation in Beirut was very unstable. On one occasion I was in a shop in the Humra area when there was a huge explosion several blocks away: an attempted assassination of the Druse leader, Walid Jumblat. Car bombs were becoming a frequent occurrence, and walking past parked cars was an unnerving experience. Palestinians were 'disappearing'; people in the camps were being harassed; efforts continued to dismantle the PRCS. The PRCS was prevented from obtaining work permits for foreign volunteers, and without work permits visas were not possible. This situation forced volunteers to leave at a time when special assistance was particularly needed.

The PRCS had, however, managed to obtain a legal work permit for me. On the morning of Wednesday, 6 April, I went by taxi to collect my visa. Before setting out I had organised staff to stay with Dalal and Hamoudi, and arranged that Dalal be ready to go shopping for new clothes as soon as I returned. She was excited about the outing and I left early, expecting to return very quickly to make the most of our shopping time.

I was relaxed as I waited at the visa office for my passport, with the work permit, to be returned because I knew everything was in order. My feeling soon changed to one of anxiety when the officer asked me to go to an adjacent room as there was something 'not complete with my papers'.

After some time another officer came in and asked me to sign a paper. I had no idea what was on the paper – my ability to read Arabic at that stage was extremely limited. He told me that it was just the information I had given him when he asked about my name, work, etc. Unfortunately I didn't think quickly enough to include a statement with my signature that I didn't understand the document I was signing.

Another lengthy wait. I got permission to go out (under guard) to the taxi waiting for me to tell him not to wait any longer. I also asked him to tell the PRCS that I was in trouble. I was feeling increasingly worried and didn't know what was going to happen to me. I was even more worried about Hamoudi and Dalal as I knew that the staff with them would need to leave by 5 pm as the situation for Palestinians was still very insecure and dangerous.

At about 11 am I was told to go down to a waiting car to be taken to the General Security building in central Beirut. On arrival, my name was entered into a book and then I was taken across the corridor and locked in a room with about forty other people of different nationalities, all men except for two women – one Asian and the other Arab. I wasn't questioned, and my request for contact with the Australian Embassy was ignored.

I was only in this situation for about eleven hours, but for me it was a major study of human behaviour. The over-riding atmosphere in the room was one of caring and concern. One of the men – I think he was from Ghana – spoke good English; he could see that I was worried and tried to encourage me to be strong. He had been there for a couple of weeks and the guards would not make contact with his embassy. A little later when guards opened the door for a person to come in with sandwiches and drinks, I refused to buy anything – I was worried and angry and had no interest in food. My Ghanaian friend intervened, telling me that I must eat to keep strong. A group of men, I think Pakistani, sitting along the far wall also refused to buy anything. Several others were concerned about them and offered to buy items for them. It turned out they wanted to go to the toilet and were afraid to take in any food or drinks.

The guards behaved very cruelly towards a man who was obviously mentally disturbed. The man was sitting on the floor, and as a guard waited for the sandwiches and drinks to be sold he trod with his boots on the man's bare feet. The man said that he wanted to go to the toilet. The guard laughed at him, verbally abused him and hit him. The sandwich seller and guards left, closing the door. The man went berserk, throwing himself around in the limited space, and then urinated over the door. This brought the guards back into the room and they dragged the man out. I never found out what happened to him. The rest of us were taken out of the room while it was cleaned, and finally were allowed access to toilets, under escort. I elected to go to the toilet, and one of the women came with me because she said she wouldn't leave me alone with a guard.

Some time later I was taken to a different area for questioning. En route I saw in the far distance an Irish nurse I knew. I asked the guards for contact with my embassy and said that I was concerned about two disabled children who would have nobody with them after 5 pm. There was no response to this request; nor again when I repeated it at the end of the questioning session.

The questioning itself was somewhat problematic because of language difficulties, but the pattern was roughly as follows:

Officer: Are you a Communist?

Me: No. I do not belong to any political party.

Officer: Are you a socialist?

Me: No. I do not belong to any political party.

Officer: You hate the Israelis.

Me: No, but I do not like what they are doing.

Officer: You hate the Lebanese.

Me: No, I work with many Lebanese people.

Officer: What do you think of the PLO?

Me: The PLO is the organisation that represents the Palestinian people.

Officer: You think the Palestinians are in a bad situation right now?

Me: Yes.

Officer: You write Arabic?

Me: I can write my name, the days of the week and a few other words only.

Officer: You spoke to the Australian media last September.

Me: Yes.

Officer: What did you say?

Me: I did not say anything different from what many others have said.

Officer: Who were the soldiers who came into Akka Hospital?

Me: I do not know.

Officer: Did they speak Arabic?

Me: Yes.

Officer: What did they do?

Me: They made us come up to the ground floor. They were going back and forth and they exploded the doors of locked rooms.

Officer: What did you see?

Me: I saw doctors being taken away at gunpoint. Otherwise nothing, as we were kept inside the hospital.

Officer: Where will you go? Which country? Jordan? Egypt?

Me: I wish to stay in Lebanon.

Officer: You must be out of the country within three days.

Me: But why? I can't. Please contact my embassy.

The interview was over and I was escorted back to the room.

Some time later – I think around 5.30 pm – the guard opened the door and there was Jackie McKenna, the Irish nurse I had seen when I was taken for questioning. Jackie, a tall woman with red hair, stood with one foot inside and the other foot outside the room and alternated her gaze between me and the guard. 'What's the matter, Jean?'; then to the guard, 'Don't close the door!' 'What can I do?'; then to the guard, 'Don't close the door!'

'Please,' I said, 'try to contact my embassy, and please try to contact people at PRCS as no one will be with the children after five.'

The encounter was no longer than a few minutes, but it gave me tremendous hope.

The impact of it on the other people in the room was amazing; they were fascinated and so happy for me. They thought Jackie was my sister and that everything would be okay for me. This reaction was very humbling. Some of these people had been locked up for weeks, with no contact with their embassy, no contact with people outside. Some of them were in a terrible situation, and yet they could be happy at the possibility of my being all right, when I had been in the room for only hours.

At about 9 pm a guard called us out of the room and ordered us to form a line for transfer to a prison elsewhere. The men were hand-cuffed but the two other women and I were not. I was called out of the line and escorted to an adjacent room; I had no idea why. I stood in the doorway and saw about six desks, each with a man lounging behind it and looking at me. I didn't know where to look or what to do. The line of people I had been locked in the room with were escorted away. Still no one spoke to me. It was very unnerving. I remained standing in this manner for some time, and then an officer came to escort me across the corridor to another room.

In this room there was a small stage to the left of the doorway that held a large desk. Two official-looking gentlemen sat at it, watching my entrance. On the other side of the room, facing the doorway, was Perry Nolan, Chargé d'Affaires of the Australian Embassy, with his secretary Magda. My relief was beyond description.

Perry was concerned to see that I hadn't been physically abused in any way. Once he was assured that I was okay, he spoke to the officials about obtaining my release. It seemed Perry and Magda had been there for some time trying to see me and to gain my release. The security officials told Perry that I must leave the country by Saturday. They didn't want to release me before then, but Perry insisted, assuring them that he would be responsible for me and that I would leave by Saturday. The officials refused to return my documents to me.

Perry asked why I had been detained and was to be expelled. The reply was: 'Because she has been interfering in the internal politics of the country.' This was quite a statement considering it was very well known that I worked twenty-four hours a day, seven days a week with disabled children and that I had never attended any sort of political meeting. I told Perry that I really needed to check on the children. He told the security officials that I was concerned about the children and that they were in the Akka Hospital complex, to which the officer replied, 'She can go anywhere, but you are fully responsible for her.'

As we left, Perry explained to me that it would be possible to challenge the expulsion, but he advised against it. He said, wisely, that the situation in the country was so very unstable that to pursue the matter could result in greater problems for other people and might mean that I would never be able to return to Lebanon.

I was frantic to get to Hamoudi and Dalal; I didn't know if anyone would be with them. When we arrived we found them in bed, looked after by one of the staff, a young nurse, Mohammed, who had been able to stay with them. The Irish Embassy had informed both the Australian Embassy and the PRCS of my situation, thanks to the chance encounter with Jackie McKenna.

When I entered the flat the children woke immediately and there was general relief and happiness all round. Dalal said, 'It has been a sad day!' Hamoudi was just full of smiles.

When we told them gently that I would have to leave, Dalal began to cry. 'But I thought that the President loved all of the children in Lebanon,' she said, referring to a local television program for children, which we often watched, about the Lebanese President and how he cared for the children in his country.

The following morning I began making plans for Hamoudi and Dalal's care during my absence. That evening, friends came to say goodbye, and one friend brought a suitcase to help me pack the few possessions I had for my enforced journey.

I had been able to organise people to look after Hamoudi and Dalal, but I wondered about Khadija and her family and how they would continue with her rehabilitation. Would they still visit the PRCS physiotherapy department? How much progress would Khadija make? How would the family continue to cope? Many questions. No answers.

On Saturday, 9 April 1983, Doug Wright, the Australian consul, took me to the special security office at the airport. One of the officers escorted me through procedures at the airport and saw me aboard a flight to London. I called Clarice, Alan and Mum from the airport to say that I was on my way and that I would explain my unexpected arrival when I saw them.

The events that followed were like something out of a novel. There were many telephone calls from the media in Australia and some of their correspondents in the UK. I answered questions on the phone, and agreed to give an interview in London. I also received a call from the office of the Australian Foreign Minister, Bill Hayden. The secretary explained that Mr Hayden had wanted to phone himself but was very busy and didn't want the call delayed. His message was: 'Firstly, are you okay? Secondly, tell me what happened.' I was very moved by this level of concern.

Dr Fathi Arafat, President of the PRCS, contacted me from the new PRCS headquarters in Cairo, where the organisation had moved at the time of the evacuation from Lebanon of the PLO. He was keen for me to continue my work with PRCS, and I was keen to stay. We were both very worried about the situation in Lebanon in general, and particularly about the welfare of Dalal and Hamoudi. Dr Fathi asked me to go to Cairo to discuss the most appropriate place for me to continue my work in developing services for disabled children. There was a great need for such work in Cairo and in Syria, he told me, both places where the PRCS had hospitals and a range of health and social services and programs.

I explained to Dr Fathi that it was very important that I travel to Australia first, because of the support the government had given me and because of the media attention. I felt I needed to be on the spot; to thank people, but also to show my legal documents and to directly counter some of the statements that had been made that questioned my integrity in relation to my work and my presence in Lebanon. Some people had claimed that I had entered Lebanon illegally; others that I wasn't really working with disabled children but rather wandering around the country to no good purpose. We agreed that I would meet with him again in Cairo in about a month's time.

I left Cairo on the Sunday and was scheduled to arrive in Sydney on Tuesday, with a stopover in Dubai. Our flight was delayed so long that when we finally took off we were advised that we would be stopping in Karachi instead of Dubai and then Singapore. We had to spend a day and a night in Karachi before it was possible to fly to Singapore. I asked the airline office to make contact with the air company in Sydney, but they didn't and I had no other way of contacting anyone. This gave the media more material for speculation: 'Calder missing' was apparently a headline in one of the papers.

By the time we arrived in Singapore, I had missed my flight to Sydney and had to wait a further night and a day in Singapore. At last I boarded the plane to Sydney. As is my custom, I settled down to sleep during the night. When I woke in the morning it was to an announcement from the cockpit: 'Due to heavy fog along the eastern coast of Australia it has not been possible to land, so we have turned back north and will land in Darwin.' Darwin? I thought. That's nearly back to Singapore! We spent some time on the ground in Darwin before the flight continued. We weren't long back in the air when there was another announcement from the cockpit: 'Because we have been so delayed, the plane will fly to Melbourne first and then go on to Sydney.'

It was a Thursday evening when I finally arrived in Sydney. I heard later that at 6 am Tuesday – my expected arrival time – there had been a large group waiting to welcome me, including press. On Wednesday and Thursday mornings, the group waited again, the numbers decreasing each day. By Thursday evening, the group was much smaller, but still included some press.

The days that followed were hectic: press, radio and TV interviews and some speaking engagements. I went to Canberra and was able to meet people at the Foreign Minister's office to express my thanks, show my legal documents and provide further information on the situation. In Melbourne I met with people from the Australian Council of Churches (ACC) who had been supportive of me following the violent massacre at Chatila and Sabra and during my expulsion period. Greg Thompson of ACC accompanied me to meet the

Lebanese consul, who was very understanding of the situation and keen to assure me that such unfortunate occurrences were a result of the civil war and the Israeli invasion of Lebanon. He knew of my work and hoped that some day I would be able to return to Lebanon.

In Sydney I met with Bishop Gabriel Gilbran, then President of the ACC and originally from Lebanon. He was anxious to discuss the details of my situation and those of the people around me in Beirut at the time that I left. He said there were some articles appearing in the Arabic-language newspapers making false claims about my activity in Lebanon, and that he wanted to correct the untruths so that people of Lebanese origin who read these newspapers would receive accurate information about me.

I was also able to spend some time with relatives and friends, which was wondeful, and flew up to Mackay for a weekend to visit family there. This reconnection with family and friends was important to me. Their support, and the familiarity of home territory, helped me put my recent experiences into perspective and gave me the additional strength I needed to continue on my chosen path.

When I left Australia I flew to the UK in order to spend another week with Mum, Clarice and Alan. Then I set off for Cairo and my meeting with Dr Fathi. I was ready to return to my work with the PRCS, and to find a way to bring Hamoudi and Dalal out of Lebanon to live with me in Cairo.

SEVEN

I ARRIVED IN CAIRO IN JUNE 1983, to work once again with the PRCS
to develop services for children and adults with disability. Much had
changed after the evacuation of the PLO from Lebanon in 1982; its
headquarters were now based in Tunis. The PRCS had also suffered
during the war in Lebanon, and had established new headquarters
in Cairo in the Palestine Hospital in the suburb of Heliopolis. The
PRCS had run some small clinics in Egypt for many years, serving
Palestinians who were living there, but open to anyone seeking help.
Although there were no Palestinian refugee camps in Egypt, there
were many Palestinian refugees – part of the Palestinian diaspora –
living in different parts of the country. For many, the PRCS was a
link with their identity and an opportunity to contribute towards a
future Palestine. For Egyptians and other nationals, it was a means
of sharing in the efforts of the PRCS to serve Palestinians, Egyptians
and others in need. At the time I arrived, the PRCS was extending
and upgrading Palestine Hospital; eventually it had seven floors –
clinics and offices on the lower floors; four floors of hospital, including
a geriatric unit; guest accommodation on the fifth floor; and an
educational and cultural centre on the sixth and seventh floors. In
other locations were a kindergarten, a nursing school, a heritage
centre, and later the Ain Shams Rehabilitation Centre, as well as several
small clinics in other areas.

Cairo, the capital of Egypt, with a population of more than 16 million people, is a city bursting with people and traffic, day and night. It is a city of incredible complexity and contrast, combining a great heritage with the latest technology; absolute wealth sits alongside absolute poverty. The colour of the desert is reflected in the light brown colour of most of the buildings, and the desert dust encroaches on the city, even coating the leaves of the trees. It bothered me at first to have to blow the dust off my purchases from the small store near the PRCS guesthouse where I was living, but, like everyone else, I soon became used to this endless dust invasion.

The heavy traffic in Cairo is notorious for its lack of rules. When driving I discovered a system in the seeming lack of it: I had to expect anything at any time, drive with caution, and cope with whatever happened. Whenever I needed to drive across a very busy intersection, I tried to tuck in beside a bus or truck – any vehicle big enough to bring the cross traffic to a halt. On one occasion I saw a donkey cart push into the traffic with great authority and confidence, and so drove out alongside it, amused at the picture of my modern car being protected by the old-fashioned cart. I always wanted to look away, however, when I saw entire families on a motorbike, zigzagging between the cars with children perched front and back and not one of them wearing a crash helmet.

The people of Cairo are special – fun-loving and friendly in a non-intrusive way. I was often invited to attend weddings and feast day celebrations, and decided that the Egyptian people took their celebrations seriously – everyone participates and the aim is to have fun. Each time I left the country and returned, I had the very warm feeling of returning to a place where I felt at home. I also felt safe in Cairo, which was in sharp contrast to the underlying tension and sometimes fear I'd experienced when living in Beirut – although my desire to return to Beirut remained strong. I longed to return to my work there, and of course I worried a great deal about Hamoudi and Dalal. From time to time, I was able to get some general information about the children via the PRCS, and several times I was able to speak to Dalal briefly by telephone when she was at her school. It was contact, but without any details about their living conditions.

Two very different but equally strong feelings overwhelmed me during this period in Cairo. One was a feeling of love for people in general and the accompanying need to contribute to the improvement of life of those in difficult situations. The feeling was all the more powerful because I felt I was in a situation where I was unable to fulfil such a role. I found it frustrating to be working and living in an affluent area after my experiences in Lebanon, where the conditions were very basic but I'd felt I was helping those truly in need. It was difficult to deal with, and there were very few people I could talk to about it. It seemed foolish to have such a depth of feeling; to feel so impotent in terms of contributing to a better world.

The other strong emotion that I experienced soon after arriving in Cairo was an overwhelming feeling of anger. Anger at all that had occurred in Lebanon during the war, during the massacre; anger at the condition of war in general; anger at being expelled from the country, linked with fear for the safety of the children. I'd never experienced such anger before – or since – and while it only lasted for minutes, it took me longer to recover from the confusion such feelings caused in me. I think that when I was dealing with the range of traumatic events in Beirut, I was too busy, too involved in the 'now' of survival, to fully experience the emotions. It was only after I had left the scene, when I was living in more comfort, that I had time to reflect on the events, and all of the buried emotion surfaced.

The past returned in other ways too. I had the opportunity to attend Arabic language classes in Cairo, and one evening we were all intent on the lesson when a sudden gust of wind caused the classroom door to shut with a loud bang. I think I lifted six inches off my chair, scattering books and pens across the floor. I was very surprised at my reaction and somewhat embarrassed by the confusion I caused. Fortunately my teacher and fellow students were aware of my recent arrival from Beirut and expressed support and sympathy for me – '*Maskeen ya* Jean'.

Dr Fathi, knowing my interest in working in disadvantaged areas, took me to visit the small PRCS clinic in Ain Shams, a crowded, noisy, poorer suburb of Cairo. I set up a service for disabled children there, using a small room in the clinic furnished with an old desk and a broken bench, and I bought some educational toys and simple equipment. I began working with seven Palestinian and Egyptian children within the first week: a boy severely disabled with cerebral palsy; a girl physically disabled from polio; two brothers with muscular dystrophy; three other children with various degrees of intellectual disability. I developed programs of physical, educational and daily living activities relevant to each child's needs, and felt so much better myself now I was directly involved with individual children who were also disadvantaged. I enjoyed seeing their progress, their happiness and pride in their achievements, and the encouraging response of their parents. For me, it was also a challenge: how to reach more children, how to build the services needed.

Around this time, Dr Fathi found a bigger location for the PRCS clinic on the main road, Shara Ahmed Ismat, and organised a large flat in the same building for the rehabilitation work. This flat would also be a residence for me, and for Hamoudi and Dalal when we managed to bring them from Lebanon. It was an exciting period. The children I had been working with in the old clinic came to the new centre, along with additional children. The PRCS employed a woman, Um Ahmed, to cook and clean. Um Ahmed was an intelligent and capable woman, but had not had the opportunity to go to school and so she was illiterate. I always thought she had unrealised potential; if she'd had the opportunity, she could have been qualified to work in a managerial capacity. She had several children, lived in very poor conditions and had a generally unhappy home life; however she seemed to really enjoy working in the centre and sharing in our early developments. Sadly, Um Ahmed died a few years later of a brain tumour. The other key helper during the centre's early years was Hana Dajany, a Palestinian woman who was a long-time friend of Hadla Ayoubi and other PRCS personnel. She contributed so much as a translator, adviser and supporter.

It was obvious that with the increased number of children I needed professional staff too, in addition to a full-time physiotherapist and other visiting specialists. The PRCS agreed to send people to assist me, and several young women arrived. I had wanted both male and female staff, but because of cultural sensitivities the PRCS officials thought it might create problems if there were men and women working together, especially in these early stages. The girls who came didn't have any background in working with children nor in the field of disability. They had completed secondary school and were, in fact, seeking work as secretaries. I had to explain that there was no such work available, but that I needed assistance to work with children. I continued to work with the children myself, teaching my new assistants some of the necessary techniques and skills 'on the job'. Hana's help during this period was invaluable. Fortunately they were all very pleasant young women who liked children and were prepared to work, but it was obvious they would need some formal training in order to contribute to the development of the centre.

I ran the centre with an open-door policy; it seemed impossible to me to restrict acceptance to a narrowly defined type of disability. There were limited numbers of relevant specialists in the country, and given the numbers of children likely to need services, the staff had to be trained as generalists – people who could work with children; who knew how to deal with different types of disabilities; and could identify the type of specialist assistance needed and where to get it. Most importantly, however, I wanted people who respected the dignity of the individual.

The PRCS responded positively to my request to establish a training program for the staff, and we began to build up an excellent team of people with professional expertise in rehabilitation. The training program was a major undertaking and the potential for it to develop into a well-structured on-going program became evident. I estimated that if we were able to complete the year of study as planned, with structured examinations and a graduation ceremony, we could go on. In contrast to my excitement, however, the young women weren't so impressed. Lectures, study? It was all a bit too much! To help them get into a study pattern, I introduced set hours for supervised study time during the work period. Our reluctant starters, much to my delight, began asking for further studies. The program was a success, and soon we were preparing for a new intake of students.

Although my work in Cairo was going well, I was always thinking about the conflict in Lebanon, with particular concern for Hamoudi and Dalal who were still in Beirut. I loved these two children and it was very distressing to know that they were in such a vulnerable situation. They had no special residence and no one to give them the care they needed. The PRCS ensured their basic care, but the organisation was still in a very difficult situation in Lebanon. Dr Fathi and other senior PRCS personnel were working at bringing the children to Cairo but it wasn't an easy task. I was in contact with the Australian Embassy in Beirut and with Save the Children UK, both of whom shared our concern for the fate of these two children and were anxious to assist in enabling them to move to Cairo.

It was during this time that I realised that while I had always been fascinated by people and places, I had avoided having 'anchors' in my life. I loved my family and valued my many friends all around the world, but I'd always felt the need to be free to travel, to explore, to learn, to be ready to help as the need arose. Now, without my even realising it, very strong 'anchors' had appeared in my life. It was important to me to have Hamoudi and Dalal with me and to ensure they had the love, care, opportunity and security they needed.

In September 1983 I told the PRCS that I wished to legally adopt the children. I had no idea if this would be possible, nor how I would manage, but it seemed the best way to ensure their safety. As for me, I would have the privilege of legally having two wonderful kids.

Both Dalal and Hamoudi, now around nine and eleven respectively, had an individual history of survival, courage and resilience. They were so different from one another, yet I could see a very strong and special bond and understanding between them. It was interesting to watch the way their love of life and their care for one another – and for others – developed. My life is certainly richer for sharing so much with them.

On 5 October I was advised by the PRCS administration that permission had been granted by the PRCS for me to go ahead with the necessary procedures to adopt Hamoudi and Dalal. I was overjoyed, and immediately made contact with embassy personnel in both Cairo and Beirut, Save the Children UK, government officials in Australia, and family and friends in Australia. I was advised that the whole process would be very difficult indeed: Dalal and Hamoudi were Palestinian, orphans, origin unknown, disabled, and without any identification papers. I became aware at this time that unless one had a 'paper', one did not exist. On 10 November I was advised by the PRCS administration that it wasn't possible for me to adopt the children, that there had been a mistake in the information previously given to me. It was explained that as they were wards of PRCS, they could not be adopted. I was told that adoption is not a common practice in Palestinian culture, and it is near to forbidden for a child to be adopted outside the culture.

I felt shattered. Fortunately, I was also advised that the PRCS wished the children to live under my care in Cairo, and that I could continue with this process. The children would be fully under my care, but not adopted. I didn't have time to dwell on my disappointment as I needed to continue contributing to efforts being made to obtain papers to enable the children to move from Lebanon to Egypt.

By mid-December 1983, PRCS received information that the necessary approval had been obtained for the children to move, and the International Red Cross advised that it would take about three weeks. Once all had been cleared at the Beirut end, permission had to be secured from the Egyptian government to accept the children. Again the Australian Embassy personnel in both Beirut and Cairo were very helpful, as was Save the Children UK.

By mid-January 1984, the Egyptian government had agreed to the children entering Egypt, but there was some delay concerning the type of travel document needed. The discussion concerning what papers the children required to enter Egypt and who should sign what went back and forth for another month. The PRCS, the Australian embassies in Cairo and Beirut, Save the Children UK and the ICRC continued to follow up on this and that contact; nevertheless, I was feeling very frustrated about the whole process and began to think that Dalal and Hamoudi would never come. Finally, we were told that the children would be given an entry permit, but for one week only. Obviously such an arrangement was completely out of the question, so further follow-up was needed. Everything continued going around in circles, and then it was suggested that the children couldn't be moved until the airport in Beirut was opened again. By March, it felt as though we were back at square one. It was unbelievable. I was distressed, but even more determined to keep trying, as was PRCS.

On Thursday, 29 March 1984, the PRCS received a telex from ICRC in Geneva to say they were ready to move the children in ten days' time. On 31 March, a message came from the PRCS office in Beirut saying that the papers for the children were all ready, but as the airport would soon reopen they had decided to wait until this happened so Hamoudi and Dalal could fly direct to Cairo.

I heard on the news that there was renewed fighting in Beirut and that areas near to the PRCS complex had been hit. I immediately checked on the children and other people I knew, and was advised that all was well and the children weren't affected. But I had an uncomfortable feeling that something wasn't right and remained very anxious about Hamoudi and Dalal.

Throughout April and May the messages and queries continued. The situation in Beirut was not good, then it was improving but better to wait until the airport opened. Finally the children were on their way. We had a busy day with phone calls and telexes concerning their arrival in Cyprus, and their pending arrival in Cairo the next day. The Beirut airport was still closed so the children had travelled by ship to Cyprus with Namiti and ICRC personnel.

Now that the children were on their way, Dr Fathi told me that Hamoudi had been injured during the outbreak of fighting in March. He had forbidden staff from telling me about the situation in case it worried me. I wasn't surprised by the news as my strong feeling that something was wrong had never gone away. Hamoudi, Dalal, a staff member caring for them and some neighbourhood children were on a balcony in Akka Hospital when it was subjected to shelling. Hamoudi was injured; I didn't know exactly how, or what condition he was in now. Dalal had gone into shock during the experience but she was all right.

Thursday, 7 June 1984 – the day I had been waiting for since I left Beirut in April 1983. We arrived at the airport around 11.15 am, just as Dalal and Hamoudi's plane was landing.

It was almost routine for Palestinians to experience delays at Cairo's airport, but it wasn't expected that two disabled children, who had all the required papers to receive their permits to enter, would be held up too long. Nevertheless, several PRCS staff came and went as we waited, including Dr Fathi himself. As time went on, various people tried to get permission for me to enter the arrival area to assist with the children, but to no avail. I kept asking people coming out from the arrivals area if they had seen the children waiting inside; I still wasn't sure within myself that both of them would be there. At about 3 pm Namiti, accompanied by a guard, came out to see us. She said that they had nothing to eat or drink. She bought some guava juice for the children and returned (until this day Dalal refuses to drink guava juice). By now, I was very distressed by the situation and tried again to enter, but again without result. Other PRCS officials came to the airport, many phone calls were made, but the children were still being kept inside.

At 2 am a PRCS administrator tried to persuade me to leave the airport and return in the morning. He said there was a hotel area inside and the children were sleeping and there was nothing further that could be done until morning. I could sleep at the PRCS guest-house in Heliopolis and return early the following day. I realised there was nothing I could do, so I went to the guesthouse as he suggested. It was only afterwards that I discovered the information given to me wasn't true. There was no such hotel inside the airport. The children were sitting near the security office within the arrivals area, Dalal on a bench, Hamoudi in his chair.

At about 5 am the doorbell of the guesthouse rang. There were Namiti and the two children! They had been given permission to leave the airport at 3.30 am and had gone to the centre at Ain Shams where I lived. Not finding me there, they had woken the adminis-trator at his house nearby and he had directed them to the guesthouse in Heliopolis. The children had been detained at the airport for sixteen hours.

It was wonderful to be with them again. Words are inadequate to express the moment. There were greetings and hugs all around. Hamoudi had lost his right eye and had a number of scars, but otherwise he seemed okay. However, he was very thin and had regressed in his skills. Dalal was bright and chatty, but her first comment to me as she gave me a hug was, 'Don't cry.' She had grown, but had also regressed in terms of her independence in mobility and some daily living skills.

I was eager to get the children 'home' to the centre in Ain Shams, where everything was waiting for their arrival. But first I needed to change and wash Hamoudi; Namiti had been unable to attend to him properly by herself during the long wait. Dr Fathi and other PRCS officials arrived at the centre not long after us, laden with gifts to welcome the children and to check that all was well.

For the first three months that Hamoudi was in Egypt, I was with him twenty-four hours a day, seven days a week, as staff at the centre weren't yet trained to work with him. He had received severe facial wounds that day in Beirut. He had been in intensive care for twenty-five days, and during that period his heart had stopped several times. He had been given a tracheotomy in order that facial surgery could be carried out. I was told that a young nurse who had been training with me in Beirut had stayed with Hamoudi during his time in intensive care and had made a significant contribution to his recovery during the dangerous period. Hamoudi had an ongoing choking problem after the injuries; at least six times during his first year in Cairo I saw him turn very grey and be unable to breathe. Dalal didn't receive even a scratch during the shelling, but had been covered with blood and dirt, and was unable to walk for a week afterwards due to shock.

The centre was growing rapidly, and the arrival of Hamoudi and Dalal added another dimension to the work of the young women we were training as developmental workers. I would need staff during the night to help with Hamoudi, so I changed the work schedule to include some night duty. Some of the women refused outright to be involved, saying that it was not culturally accepted for them to sleep away from home, and it would be interpreted in a negative way by others. Meetings were held, and in some cases the parents of the young women came to discuss the matter. We tried to convince everyone that night duty wasn't unnatural work, and explained that I would be present so there was supervision and protection. There would also be some night staff working in the PRCS clinic on the ground floor. Once this hurdle was cleared, the pattern of work became routine.

Just before I was expelled from Lebanon, Badr and the other PRCS toddlers had been evacuated from Beirut. I had been told that the children were taken to an orphanage in Tunis, but I didn't know that Badr had been left in Syria because the orphanage refused to accept him due to his disability. As the PRCS in Syria didn't have a program to care for children, Badr was being looked after by one of the cleaning staff in her home near the hospital. When the director of the hospital heard that I was in Cairo he asked if Badr could be sent to me. I was overjoyed to find out that Badr was okay and that he would be joining us.

As with the other two children, the process to bring Badr to Cairo took time. It was early March 1985 when he finally arrived. I can still see him – a little boy of almost four years old coming out of the arrivals area of the airport, limping as he does, with a sandwich clutched in his hand. He was accompanied by a PRCS employee who was travelling to Cairo to visit family. He had been kept waiting for just over four hours before being allowed to leave the airport.

Hamoudi was in Palestine Hospital when Badr arrived, having been ill with a severe chest infection, however both he and Dalal were delighted to have Badr with them again. The family felt complete.

As a little boy Badr often repeated the word 'mummy' five or six times, as if assuring himself that, like the other children, he had a mother. Now a young man, he often says to me, 'Do you know what your son did today?', seeming still to need to reassure himself that he has the security of family. As far as the four of us are concerned, I am Mummy and they are my children. We are family.

EIGHT

LIFE IN CAIRO WAS GOOD. The staff quickly learned to work with Hamoudi and, most importantly, grew to like him – he was soon everybody's favourite kid brother. In addition to his cerebral palsy, Hamoudi is also epileptic and has severe chest problems. The chief neurologist working with the PRCS at Palestine Hospital came to the Ain Shams Centre to examine the children. He spent a great deal of time studying Hamoudi so as to organise his drug intake in the most appropriate way. He commented that Hamoudi was 'a textbook on epilepsy' as he had so many variations.

Working with Hamoudi taught the staff a wide range of skills and they learned to respect a person with severe and multiple disability. Initially, staff learned to play with Hamoudi, later to change him, and gradually to feed him. Sometimes he objected to a new trainee coming in to observe or beginning to learn to feed him. On one occasion he 'fussed' so much that a new trainee came out crying, saying, 'I don't think Hamoudi likes me.' I convinced her eventually that it wasn't personal. At times Hamoudi needed to exercise some control in his life and perhaps he just wasn't ready to train someone new that day.

I enjoyed seeing the staff greet parents with a severely disabled child and fuss over the child as is common with children without disability. The parents' expressions showed their surprise at this interest in and respect for their child, in contrast to the often shocked response or comments like, 'Forget about him – he is useless.' When the staff ran through the range of activities and management arrangements suitable for a child, they often used the phrase 'like we do with Hamoudi'.

Dalal had her own special challenges when she arrived. She'd had a very broken beginning to her schooling because of the war situation in Beirut; also, her self-care skills were underdeveloped. I enrolled her at the Al-Nour wa Al-Amal school for blind girls in Heliopolis, where she faced an additional challenge as she needed to be able to write Braille using a writing board to enter the second grade, otherwise she would have to begin again from grade one. At school in Beirut she had been taught to use the Perkins machine to write Braille, whereas in Cairo the Perkins wasn't introduced to students until the secondary level. Dalal was determined to succeed as she didn't want to be delayed yet another year. I worked with her and taught some of the staff how to assist her as well. She succeeded and was very proud to be able to enter the second grade.

Dalal had a special love of music and was frequently singing or tapping out a rhythm on tables or doors. Al-Nour wa Al-Amal provided a music program and had an Institute of Music that was linked to the Cairo Conservatoire of Music. Dalal stayed after school for choir, the bells group, and became a member of the junior orchestra. She was delighted when she was assigned to learn the flute, which she thought sounded 'like a bird'. Dalal demonstrated her musical skill very early. She didn't have a flute at home initially, but she did have a small three-octave toy org (a small battery-operated piano keyboard). She would say to me, 'Would you like to hear the new tune I have learned on the flute?' and transpose it onto the org. When I travelled to England to spend a few days with Clarice and Mum, I was able to buy a flute. Dalal was overjoyed at receiving her very own instrument.

Although our centre was located in a disadvantaged area of Cairo, because of its unique character parents from other parts of the city brought their children there. A father from one of the more affluent suburbs said to me one day when he came to collect his severely intellectually disabled son, 'We are so very happy with the program here for Mohammed, but do you really have to have the centre here in Ain Shams? Why not in Heliopolis, for instance, near to the PRCS Palestine Hospital?'

I said that I was pleased that he was satisfied with the program, but that it was important such a centre be located in a disadvantaged area. The Ain Shams Centre had developed its special character not only because of the 'open door' policy and the training institute, but because of the children in the small residence. Hamoudi, Dalal and Badr, and other children who stayed for short periods, provided the centre with a soul.

The centre was greatly helped by ongoing support from international organisations. Norwegian Groups for Palestine were among the centre's earliest supporters and continued with that aid over twelve years, sending specialists and assisting us to acquire equipment. I was invited to travel to Norway and Sweden to see a range of programs for children with disability. While in Norway, I visited a large rehabilitation hospital across the fjord from Oslo; the facilities and programs were of an extremely high standard. There was even a shop selling wheelchairs with an amazing range of types and sizes. I remembered the time we spent in the underground temporary hospital in Beirut and how Nour cried when the nurses asked to borrow his wheelchair; there were so many people confined to bed because of lack of a wheelchair, and it took endless effort to obtain chairs for those in need. Here in Norway, the wheelchairs seemed a metaphor for the injustices of the world: in some countries people live in comfort and security; in other places people are poor, oppressed and struggle just to survive. Why is the world this way? Why are there so many people in impossible situations, whose lives are of great suffering? The experience strengthened my conviction to work even harder with the PRCS.

The centre at Ain Shams continued to develop, strongly supported by Dr Fathi. In 1986 we began to recruit male trainees. This was an important step as the children needed both male and female life models. The men were keen to learn most of the work, but bucked at carrying Hamoudi as they considered it undignified. They felt he should be carried by workers employed to clean and carry things. They also considered that feeding him and changing his nappies was women's work. This was another challenge to face: Hamoudi and other children like him needed both male and female carers who would work with the whole child, dealing with all of his or her needs with dignity. When such a standoff occurred, I would carry Hamoudi myself. When I did, most of the men were ashamed and came to take him from me. I would refuse to hand him over, saying, 'No, we are now playing. I am a train and we are on a journey. We are having fun.' Nasr was the first of the men to establish a personal link with Hamoudi, quickly forming an important bond with him. He was keen to learn more and asked many questions. Very soon the other men learned that working with children with disability meant working with the whole child and dealing with the range of needs present. Once they passed this barrier, they not only realised the value and dignity of the skills they were acquiring, but that all aspects of the work were important and could be enjoyed.

A concept that I tried always to instil in the staff was that it was important for them to work closely together and to interact with the person with the disability, their family, and all professions involved. No one person, no one profession, no one organisation can fulfil all of the needs and provide all the opportunities that a person with disability requires. Further, in working in the field, I stressed the need for the developmental worker to approach each situation with head, hand and heart fully integrated; that is, to relate sensitively and meaningfully to all the people they worked with.

Life in Cairo seemed, on the surface, to be very stable, and I certainly felt safe, but there were undercurrents of dissent. In 1985 there was a tense period due to an army revolt, and our area was placed under curfew. We first became aware of the problem when one of the staff arrived looking rather distressed and announced there were tanks across the main road out of Cairo. Dalal had already gone to school, so Amal, one of the staff, went with a driver to bring her home. We maintained a calm atmosphere around the children, who didn't fully understand what was going on. The situation lasted only a few days but it was unnerving, bringing back memories of our experiences in Lebanon.

There was a buildup of tension in Lebanon too, with the camp wars of 1986, and in 1987 the first Intifada (uprising) broke out in the Occupied Palestinian Territories. The Palestinians in Cairo often spoke of their concern about the situation and for their families. I shared their concerns and felt very sad at the deterioration of the conditions of the Palestinian people under occupation. The Intifada was the Palestinian response to what people felt was a lack of progress in dealing with their difficult existence, and began with demonstrations and riots against the Israelis. The Israeli government reacted by closing universities and arresting and deporting many people. By December 1987 the situation had escalated, with young people throwing stones at the Israeli soldiers, who would shoot or arrest them. A significant aspect of the Intifada was the involvement of women, with various women's organisations contributing to the resistance in different ways. From its spontaneous beginnings, it soon came under the leadership of the National Command of the Uprising, which had links to the PLO. People in the Canada refugee camp in Egypt could see the smoke and hear the gunfire and ambulance sirens and worry about what was taking place across the divide.

Dr Fathi suggested forming a parents and friends group for the Ain Shams Centre, saying, 'If we form such a group, they will be able to assist us in many ways; and also they will be able to carry on with the work if anything should happen to the PRCS.' What the effect of the Intifada within Occupied Palestinian Territories and throughout the Palestinian diaspora would be was still unknown, but Palestinian people and their services are always at risk and face uncertainty. In order to establish a formal society it was essential that the people forming the group were Egyptian. We organised a meeting of parents and friends and there was great interest in the idea. It took some time to complete all of the paperwork for the society, but the group was very active and Al-Ghad Al-Mushreq (A Better Tomorrow) later became one of the leading rehabilitation centres in Egypt.

Other, more personal events also took place during this period. In November 1987 my thoughts were very much with my family as it was Mum's ninetieth birthday. Auntie Rene, who was now eighty-three, travelled to England to visit Mum and to share this special birthday with her. Unfortunately it wasn't possible for me to be with them.

In early June 1988 I was delighted to hear from the Australian Embassy that an Australian parliamentary delegation would be visiting the Ain Shams Centre. Dr Fathi and representatives from Al-Ghad Al-Mushreq came to the centre to receive our visitors, and the staff were proud to have the opportunity to show others the work they were doing.

Around the same time, the Australian Foreign Minister, Mr Bill Hayden, made a visit to Cairo. Because of the political situation it wasn't possible for Mr Hayden and Dr Fathi to meet, but the embassy was able to make an appointment for a meeting with personnel from his delegation. After the meeting, we had a chance encounter with Mr Hayden in the passageway. I appreciated being able to thank him for the support he had given me during my problems in Lebanon, and I was especially pleased that he and Dr Fathi were able to meet, even so briefly.

The work at the centre was constant, and at times difficult, but there was a warm family feeling about the place, both amongst the employees and with the clients and their families. In addition to accepting more clients, we were also increasing names on a waiting list. Dr Fathi, in his eagerness, was acquiring additional apartments adjacent to the original residence where Hamoudi, Dalal, Badr and I lived.

Our in-service training program had become more formalised and was now the Institute of Rehabilitation Studies, with a contributing team of Egyptian and Palestinian specialists in the field. The students were mostly Palestinians living in Cairo or the Canada camp, but there were also some Egyptian students. People selected to enter employment as developmental workers at the centre attended lectures three days a week and worked as assistants in the centre's programs over another three days until they completed the course. In addition to meeting the needs for the work and development of the Ain Shams Centre, we were able to design intensive courses, usually about a three-month duration, to give training to staff from other organisations. We were fortunate to continue to have the interest and support of specialists from different countries, mainly Norway and the UK. These young women and men worked together with the staff for some months, or even a year, and contributed a great deal to the staff's development of their knowledge and skills.

The number of children who took advantage of our short-stay facilities increased. Sometimes they came alone and sometimes with their mother. Each of these children had their own story, but three of them in particular had very special situations, and taught the staff working with them many lessons.

Yasser was a boy of about eight years old from the Gaza Strip who had a severe hearing problem. He stayed with us for about a year. Developing a program for Yasser was the primary task, but dealing with his behaviour became our first priority. A bright boy, but with limited communication skills and little education, he presented a major challenge to the staff. Whenever he didn't receive what he wanted he screamed and stamped and pulled away from anyone trying to approach him. We thought our neighbours must imagine that terrible things were happening to him. In the evening when we were settling Hamoudi to sleep, Yasser would delight in going into his room and adjoining rooms and turning on the lights. Luckily, Hamoudi loved Yasser's naughtiness and would laugh heartily as he dodged around the flat upsetting all in his way. The staff worked in a caring way to assist Yasser to learn communication skills and to open avenues of learning and discovery for him. Gradually his behaviour improved, and as he became more involved in activities and learning, and felt the warmth and care surrounding him, he began to respond in kind. Indeed he became a delightful well-mannered little boy full of curiosity and joy. Having lived in the Gaza Strip under Israeli occupation with the ever-present army jeeps, soldiers and confrontations, he had many stories to tell and his mimes and dramatisations of his experiences were pure theatre, presented with much feeling and action. When Yasser left with his father to return to the Gaza Strip there were sad farewells, but we all felt confident that he would be able to interact successfully in his environment and pursue his education.

Rusha's story is almost like a fairy tale – at least in some part. Rusha is an Egyptian girl who, at about the age of five, was found abandoned on the streets of Cairo near a mosque. She was severely disabled: her whole body was very floppy and she was unresponsive to any stimuli. The people who found her took her to a nearby centre for children with disabilities, but it wasn't equipped to manage such a child. I received a phone call from a representative of Oxfam asking if I could send a doctor from the PRCS Ain Shams Centre to look at Rusha. Dr Jamal and Mahmoud, an administrator who was also a social worker, made the visit. They considered that Rusha was old enough and aware enough to realise that she had been abandoned and was also experiencing the trauma of her situation. We organised some visits for Rusha to Ain Shams – which was quite some distance from the centre where she was.

Not long after this, Rusha broke her arm. The condition of the arm worsened, progressing to osteomyelitis (inflammation of the bone), and the whole of her arm from the shoulder swelled up. It was a serious situation, possibly needing an amputation to save Rusha's life. It was essential that she be hospitalised. Staff at the centre where she was staying weren't prepared to stay with her in the hospital, and she needed someone with her at all times. Our staff had often stayed in the hospital with Hamoudi, so we hastily arranged a schedule for some of the young women to stay with Rusha. A couple of days later when the doctor came to inspect Rusha, one of the staff with her said to him, 'Rusha seems to be epileptic. She had a fit this morning – here is where I have written the information in the day book.'

The doctor looked at her with surprise and said, 'How do you know that she had a fit? What do you know about epilepsy?'

'Oh,' she said, 'we work with Hamoudi and he has epilepsy with different types of fits. Also, there are other children at the centre who are epileptic – and of course we learn about epilepsy in our lecture course.'

'I had no idea there was such work in the PRCS,' the doctor said. 'I am impressed.'

The staff were delighted by this response, and were very keen to recount all when I went to check on Rusha.

When Rusha passed crisis point and it was time for her to go home, it wasn't possible for her to return to the original centre because she still needed very careful handling. We agreed to care for her at Ain Shams until it was possible for her to return – we expected it to be about four months. In fact, it was five years. Rusha provided an important lesson for the staff, too. It took over a year for her to be toilet trained, which the staff found difficult. On several occasions I said to them, 'You talk of giving up on Rusha becoming toilet trained. It is taking a long time, but we must never give up. How often have you told a mother not to give up? Now you know how much persistence it needs to keep going against all odds.' Eventually, there was success.

To see Rusha during that period was like watching someone come alive. From a flaccid, non-responsive child, seemingly unaware of her surroundings, she evolved into a delightful little girl, able to express her feelings towards her friends, her concern for others, and full of joy in all of her activities and keen to learn and succeed in simple tasks.

Khaled was around seven years old when he came to us from Lebanon in 1989. His family was very poor and he came to Cairo with a PRCS employee who brought him to the centre. Khaled was obviously very bright, but he was also severely disabled with cerebral palsy. The challenge for the staff was to find a way to enable him to follow an education program and learn skills to assist him in life. We usually began with speech therapy and physiotherapy but Khaled didn't have speech, nor did he have sufficient control of his limbs to enable him to walk or to use his hands in a controlled manner. Fortunately, through the Norwegian Groups for Palestine, our staff had had the opportunity to take a course in Bliss symbols, a system that requires the user to point to symbols arranged on a board. Khaled was a very intelligent child and the system opened up his world and enabled him to hold two-way conversations. I can still see the joy on his little face as he pointed out a question or statement on his board, which then resulted in interaction and communication with others.

Although we occasionally received news about Khaled's family through a PRCS social worker in Lebanon, there was no direct contact from them for more than five years. This was stressful for Khaled and he often used his Bliss board to speak of his father. Then out of the blue in early 1994 there came a phone call from Khaled's father. One of the staff spoke to him, giving him news about Khaled and translating questions and comments from Khaled himself as he pointed them out on his board. Khaled also listened to the voice of his father, mother and other family members and made some sounds in response. This was a most emotional experience for all present, and several of the staff on duty that evening couldn't contain their tears. We all felt, *Inshallah*, there was hope that one day Khaled would be able to rejoin his family.

New opportunities were also becoming available for Dalal and Badr. In the summer of 1988, Dalal (now about thirteen) and Badr (about eight), together with seven other children made up part of a PRCS delegation to participate in a ten-day summer camp in Finland. I was the leader of the group, and there were three other PRCS mothers with me. The camp was situated in a forest on the edge of a beautiful lake and one of its themes was to span the world with friendship. Dalal and Badr were the only two disabled children. Dalal was delighted to learn phrases in different languages from children from different countries, and as always everyone was amazed by her immediate recall of the words and phrases and her perfect accent. Badr had some problems keeping up on the long walks through the forest and inevitably ended up on the shoulders of one of the camp leaders. I marvelled at how Dalal and Badr were able to travel to another country and participate in such a camp. This was something far beyond imagination just a few years before when we were in the midst of the trauma of war and massacre in Lebanon.

Hamoudi, Dalal and Badr continued to grow and develop in their own way, but problems were beginning to emerge concerning Badr's education. A bright boy, he also had learning disabilities and was finding it increasingly difficult to manage in a large class. Like many disabled children with learning disabilities he was dismissed as being naughty, lazy or intellectually disabled. He used to say to me, 'I know my lessons, but in the exam it all comes out wrong.' He would fail his English exam, then come home and give a speech in English to foreign volunteers. It was fascinating to watch him teaching himself English: he would ask me for the meaning of an Arabic word in English, and then very soon after come to me with information or a question that used the new word in a sentence. The problem at school was that with so many children per class, he wasn't getting the attention he needed to overcome his learning disabilities. At this time too, learning disabilities weren't yet generally understood.

I was concerned about Badr's situation and so made an appointment to meet with his headmaster. I wanted to explain to the headmaster that Badr was bright but had learning difficulties that needed to be understood so he could receive the support he needed. During the meeting I made a point of often speaking to Badr in English. 'But he isn't mentally retarded!' was the headmaster's surprised response. Unfortunately, Badr never did have the opportunity to follow the type of program he needed to enable him to realise his potential academically. He left school in grade five and continued his education in a special program at the Ain Shams Centre.

NINE

IN THE SUMMER OF 1989 I took a couple of weeks' holiday to visit Mum and Clarice, Alan and family, in England. I asked Dr Fathi if it would be possible for me to take Dalal and Badr with me; I thought the trip would be good for them, and it would be special for me to have my family meet these two young people who had become so significant in my life. Unfortunately, it wasn't possible to arrange such travel for Hamoudi because of his general health situation associated with his disability and because he had never received any passport documents. Dr Fathi was keen for the children to make the trip, but asked us to travel to France first because he wanted Dalal to play the flute at a special cultural program at the UNESCO theatre in Paris.

Dalal, dressed in her Palestinian embroidered dress, opened the concert with her flute rendition. We spent a wonderful few days in Paris where we were very well looked after by the PRCS office there and other friends. We took a tourist boat along the river Seine and Dalal was delighted to be able to detect when the boat was passing under a bridge. The low arches of the bridges across the Seine created a change in pressure that Dalal was sensitive to, as well as changing the quality of people's voices.

Next stop was London where, again, people from the PRCS office there took great care of us, along with staff from the Medical Aid for Palestinians (MAP) organisation. We then had a wonderful time with my family in Newton Ferrers. Clarice had arranged for the two children to attend the local school for three days, where Dalal was invited to play flute with the school band and also to play at a farewell party for one of the teachers who was retiring. Badr loved taking part in a swimming lesson and was fascinated that children could learn such things at school. Mum, who was in her nineties now, was delighted with Dalal and Badr. 'I think that God has let me live this long so as to give these children a grandmother,' she told me.

In August 1990, Mum died. She was ninety-three and had been getting increasingly frail over the past couple of years. She had moved from her flat to a residence for aged people that was just five minutes' walk from Clarice and Alan's home. I kept in close contact with Mum and Clarice by telephone over the years, but it was often difficult to get a connection. It is a strange feeling to be away from family at such times. Mothers are so very special, and our mother was more than special. By some miracle I was able to share her last moments. I had phoned to speak to Mum and was advised that she was in a critical state. Clarice was soon by her side and phoned me back. 'Mum is very low,' she told me. 'She isn't able to speak at present, but she can hear and is responding to our voices. If you speak to her she will know that it's you.' What a precious moment. I was able to speak to Mum, and Clarice told me that she smiled and obviously recognised my voice.

A short time later, I had a telephone call from Alan to say that Mum had quietly passed away. It wasn't unexpected, but still a shock to deal with. I was able to fly across to England to spend some time with Clarice and Alan and to attend Mum's funeral.

When I returned to Cairo, Dr Fathi told me that he wanted me to make a visit into the Occupied Palestinian Territories (West Bank,

East Jerusalem and Gaza Strip) to visit the facilities providing re-habilitation services, and at the same time to look at programs for early childhood education and services for the elderly. My excitement at making the trip was tinged with guilt, however. My Palestinian colleagues – concerned about relatives and keen to visit Palestine – weren't permitted by Israel to do so, just because they were Palestinian. I, as a foreigner, could make the visit. I was to experience this feeling of guilt many times over the years.

It was a wonderful but sad experience to travel to the Occupied Palestinian Territories (OPT). The living conditions under occupation were both difficult and dangerous, but the people's spirit was most impressive. I was able to visit all of the programs in the Gaza Strip, as well as in the north, south, and middle areas of the West Bank. The professionals and volunteers working in the field of re-habilitation for people with disabilities were enthusiastic about their work and had developed a number of non-governmental organisations (NGOs) with a range of good centres. I met many people from a range of different professions and received the most wonderful hospitality throughout.

It wasn't always easy to move around in the OPT. Sometimes there were strike days when all the shops would be closed as a protest against the occupation. The Israeli army imposed curfews and people weren't permitted to leave their houses. There were military jeeps cruising along the roads. On one occasion I was in a car behind an army jeep for a considerable length of time and could see two boys – about ten to twelve years old – in the jeep, seated between the Israeli soldiers with their guns, their hands tied. The children had probably been caught throwing stones at the jeep and were being taken into custody. I'm sure my intense feeling of helplessness regarding these children was far more pronounced within the Palestinians in the car with me.

At that time, passing through Erez – the Israeli-controlled border crossing between the northern end of the Gaza Strip and Israel –

was a somewhat tense procedure, and Palestinians were often prevented from passing. As this was the only route available to travel to the West Bank, it created many difficulties for Palestinians. On one occasion, Israeli soldiers stopped the share taxi I was travelling in to check the passengers' IDs and passports. All of the men were required to get out and stand in line. The driver was ordered to collect the documents and pass them to the soldier; I could see his hand shaking as he attended to this task. I was the only female – and also the only foreigner – so was left to sit in the car. One of the soldiers came to the window and wanted to know what I was doing there. He said that I should get out as I would be safer with the soldiers. I insisted that I was perfectly okay, at the same time praying that I wouldn't be forced to leave the taxi. By this time, the men's documents had been checked and returned and they came back to the car. As my passport had not yet been returned, and there seemed to be discussion going on between the soldiers, the taxi had to wait. The atmosphere was tense. Eventually, my passport was returned and we were on our way. As soon as we cleared the crossing, an almost party atmosphere of relief filled the car. Some of the passengers produced sandwiches or biscuits, which were passed around. All were curious as to why I had received so much questioning and delay. Where did I come from? What was I doing?

On 8 October 1990 I visited the Al-Maqassed Hospital in occupied Palestinian East Jerusalem with Dr Jawad. Al-Maqassed is located on the Mount of Olives overlooking the old city, with the Al-Haram Al-Sharif (Dome of the Rock) in the foreground. It is the main Palestinian hospital for management of spinal cord and head injuries, and during the conflict of the first Intifada there was a great increase in both types of injury. Soon after we arrived, major disturbances began taking place on the Al-Haram Al-Sharif. I could hear ambulances approaching the hospital and saw staff hurrying to the emergency department. We went to the windows to look down towards the old city, which was a scene of confusion. People were running in all directions across the Al-Haram Al-Sharif and the sound of gunfire and helicopters became louder. Dr Jawad said, 'I must get down there as quickly as possible so that I can help with the wounded.'

We hurried down to the old city, but got caught in the heavy traffic as people fled, and cars ferrying the wounded tried to reach the hospital. I told Dr Jawad not to worry about me as I could walk around the conflict area and avoid the problem. I got back to the YMCA in time to join a group that was preparing packages of bandages and other items for the emergency workers. There were many injuries and deaths that day, which became known as 'Black Monday'.

Throughout my five-week visit to the OPT, I met people working in the field of rehabilitation and was also able to learn about the difficulties faced by the Palestinian people during the Intifada. One girl told me how she had been confined to her house over several days during a curfew. Watching from her window she saw a cat running from house to house. 'This made me feel very mad,' she said. 'I realised the extent of our confinement, and the freedom available to the animals around us but not to us.'

Israeli soldiers carried out evening raids on people's homes, and sometimes took a family member away to an unknown destination. There were additional problems if there happened to be a Palestinian flag in view, or books on the shelves not to the liking of the soldiers. Outside, there was often thick black smoke and a terrible smell of tyres burning.

As I travelled through the country I was amazed to see so many Israeli settlements scattered across hilltops, clearly recognisable by the rows of red-roofed houses. The spill-out of settlements from the area of Jerusalem were beginning to look like cities, with high-rise buildings and tall cranes showing further construction.

One young woman, Iptisam, whom I met on this and subsequent visits, was especially concerned that the Palestinian children had become obsessed with a game they called 'People and soldiers', which they played in the streets, in the school grounds and at home. The 'people' threw stones and the 'soldiers' attacked them. As no one wanted to be a soldier, the game was always organised so as to enable the children to take turns: everyone had to be a soldier for a specified period. Apart from the problem of this activity overshadowing traditional and creative play, at times it was also extremely dangerous. Sometimes when the children were involved in the game, real soldiers would suddenly appear in jeeps and the game would turn into the real thing.

During my time in the OPT, I kept in close contact with the children and the staff at the centre; I enjoyed listening to Dalal and Badr chat about their doings and hearing Hamoudi's babble and laughter. When I returned to Cairo, we organised a holiday at the beach for the children in residence, booking into a holiday complex at Faed on the Suez Canal. Several of the staff came along too, and we spent a wonderful few days enjoying the relaxed but active time that is so special to beach holidays. I always felt a sense of wonder that we were able to provide such experiences for the children.

In May 1992 we organised an international conference on the academic program of the Institute of Rehabilitation Studies. From its simple beginnings as 'on the job' training for new staff, the program had become a two-year intermediate-level certificate followed by a two year diploma. This was a significant achievement based on years of work and I felt very proud of everyone's effort and commitment in getting us this far.

The activity of the PRCS Ain Shams Centre had developed a great deal too, both in terms of services to children and adults with disabilities and their families and staff training. Some of the original staff now held senior positions in the centre and were responsible for many aspects of the work. By now there were approximately four hundred clients receiving services, but unfortunately there were still hundreds on the waiting list whom we weren't yet able to include. The services offered ranged from baby and parent programs, to education and training programs, and adult vocational training. Physiotherapy and speech therapy were given to clients who needed them, and the medical staff carefully monitored health issues.

The physical facilities had increased accordingly. Programs now took place in four buildings, comprising twenty apartments, and there were two small residences. Dalal, Rusha and I lived in one flat, along with Hamoudi and the women who looked after him during the night. Badr, Khaled and Salah (a deaf boy in residence during the week who returned home at weekends) lived in the other flat, with male staff on duty. The centre had become recognised throughout Egypt for its inclusion of children with different types of disabilities, and for its particular expertise in working with children with cerebral palsy and those with severe multiple disabilities.

I had arranged for Azza Mohammed Ali to teach an English language course to our staff. Azza was a remarkable young woman, full of fun and warmth, who was able to accomplish a great deal despite being severely disabled with cerebral palsy. She had always received a lot of support and care from her mother, and with a PhD in English literature she had much to give. This was a very important arrangement as not only was Azza a good English language teacher, but the staff had the opportunity to learn from a teacher with a disability. Azza also became a consultant to our parent and baby program, assisting staff and parents with ideas in working and playing with their babies and toddlers who were cerebral-palsied.

On the political scene, it was obvious there was something going on. The Intifada, internal Israeli politics, the Gulf War following the invasion of Iraq into Kuwait, and the PLO's support of the Iraqi position all made for a very disturbing situation. The Gulf States ceased their funding of the PLO due to its support of Iraq, which had implications for the work of the PRCS. There was a period when employees' salaries were delayed by months, and there were many restrictions on purchases. Until this point, the PRCS hadn't charged any fees for disabled children and adults attending the centre. However, with this financial difficulty it was decided that a small nominal fee would be introduced, but only for those families who could afford to pay something. Less than half the clients were able to pay, but those who could were willing to contribute in this way. As always, we did what we could with what we had, and, like many problems in life, the difficulty was weathered and it passed.

In October 1991, the US Secretary of State, James Baker, was able to arrange an Israeli–Palestinian peace conference in Madrid, but PLO officials were banned from any involvement. This was the beginning of several meetings with a somewhat complex agenda and with obvious differences in expectations between the Palestinian and Israeli positions. The Palestinians at the Ain Shams Centre and the Palestine Hospital followed the events closely, with rising hopes of a Palestinian state – in spite of the continued expansion of Israeli settlements and Israel's position of autonomy for the Palestinians rather than statehood. When we were advised that the Palestinian delegation to the Madrid conference would be visiting the PRCS and would make a presentation to staff at the Palestine Hospital, there was great interest. I attended the meeting, and took Dalal who had been asked to play flute on the occasion. She was very excited to meet all of the people, especially the three key negotiators, Dr Haider Abu Shafi, Dr Hanan Ashrawi and Feisal Husseini.

There was great shock and concern in April 1992 when news broke that the small plane Yasser Arafat (Abu Amar) was travelling in had crashed, possibly during a sandstorm in the desert over Libya, and its whereabouts were unknown. For the Palestinians, it seemed unthinkable that they should lose their esteemed leader, and at such a crucial time. For the PRCS, the fear for Abu Amar's safety was intensified because we were all concerned for Dr Fathi as he worried about the fate of his brother. It was with great relief and joy that we greeted the news that Abu Amar had been found and was safe. Sadly, however, two of his companions had died in the crash.

In September 1992 I was again in the OPT, participating in a conference on rehabilitation. The people from the rehabilitation centres throughout the West Bank were present, but it hadn't been possible for workers in the Gaza Strip to get permits from the Israelis to attend, as was often the case. At the conference I met up with Yusif and Akram, both physically disabled and founding members of the Arab Society for the Physically Handicapped (ASPH). They invited me to spend a couple of days in a recreation camp they'd organised, which was being held near the border between northeast Israel and southwest Syria. 'But how can you go to a camp inside Israel?' I asked. 'Can you get permits for that?'

They explained that the camp site – at the location of Jesus's Sermon on the Mount – belonged to a German order of monks. About a year before, some of the monks had visited Al-Maqassed Hospital and were concerned to see so many young people disabled because of injuries sustained from the Israeli army. They felt these people would benefit from the opportunity to spend some days away from the hospital in a relaxing and beautiful environment on the shores of the Sea of Galilee. Yusif and Akram had been able to make special arrangements with the Israeli authorities to allow the group of disabled people and their attendants to travel to the site and spend some days at the camp.

I drove up there with Yusif and Akram. It seemed unreal in many respects to be in the area that was of special significance in the life of Jesus and his teachings. There was an outdoor chapel at the edge of the water with an atmosphere of serenity and reflection – in contrast to the activity of the camp site behind it.

Each time I visited the OPT, I was able to gather further information on the rehabilitation services available and the needs of people with disabilities. The PRCS needed this data in order to assess the overall status of health and social services for the people in the OPT in order to develop a National Health Plan, which would later be used by the Palestinian Ministry of Health. I was asked to contribute to this work by developing a National Rehabilitation Plan, drawing on my visits into the OPT, together with my work in Beirut and Cairo.

In February 1993, with the International Cerebral Palsy Society, we conducted an international workshop called 'Quality of Life – In Spite of Cerebral Palsy'. Leaders in the field from different professions spoke, but, most importantly, so did parents of children with cerebral palsy. One of the speakers was Dr Yousria, mother of Mohammed, fifteen, who was severely cerebral-palsied but highly intelligent. Mohammed had attended the Ain Shams Centre since he was five, and was now preparing to sit for school examinations. He eventually went on to earn a baccalaureate degree in business management and to run his own small business. At the conference his mother spoke about how she and the family had accepted Mohammed's situation and sought how best to assist him in life. 'My harsh experience taught me a great deal,' she said. 'Through Mohammed I learned how to love people more, and how to help them to overcome their difficulties and problems. By his success and self-assertion he helped us, and made us all share our responsibilities and emotional problems to be able to find the right path.'

Azza also presented a paper, in which she made a strong plea for greater recognition of and opportunities for people with cerebral palsy. She noted that 'with cerebral-palsied children – they do not need braces or artificial limbs or splints. We need human communication, human contact and love.'

I was very moved by a comment made by Aida Gindi, senior adviser to Mrs Suzan Mubarak, wife of the Egyptian President, and previously responsible for the African division of UNICEF. 'You know, we were afraid of working with children with cerebral palsy,' she said, 'but you have shown us that, after all, they are just children. We have a duty to address their needs also.'

I had the privilege of working with the team headed by Aida as they developed a centre for children with disabilities in a disadvantaged area of Cairo, very near to Ain Shams.

On 13 September 1993 the Oslo Accords were signed on the lawn of the White House in Washington DC. This was the beginning of what was heralded as the 'Peace Process' between Israel and the PLO. President Bill Clinton, President Yasser Arafat, Prime Minister Yitzhak Rabin and Shimon Peres were the key figures on this historic occasion. At the PRCS Ain Shams Rehabilitation Centre, we all gathered around the television set to watch the ceremony take place. The atmosphere was one of tension, excitement and anticipation. Discussion centred on a dream for the future – Palestinians returning to live in Palestine.

In simple terms, the Oslo Accords called for the withdrawal of Israel from the West Bank and Gaza Strip, and the Palestinians' right to self-govern through the Palestinian Authority (PA). It left big issues like the future of Jerusalem and the right of return for refugees until later discussion.

There was also controversy about the Accords. Professor Edward Said, a leading Palestinian academic, was a sharp critic, considering that it left the Palestinians in too vulnerable a situation. Others pointed out that the base of the Accords – UN Security Council Resolutions 242 and 383 – was much too vague to ensure rights and justice for the Palestinian people. They considered the signing of the document to be a surrender by the Palestinian people to the demands of the more powerful Israel backed by the US, and warned that such a situation could only lead to further oppression and the denial of Palestinian identity and rights. Hanan Ashrawi records in her book *This Side of Peace* the disappointment that she, Feisal Husseini and others of the Madrid group felt about the situation. However, they remained committed to the legitimacy of the PLO and the unity of the Palestinian people, and gave their support to the developments that followed. For those watching the ceremony on television, however, the different reactions, the controversy, weren't the issues in mind. Their thoughts were wholly on the chance to return to Palestine at last.

Dalal and Badr were affected by the mood around them and talked happily about moving to Palestine. I felt pleased for the recognition that was being given to Palestinians, to their historic link to the land and their right to be free of occupation, but at the same time I wondered just how it would be implemented. Would there emerge a just peace, with Israelis and Palestinians living side by side in harmony and security as the Oslo Accords promised?

This was an especially interesting time for the PRCS as, under the auspices of the International Federation of Red Cross and Red Crescent Societies (IFRC), it could now begin to bring together the various independent Red Crescent Societies and the branches of the diaspora. The PRCS headquarters would eventually be moved into Palestine – initially Jericho, later Ramallah, with an ever-present aspiration to finally be located in the Palestinian capital of East Jerusalem.

I wasn't directly involved in this work, but I was very excited to have the opportunity to attend one of the meetings in Cairo. I marvelled that people who previously weren't able to meet were now working together with much enthusiasm and skill to establish the united Palestine Red Crescent Society. Now it was possible to involve the whole community in services for its people. It felt that endless opportunity was ahead.

In 1993, our Institute of Rehabilitation Studies held a seminar on special education in our small lecture theatre. Afterwards, Dr Fathi invited the attendees to a reception at the home of his sister, Hajjah Inam, in the Roxy area of Heliopolis. Hajjah Inam was the eldest in the Arafat family and played a key role in the life of her siblings, as she had taken responsibility for them when their mother died very early on in their childhood. She continued to support them as adults and radiated love and pride whenever she was with them.

The PRCS had a cultural museum, Heritage House, on the ground floor of the building where Hajjah lived; it held an extensive collection of costumes, paintings and items that displayed the varied culture of the Palestinian people. During the reception, there was unusual movement in the street below. I moved to the window with the others to look down onto the street. There was much surprise and excitement: the PLO Chairman, Yasser Arafat, was coming to visit his sister and brother. We watched the police and security men clear the way for his car, and caught a glimpse of his characteristic headdress as he climbed out. Soon he was in the room with us.

Family greetings were exchanged, and then he sat down with the guests and expressed his interest in the activities they were involved in and his appreciation for their assistance to the Palestinian people. It was a relaxed and friendly time, and then just as suddenly he left. Watching from the window again, we saw there was the bustle of security men running beside his car and then jumping in as it moved along, and the police organising the traffic.

It soon became clear that the Peace Process was not going to bring the hoped-for results without difficulties, despite the international recognition given to the achievement of the Oslo Accords with the awarding of the 1994 Nobel Peace prize jointly to the Palestinian and Israeli leaders. In the OPT, the mood swung between hope and despair, but the people met setbacks with resilience.

Among those setbacks was the action of an Israeli settler, Baruch Goldstein, on Friday, 25 February 1994. Goldstein opened fire in the Al-Haram Al-Ibrahimi Mosque in Hebron during dawn prayers, killing twenty-nine worshippers and wounding many others. The Israeli army added greatly to the number of wounded and killed during the demonstration that followed.

TEN

EARLY 1994 BROUGHT A VERY SPECIAL FAMILY EVENT FOR ME – the visit of Clarice and Alan to Cairo. This was the first time my family had visited me since my arrival in the Middle East, and it was so special for me to show them the centre and introduce them to my colleagues and the children. Clarice and Alan had met Dalal and Badr when we visited the UK some years earlier, but it was their first meeting with Hamoudi. He was now about twenty, while Dalal was eighteen and Badr was thirteen. All three were excited about the visit and, as usual, Hamoudi charmed Clarice and Alan with his personality. They were also delighted to see the progress that Dalal and Badr had made and what fine young people they were becoming.

Around the same time as this family visit, there was much tension and excited anticipation amongst the centre's staff as the date for Yasser Arafat's entry into Palestine approached. As per the agreements of the Oslo Accords, the Gaza Strip and the Jericho area of the West Bank were to be granted interim self-government as part of the process for negotiations on the permanent status to lead, within five years, to the implementation of UN Security Council Resolutions 242 and 338.

The Palestinian people place a great deal of trust and hope in these two resolutions, but unfortunately they are worded vaguely, which leaves them open to different interpretations. The Palestinians read them as a promise of a Palestinian State, comprising the West Bank, East Jerusalem and Gaza Strip, with borders according to the armistice line following the 1967 war. The Israelis don't recognise this interpretation; their interpretation is that they withdraw from 'some' of the area occupied during the 1967 war, according to their interests. Further, they consider that their withdrawal from the Sinai is the major part of this obligation, which doesn't recognise any Palestinian claim. The same words are given very different interpretations, resulting in a stalemate in any attempt to address the issue realistically.

On 1 July 1994, Yasser Arafat made a triumphant entry into the Gaza Strip, where he was to set up his first provisional headquarters to establish the Palestinian Autonomous Region. Crowds thronged to cheer him and make him welcome. Again, the staff at the centre were keen to watch this event on television, and saw it as an important milestone towards a realisation of the State of Palestine.

Most of the Palestinian staff at the centre had made application to the Israeli department responsible for processing permits and were waiting anxiously for a response. The PRCS had applied for permits for Hamoudi, Dalal and Badr, and they, like all around, were excited about the prospect of moving to Palestine. Dalal spoke about the importance of living in 'her own country' instead of always being the foreigner in another country. I was caught up in the general excitement too, but couldn't help wondering how it would work out. How would we manage in Cairo if most of our staff moved back to Palestine? Would the children receive permits? And if they did, when? What would happen to the Ain Shams Centre once we were gone? What would life be like in Palestine?

My trip to Palestine in January 1995 was very different from my previous visits. The Palestinian Authority was in place; the concept of 'Jericho and Gaza first' was being implemented. At the same time, the implementation was not going according to Palestinian expectations. Amongst numerous problems, the construction of Israeli settlements intensified, taking more of the land Palestinians envisaged as being within the future Palestinian State.

Dr Fathi had advised me that the Khan Younis municipality had donated an area of land to the PRCS and that the organisation intended building a community centre there, with a focus on the integration of people with disabilities into the community. Dr Fathi explained that he had selected Khan Younis for this project as the south of the Gaza Strip had been very isolated and disadvantaged, in contrast to the range of services and programs available in Gaza City. Khan Younis was the second largest town in the Gaza Strip, with a population of about 200 000, evenly distributed between the town, the refugee camp and the eastern villages. Israeli settlements surrounded three sides of the area of the town and the camp, and Palestinians had to pass an Israeli army checkpoint to go to the beach.

Dr Fathi asked me to go to Khan Younis to check on progress in establishing a training program and planning programs and services for children with disabilities, to visit the various centres for rehabilitation throughout the Gaza Strip, and to make contact with staff who had trained in Cairo but were now working within the Ministry of Health.

I was able to spend some time with Dr Najat Al-Astal, who was to coordinate the development of the PRCS Institute of Rehabilitation Studies in Khan Younis. She had a copy of the curriculum from the Ain Shams Centre Institute, which we discussed, and I met briefly with the group of twenty-six young people who had enrolled in the course.

The atmosphere in the region was much more relaxed than on my previous visits, especially in Gaza City, where there was a definite air of anticipation. Israeli soldiers were still present, but more related to the several Israeli settlements than to the land in general, and were often seen together with Palestinian army personnel in joint patrols. It was a very emotional experience to see the Palestinian flag flying freely on some of the buildings; I wondered how many young people had been killed during the Intifada for daring to raise the Palestinian flag.

Back at the Ain Shams Centre in Cairo, the atmosphere was one of rapid change and a mixture of excitement and uncertainty. Staff and some clients left at regular intervals as their names appeared on lists with permission from the Israeli government for them to travel into the Gaza Strip. The same was happening in other PRCS facilities in Cairo. Who would leave next? How would we fill the vacancies? Which services would continue and which would stop? It seemed to me that the PRCS would eventually close the Ain Shams Centre, as most of the staff and some of the children were leaving. The majority of children attending programs were Egyptian and many of them were transfering to the new Al-Ghad Al-Mushreq Centre, as were some of the staff – Palestinian and Egyptian – who weren't leaving Egypt.

All people going into Palestine (including myself on visits) were asked to carry a carton of books from the institute library in Cairo to place in the new institute in Khan Younis. It was a very strange period, with many mixed feelings.

Amidst all the excitement, we were also waiting anxiously for the publication of the *Sanawi aam* examination results for final-year secondary students. Dalal was one of the many thousands of students in Egypt waiting to know her results. It was exciting to see her name on the list of those who had passed. *Al-hamdu lillaah* (Thanks be to God). We were thrilled, and Dalal was radiant – in spite of all odds she had been able to achieve this goal. I felt very proud of her and excited about the opportunities now open to her. She began to gather information about university studies.

We expected to be able to travel into Palestine soon, so we focused our search on courses and requirements for Palestinian universities. I hoped, *Inshallah*, that we would be able to travel before the commencement of the academic year, so that Dalal could begin her studies and not be delayed until the following year. After much research, Dalal decided to enter the degree course in English Literature at the Al-Azhar University in Gaza City.

In August 1995 I again travelled to the OPT, but this time, instead of going by tourist coach to Jerusalem, where I usually established my main base, I took the local bus to Rafah on the Egyptian border and crossed over to Khan Younis in the Gaza Strip, which was to be my main base from now on. The purpose of this trip was to make arrangements for the expected transfer of Hamoudi, Dalal and Badr to their new home in Khan Younis, to check on the progress of the institute, and to begin rehabilitation services for children and adults with disability.

This time I stayed in the flat that was to become our home when the children arrived from Egypt. It had three bedrooms, a lounge, a guest room, a kitchen, one main toilet and bathroom, and a second *baladi* toilet with a shower. I requested a dividing wall and door between the guest area and the rest of the flat, which would become Dalal's and my space, with the remainder of the flat for the two boys and the male staff looking after them.

A couple of hundred metres down the street was a large area of land donated to the PRCS by the Khan Younis municipality, where construction of the future community centre had already begun. It was a few minutes' walk from the back of the flat to the two adjacent garage areas that PRCS had acquired and was now using for the institute. The institute took up part of the space; the remainder was to be set up as a rehabilitation centre for children and adults with disabilities. The students in the training course already had a waiting list of children wishing to attend a program. Potential staff were interviewed and several were hired, so I was able to set up the centre, relying on a nucleus of staff from the Ain Shams Centre in Cairo who were suitably experienced to keep the place running until I returned permanently.

On my return to Cairo, it was necessary to make arrangements for the children who would not be accompanying us to Khan Younis. Khaled's family had been in contact with the PRCS, and agreed to come to Cairo for some weeks in order to learn the skills necessary to manage Khaled and then to take him home to Lebanon. If Khaled moved to the Gaza Strip it would be impossible for his family to visit him, as Palestinians from Lebanon always experienced great difficulty in obtaining a permit to travel into the OPT.

Dr Fathi had included Rusha in the plans to move to Khan Younis and we had commenced the process of obtaining an Egyptian passport for her. However, I realised that, unlike our situation in Cairo, it would be difficult to arrange for women staff to work in the residence overnight, which was necessary for Rusha's care, and the residence was very small. Rusha was Egyptian and it didn't seem suitable to move her into such an uncertain situation. Eventually we found a centre for her in Cairo that could care for her properly.

In October 1995 Hamoudi, Dalal, Badr and I set out to travel to Khan Younis. I felt sad to be leaving Khaled and Rusha, but could only hope that they would be okay. This was a major journey for us all, a journey into a new life in Palestine. The children were excited about going to their homeland, and as they were now approaching young adulthood – Hamoudi was about twenty-one, Dalal nineteen and Badr fourteen, there would be other changes in their lives too. Dalal would begin university studies and Badr would soon need to begin a vocational training program. Hamoudi would experience a change to his pattern of care and training from female staff to male staff. A whole new world seemed to be opening up. I shared their excitement and anticipation, but also wondered what life would be like in the Gaza Strip.

Although I had been to the Gaza Strip several times, I didn't know a great deal about it; I had spent more time on the West Bank, the larger of the two Occupied Palestinian Territories, during my visits. The Gaza Strip is a small area bordered by the Mediterranean Sea to the west, the 'green line' (the armistice line, following the 1948 war, and again following the 1967 war, that separates it from Israel) to the north and the east, and Egypt to the south. In 1995, with a population of almost one million, the Gaza Strip was considered to be one of the most densely populated areas of the world.

My early views of the region, with its beautiful coastal strip, the eucalyptus trees lining the central north–south road, as well as hibiscus, bougainvillea, jacaranda and poincianas, reminded me of my Queensland home. It was magical to drive along the beach road in the late afternoon and watch the sun sinking into the sea, radiating pink, orange and yellow into the clusters of grey clouds. It wasn't all beautiful though: the main part comprised densely populated areas, which was intensified in the overcrowded refugee camps. In the shopping areas, metal doors enclosed the shop windows, decorated with graffiti. Donkey and horse carts mixed with cars, minibuses and commercial vehicles on the busy roads. Rubbish lay piled at the sides of the streets and torn kites dangled from electricity and telephone wires. On my visits during the first Intifada, I'd seen the remains of burnt tyres on the roads, Israeli army jeeps everywhere, and sensed the fear. Nevertheless, the people I met were exuberant, kind and hospitable, and industrious and creative in their approach to their work. The contrast between such beauty, the modern developments and great disadvantage gave me a glimpse of the complexity of the place.

I was always fascinated by the difference in character between the Gaza Strip and the West Bank. The topography is very different, and whilst a large percentage of the West Bank is rural, only a small percentage of the Gaza Strip is. Both have a substantial urban population. It is estimated that approximately 32 per cent of people in the Gaza Strip live in refugee camps, while in the West Bank it is approximately 5 per cent. Although initially displaced Palestinians were provided with tents as refugee camps were established, over time the camps have become a mixture of crowded cement block structures with asbestos roofing and buildings with three or four storeys. Many of these multi-storey buildings remain unfinished.

An interesting aspect of the population of the Gaza Strip is the existence of four distinct Palestinian groups: the original residents of Gaza; the Bedouin; and post-1948 and post-1967 Palestinian refugees from what is now Israel. In the 1990s, there were also Palestinians returning from the diaspora following the Oslo Accords, creating a division between insiders and outsiders. The population of the Occupied Palestinian Territories is also known for its youthfulness; in the Gaza Strip, more than 50 per cent of the population is younger than fifteen.

The Gaza Strip, as we know it today, is an entity that came into being only after the 1967 Israeli–Arab war. The British Mandate of 1920 to 1948 defined a Gaza District, which spread from the coast eastward beyond Beersheva. Prior to this, the various occupying powers defined areas under their control, including not only what is now Israel, West Bank and the Gaza Strip, but also parts of what is today Lebanon, Jordan, Syria, Egypt and beyond. Gaza was an important trade centre and had a rich hinterland. However, with the drawing of armistice lines in 1949, Gaza was cut off from its hinterland. Night raids by the Israeli army into Gaza City and other towns during the 1950s, with many Palestinians killed, wounded or detained, increased the resentment of the Palestinian people towards Israel. Following the 1967 war and Israeli occupation, the Gaza Strip became completely isolated and considered somewhat as a 'backwater'. All aspects of life in the Gaza Strip came under Israeli military control, including access to water and electricity and the movement of people and goods in and out of the area. Palestinians often described the Gaza Strip under Israeli occupation as the largest prison in the world.

Another difficulty for Palestinians in Gaza was that more than a third of the coastline and other areas in the centre and north were Israeli settlements, built post-1967 when Israel occupied the area. There were twenty-one Israeli settlements in the Gaza Strip, housing approximately 8600 settlers strategically placed to the north and south of the region. The largest spread of settlements, in Gush Katif, partially surrounded the refugee camp and town of Khan Younis and also parts of Rafah. To reach the small section of beach that Palestinians were permitted to use, adjacent to Khan Younis, it was necessary to pass through an Israeli army checkpoint. Once through, Palestinians needed to quickly cross the settlers road to the far inferior Arab road leading to the Palestinian area of Al-Mawasi, a rural and fishing area, and through to the beach.

A people with a long history of being subjected to conflict, displacement, dispossession and occupation, Palestinians have not lost their spirit for survival. It is not surprising that the first Intifada, which began in December 1987, was an outbreak of mass feeling against oppression and began in the Jabalya refugee camp in the northern Gaza Strip. For most Palestinians, the Peace Process seemed to offer the chance to develop their own country and look forward to a future of peace and opportunity. The possible flaws in the agreements weren't issues that concerned the majority of the people, who just wanted to be able to carry out activities required for their day-to-day living.

As we set off on our journey from Cairo to Khan Younis, however, my thoughts weren't on the history of the Gaza Strip, but on the practical matter of getting us there. I was worried about how we were going to manage the move with Hamoudi. The arrangement was for the PRCS minibus to transport us to the border at Rafah, where we would make the crossing into the OPT. Two of the staff – Nagwa and Mahmoud – were able to obtain permits in time to travel with us and so assist during the journey. They made this arrangement on their own initiative, which was a kind gesture on their part and certainly made me feel more relaxed. Mahmoud had actually made the seven-hour trip to the Rafah crossing the day before, to accompany his wife and children, before returning to help us. Also with us were Dr Ismaeil and a nurse, Mohammed.

We decided to travel at night as, hopefully, the children would sleep and there would be fewer problems organising meals and medicines. It would also be more comfortable crossing the Sinai Desert region without the hot sun overhead. We were all packed and ready to leave at around 10 pm; all that was left to be done was to speak the common Arabic expression that asked for God's blessing on our journey: *Bismillah Al-Rahman Al-Raheem* (in the name of God, the most merciful, the most compassionate).

Hamoudi seemed a bit bothered by the unusual situation – the lateness of the hour, the packing, the noise, the general atmosphere of people saying their goodbyes. Suddenly, he began to vomit. Oh, help, I thought. We had a journey of about seven hours ahead of us and Hamoudi was in trouble before we'd started. Fortunately, Dr Ismaeil gave him an injection to arrest the vomiting. He seemed okay once we set off, but I couldn't get him to settle to sleep. No doubt everything felt very strange to him. Although we had spoken about the move many times, he may not have fully understood what it would mean. The mixed emotions, together with the major change to his routine, was obviously disturbing him. The other children were okay, although nobody actually managed to sleep.

At one point we lost the truck that was supposed to be travelling in convoy with us, which caused some delay until we found it. It was loaded with furniture, bedding, wheelchairs, various other essential items and clothes, so we couldn't afford to lose it. Eventually, we arrived at the Egyptian side of the Rafah crossing at about 7 am. Fortunately it didn't take long to exit Egypt, and we were also able to feed Hamoudi and give him his medicines. The level of excitement amongst the children and staff was mounting as we were now very close to the realisation of their dreams: entering Palestine.

We moved out of the hall to find our transport to the Israeli border control. Dr Jamal had organised for a minibus to take the children, myself, Nagwa and Dr Ismaeil. Mahmoud and Mohammed were organising arrangements concerning the truck and would continue their journey later. (In fact, getting all of the luggage through took Mahmoud and Mohammed several days.)

It was late morning by the time we had cleared the Israeli procedures. The minibus then took us out of the area to the Palestinian entry point. There were two PRCS ambulances waiting to take us to Khan Younis. Dr Jamal had taken the precaution of arranging them as we had all been concerned about how Hamoudi would manage the seven-hour journey from Cairo to the border. *Al-hamdu lillaah ala al-salama* (thanks be to God for safe arrival), Hamoudi was okay and didn't need medical attention.

We arrived at the flat in Khan Younis tired but fine, and found staff waiting to greet us. Some we knew from Cairo days, others were new to us, but all were excited to see us. It was difficult to believe that we were now in Palestine.

Dalal and Badr excitedly explored their new home and exchanged kisses and hugs with all who greeted them. Hamoudi was happy and responded well to all the fuss, but at the same time seemed a bit uncertain about what was happening around him.

Once I was assured that there were suitable arrangements in place for the care of the three young people, I went to check on the progress of the institute and the rehabilitation centre. I could see that although construction had begun on the new building, there was little advancement beyond the foundations and ground floor. The garage space we were using temporarily for both the institute and the rehabilitation centre, however, although small and very basic in design, was serving our purpose very well. It was crowded, as the institute had more than twenty first-year students and the rehabilitation centre now had ten staff and approximately one hundred children and youth attending, but I was pleased by the way the staff had managed since

I had set up the program in August. I felt that we had a sound base from which we could develop further.

There was a constant flow of people seeking places for children and adults with disabilities in our programs. Although we were limited in the number of clients we could accept and the number of staff we could employ, I was looking closely at ways to meet the needs of more of these people. Now that I was present, and with the assistance of Nagwa and Mahmoud, both experienced senior personnel, such planning was possible. Initially, I spent time working with individual children and closely monitoring the programs being developed by staff, but I gradually passed over these responsibilities when possible. At times a parent would come to the centre insisting that I, personally, see their child, but in such cases I would meet the family but arrange for the social worker and developmental workers to follow up, explaining that these people had the skills to give the assistance required, and could deal with their needs even better than I could. I was keen to dispel expectations that a 'foreigner' would automatically provide better service than local staff. At the same time, I was re-establishing my links with the other rehabilitation centres in the Gaza Strip, most of them located in Gaza City.

One of the features that has always impressed me – in Australia, in other countries, and now in Palestine – is the way in which many families give so much care and attention to their family member who is disabled. There are so many stories, so many families, that I bring to mind, but there were four special families in our early days in Khan Younis that made a marked impression on me. Mahmoud, a bright boy of about eight years old, was severely disabled with cerebral palsy. He could walk with some difficulty, if he was supported. His sister, not very much older than him, took the time to walk carefully with him each day in order for him to attend a program, and then came again to take him back home. Halima, a pretty little girl of about ten, was disabled with a degenerative dystrophy, but each day her father brought her to and from the centre on his bicycle. The mother of twin five year olds, both with intellectual disabilities, walked with her children to the centre every day. Ibrahiem was a nine year old with spina bifida whose brother manoeuvred his wheelchair down a narrow stairway, and then along the unpaved alley between houses in the camp, in order to ensure Ibraheim was able to attend the special education classes at the centre. These people, and many other parents and family members, were keen to work closely with the staff to assist their children in the best way possible, and followed their progress keenly.

I was working in my office one evening when suddenly there was a commotion on the steps and a group of young men entered my office carrying another man. Mohammed was paraplegic due to a car accident some months previously. He had received some treatment directly after the accident from a neurosurgeon in Jordan and his friends wanted me to arrange for Mohammed to return to Jordan to see this doctor as they were sure that it would then be possible for him to walk again. This was an example of the unrealistic expectations people had – not only of the condition of disability but also that foreigners had the answers they sought. Mohammed looked like a bright young man but was silent. I insisted on asking him questions rather than relying on the people with him for answers. I tried to lead them to think about the reality of the situation and what we could offer in relation to that. Mohammed had been a car mechanic prior to his accident, but when I said that he must be clever with his hands and therefore able to learn suitable work, his companions weren't impressed. 'Look at him!' they said. 'What could he do?' I convinced them to come back in the morning to meet with me and the staff to look more closely at what would be the most suitable plan for Mohammed. They did, and Mohammed soon became very active in the production workshops and in sport. He travelled abroad with our sport group, and some years later got married. His life held so much more potential than his friends could imagine that evening.

I had been looking forward to more of the staff who had trained and worked with us in Cairo coming to join our endeavours in Khan Younis, but I was faced with an unexpected situation. Many of the Palestinians who had sought out the PRCS whilst part of the diaspora no longer needed this connection and support once they were able to return to Palestine. They scattered across the Gaza Strip, according to where their families were located, and quickly became absorbed in the wider community. Many of our former staff were already employed in a range of different locations – some in rehabilitation centres, but others in entirely different professions. At first, I felt disappointed, but I quickly realised that this was really a natural process of people returning to their homeland. And those who were working in other rehabilitation organisations were greatly valued and now able to share with other organisations and families in Palestine the training they had received with the PRCS.

Fortunately, some former staff members did continue to work with us and played a vital role in the establishment of high standards. I also felt it was important to include people who had been living in the area prior to the influx of newcomers, some of whom had been working for a large organisation that provided services for children with intellectual disability but had now closed. Although the majority had limited training, they brought to the centre their knowledge of the local people and conditions. Together, these two different groups worked very hard to contribute to the developments that were taking place at Khan Younis.

Badr was one of the new clients to enter the centre. He continued with a special education program, but was also involved in some pre-vocational activities such as weaving. Although Hamoudi's program was carried out largely at home, his carers brought him on visits to the centre to widen his contact with people; and twice a week he had an outing in the car. I had worried that the men responsible for looking after Hamoudi might not give him the same attention as the women had done. It was important for him to have male carers, though: at twenty-one, he needed to know more about a man's world. My worry was ill-founded. The men were every bit as caring and, in fact, involved him in a more active program.

All the men working in the rehabilitation centre were listed for night duty once a week or fortnight. Students at the institute were also scheduled to spend time learning to work with Hamoudi, which included some night duty for the male students. Two men were on duty at a time and in addition to engaging in different activities with Hamoudi – and sometimes Badr – they were responsible for attending to all of Hamoudi's needs, such as feeding, changing, supervising his positioning during the night, and keeping careful records in his day book. This system enabled the men to learn important skills, provided Hamoudi and Badr with a number of different men in their lives, and ensured there were always adequate numbers of specialised staff available. Hamoudi soon became 'our professor' once again, with more people learning skills from him that enabled them to help many other children.

ELEVEN

DALAL WAS EXCITED ABOUT ENTERING UNIVERSITY. The semester commenced within a week of our arrival, so we needed to go immediately into Gaza City – about a three-quarter-hour drive from Khan Younis – to finalise her registration in the English Literature Department of Al-Azhar University.

From the beginning, it was obvious that Dalal might face some difficulties: some of the staff tried to persuade her that English Literature was too difficult for a blind student to manage. There had never been a blind student in the department and obviously they didn't know how to deal with the situation. However, Dalal had made up her mind and wasn't to be discouraged by such remarks.

We also needed to make suitable arrangements for safe transport for Dalal between Khan Younis and the university. I went with her initially, to see her settled into a routine, but this couldn't be an ongoing arrangement. Fortunately, a relative of one of our staff had a seven-seater share taxi and agreed to take Dalal as a regular passenger. It was quite common for people to make such an arrangement with the driver of a share taxi, who would pick up his regular passengers from their homes, then take in other people to fill the seats. This worked well for Dalal, although it was a tiring day for her.

She experienced some uncertainty when she arrived at the university as she needed help to find her way to the classroom. She didn't know anybody there, and it was the first time she had been alone in an institution where all of the students were sighted. I tried to teach her to use her cane when on campus, but the place was always crowded and there were too many difficult and irregular features for safe mobility. Dalal felt it wasn't feasible and reluctantly I agreed with her.

Soon, however, she had a group of friends – very nice young women who were amongst the best students in the class – who would be waiting to meet her when she arrived, and would stay with her at the end of the day until the taxi arrived. This group of friends stood by her when there were problems – such as arrangements for a writer at examination time – and ensured that she wasn't discriminated against because of her blindness. Dalal and her friends often laughed about a later confession from one of them who said that when she first saw Dalal in their class she was afraid to speak to her as she thought people who were blind were always crying and sad. Initially, the lecturers were unwilling for Dalal to record their classes, despite her explanation that she only wanted to record main points such as they would write on the board. Instead, she asked other students if she could borrow their notes, which I could then record for her or she would copy out in Braille. Dalal soon gained the respect of the staff, however, including those who had initially suggested she take a different major. The Royal National Institute for the Blind in the UK were very friendly and cooperative in getting Braille books mailed to us quickly, which helped Dalal a great deal with much of her required reading of novels and plays.

Because she lived in Khan Younis, she wasn't able to attend music activities or enrol in French classes as these were held only in Gaza City in the late afternoon or evening. I was very sorry that she couldn't continue with music as it had been such an important part of her life and something she loved. However, she was able to join an English literature club that was held on Friday mornings (the weekend) at the British Council building in Gaza City. Fortunately, there were members living in Khan Younis who were delighted to meet her and travel together to the club activities.

Another new experience for Dalal was the university regulation requiring all female students to wear a scarf to cover their hair. Although Dalal is a sincere Muslim, she didn't normally wear a scarf. Male and female students also attended separate lectures. The main universities of the West Bank didn't have such regulations, but life in the Gaza Strip followed a more conservative pattern.

For many years, while the West Bank – especially in the central region of Jerusalem and Bethlehem – experienced a continuous flow of foreign visitors, few travelled to the Gaza Strip, and those who did usually confined their visit to Gaza City in the northern part, closer to the Israeli Erez crossing. As a result, the southern part of the Gaza Strip – towns like Khan Younis and Rafah – tended to be isolated and disadvantaged. This situation was evident, amongst other indicators, in the women's dress. Most women wore full-length skirts, and all wore a scarf to cover their hair. Foreigners weren't required to conform with this dress code, but if respectful to local customs they would be sure to dress modestly. Many residents in Gaza City who did not usually wear a scarf would wear one when visiting the south.

Since the establishment of the Palestinian Authority, however, Gaza City was changing. The atmosphere was becoming more open, there was a great deal of development taking place – the building of hotels along the beachfront in anticipation of increased tourism, for example – and an increasing range of items available in the stores. Dress styles for women were changing too; some women continued to wear scarves, but just as many chose not to. The situation wasn't at the same level as cities such as Jerusalem and Ramallah on the West Bank, but things were obviously changing and the region was full of hope.

It was the disadvantaged status of the southern part of the Gaza Strip that had influenced Dr Fathi's choice of Khan Younis as the location of the first of the new PRCS developments in Palestine. Dr Fathi met with me on several occasions to stress the importance of the work he had asked me to do in developing the rehabilitation services and the institute's program. His vision was for people with disabilities to be fully integrated into the community, and to be an integral part of the centre and so have the opportunity to serve their community in addition to receiving services themselves. He saw the centre as being for all people, noting that everyone needed an opportunity to develop their abilities.

In keeping with this philosophy, several young men with hearing impairment were employed in the PRCS carpentry workshop to make the fittings and furniture for the building. There were many young women, some with hearing impairment and some with physical disability, working in the traditional embroidery (*tatrez*), knitting and sewing workshops who also contributed to making fittings and other items for the centre. Additional workshops were established, and some of the people with disabilities became responsible for managing these areas.

Construction of the PRCS building had come to a standstill for a time, but by the end of 1995 it was beginning to take shape. I was horrified, however, to see a set of stairs at the main entrance. I expressed my concern to Dr Fathi and the engineers, and an attractive curving ramp was added to the design, making the building readily accessible to wheelchair-users.

There was considerable discussion about what name to give the centre; the final decision was Medina Al-Amal (Hope City) – Centre of Ability Development. The main complex had four floors, with a tower above the back section that went up to ten floors. The tower housed a hotel, with about seventy rooms, that would provide accommodation for international volunteers, and for participants in conferences. There was no other hotel in the south of the Gaza Strip, so it would also be available to anyone seeking accommodation. In the main building was the rehabilitation centre, a college, workshops, a cafeteria, a restaurant, two theatres and a museum; adjacent to it was a market place, sports hall, all-purpose hall, and a hospital and emergency medical services station.

A committee was established to monitor the developments taking place in Al-Amal City, and I was appointed as deputy chair. The chair was the PRCS Director General, Younis Al-Khatib, but as he was based at the PRCS headquarters in Al-Bireh and was seldom able to travel into the Gaza Strip, I actually had full responsibility for organising and conducting the meetings. This wasn't an easy task as few of the committee members had experience with teamwork, nor had they yet grasped Dr Fathi's community centre vision. Their view was more focused on position and authority. Fortunately, there were some who had a much broader view and they worked with me to fulfil our responsibilities.

Living so close to the sea, I was able to make arrangements as summer approached for us to take the children to the beach on the weekend (Friday) and sometimes in the early evening on other days. I often went into the sea with Dalal and Badr so they could experience the joy of playing in the surf – something I was keen to do myself too. Dalal and I needed to be fully dressed in jeans and a top to swim, but this didn't interfere with our enjoyment. Sometimes we would hold Hamoudi at the water's edge so he could feel the waves splashing on his feet.

These were very special outings enjoyed by all, but there was one big problem: the Israeli settlement block of Gush Katif. One of the biggest of these settlements was at the western end of Khan Younis refugee camp, and we had to pass it in order to reach the small section of beach that Palestinians were permitted to use. There was an Israeli checkpoint on the road near the camp. A number of our staff were afraid to pass through this checkpoint, either because their initial visit permit had expired and their application for residence hadn't been approved – all controlled by the Israeli government – or they had experienced problems with the Israeli army during the first Intifada (which was the case for most of the young men who had been living in Palestine at that time).

In early November 1995, the Israeli Prime Minister, Yitzhak Rabin, was assassinated by an Israeli religious zealot who objected to the peace process. This created new tensions in the region and made it even more difficult for Palestinians to move in and out of the Gaza Strip. Such movement was made dependent on receiving permits that were granted to only a few of those who applied for them. The Israeli elections in June 1996 brought the right-wing Likud party into power, with Benjamin Netanyahu as Prime Minister. Netanyahu was known for his hawkish position in dealing with the Palestinian people, and had expressed opposition to the Labor Party of Yitzhak Rabin negotiating with the Palestinians. We all wondered what the future would hold.

Ramadan in 1995 fell in late December through to January 1996. Ramadan is the Islamic holy month of fasting, the beginning and end of which is determined by the sighting of the new moon. A senior sheik makes the sighting and the people wait in anticipation for the announcement. Fasting lasts from before the sun rises to when it sets. The people seem to form a special bond during this period, supporting one another to maintain the fast in spite of any difficulty encountered. A man walks around the narrow streets banging on a drum in the early hours of the morning, calling to the people to wake up for the *suhur*, the last meal before sunrise and the beginning of the fast. The call from the mosque at sunrise reminds the people that the period of fasting has begun. Dalal has been very conscientious about fasting since her early teens. I get up in the early morning to prepare her *suhur* and eat with her. Badr would like to fast, but because of the set times for his epilepsy medication he is unable to do so; he proudly says that he fasts for half a day. Although I don't fast, I don't eat or drink in front of colleagues who are fasting.

Throughout Ramadan people greet one another and exchange cards to celebrate the month. There are traditional drinks and foods in the shops, and lanterns, which children love to swing from side to side as they sing special songs. Paper decorations are strung across some of the narrow laneways in the camps, together with lanterns and balloons. We always have a supply of *kaak* (a date-filled biscuit) to serve to guests, and receive many packages of homemade *kaak* from visitors. In Cairo, when the children were younger, they used to work together with the staff on duty to make their own *kaak*.

During the month of Ramadan the work day is shortened by an hour, so there is a celebratory atmosphere in the workplace. Most people fulfil their work commitments as usual, but others tend to slow down during this period. Towards the end of the day, households are busy ensuring that the food for the *Fitar* is set out ready for when the call from the mosque signals the end of the fast for the day. The *Fitar* is a special time for family, or friends and colleagues, to share a meal together during Ramadan. Dalal, Badr and I are often invited to share the *Fitar* with our friends. Towards the end of Ramadan, there is a special night, Leilat Al-Qadr (The Night of Power) when the people believe that the sky opens for the prayers of the people. This is the holiest night of Ramadan. Special prayers are held in the mosques, and some devout men spend the whole night there.

Excitement mounts as Ramadan draws to its end and people eagerly await the beginning of the Eid Al-Fitar (the feast at the end of the month of fasting), with all of its activities and the greetings of *Eid Mubarak* (congratulations on succeeding in maintaining the fast during Ramadan) or *Eid Saed* (Happy Feast). On about the twenty-ninth day of fasting, the people wait in the evening to hear if the sheik has sighted the new moon or not. If there is a sighting, the feast will begin the next day. Usually there are three days' holiday for the feast. On the first morning, many men and some women go to the mosque for early prayers. Children get up early to dress in new clothes and play with the toys they may have received, and then head outside, playing on the streets to show off their new clothes. There is also a focus on the old and those who are ill, as it is important to give to people in need during Ramadan. The PRCS usually organises official visits to patients in hospitals, and some come to visit Hamoudi, Dalal and Badr. The meal of the day is a family affair, and once the feast is over everything swings back to the normal pace.

In April 1996, almost three months after the Eid Al-Fitar, came the time for making pilgrimage (Al-Hajj) to Mecca. Millions of Muslims from all over the word travel to Mecca to perform Al-Hajj so the Saudi Arabian government has set quotas for each country. Those who have applied to travel wait anxiously to hear if their name has been selected. (People can make a smaller private pilgrimage – *Umrah* – at any time of the year.) For Palestinians living in the Gaza Strip who want to make the pilgrimage, there is always the worry about getting through the Rafah crossing, which is frequently closed for long periods. Usually during this time, the Israeli army will open the crossing for a few set hours so the pilgrims can move through.

Returning pilgrims are given a special welcome and congratulated for making Al-Hajj. Now they have the right to be addressed as 'Hajj' (for men) or 'Hajjah' (for women). These titles are also used as a general form of respect when speaking to an older person, even if they have not made Al-Hajj and even if they are not Muslim. I am sometimes addressed this way, purely because of my white hair.

The pilgrims bring back gifts for family and close friends such as prayer beads, a prayer cap or other significant items. Dalal, Badr and Hamoudi have often received such gifts from staff members or neighbours returning from Al-Hajj.

TWELVE

WHEN WE ENTERED THE GAZA STRIP, the children and staff had a special visit permit issued by the Israeli authorities. The next step was to apply for residence status and obtain their *hawea* (ID), also issued by the Israeli government. The process took time – sometimes months, sometimes years – and sometimes it never happened at all. Those waiting for their ID are basically stateless, unable to move anywhere.

My situation as a foreigner is different. To enter the Gaza Strip and the West Bank, the boundaries of which were controlled by Israel, I need an Israeli visa, which also enables me to move around in Israel itself. I was given a three-month visa when we entered the Gaza Strip in October 1995. It is extremely difficult to obtain a longer-period visa and work permit from the Israeli authorities, and for those foreigners working with Palestinian organisations it is virtually impossible.

Thus, from January 1996 I have had to travel out of the area in order to return and renew my visa. For some years I maintained my residency in Egypt, which enabled me to enter and leave at any time without any problem. Unfortunately, the visa I was granted at the Israeli border as I returned to the Gaza Strip was often for one month only, which caused difficulties in relation to both time and money. Fortunately, a few of the female staff were prepared to work night duty to be with Dalal when I was away (usually the women were unable to be out of their homes at night) and the boys were well cared for, with a well-established schedule of male staff night and day.

Once Dalal and Badr had received ID cards and passports, I sometimes took them them with me when I needed to travel to renew my visa. I only took one at a time so I could give each my full attention, but also so there was always someone at home with Hamoudi so he didn't feel that we'd all left him. Unlike our Cairo days, there weren't any short-stay children to keep him company. When Dalal came to Cairo, she enjoyed seeing the PRCS staff and our family friends, and also met up with her school friends, most of them now also at university. It was easy for Dalal to enter Egypt as the Egyptian government had a special arrangement for Palestinian women to enter without a visa. It was much more complicated for Badr, as there were restrictions and regulations concerning Palestinian males from fifteen through to forty. Fortunately we were able to get permit papers for him when it was his turn to travel with me.

In spite of my heavy workload and the need to travel so often, time spent with Hamoudi, Dalal and Badr was a precious and important part of my life. Language was always an interesting factor in our time together – a strange mixture of Arabic, English and Hamoudi's sounds – but there was never any problem of understanding. Dalal's English was much better than my Arabic, so when it came to complex discussions we used English. If there were other people to be included in the conversation, Dalal easily translated. Most of the staff working with me do not speak English so a lot of my work is conducted in Arabic, and staff quickly develop an understanding of my rather quaint accent and use of the language.

In addition to my work at Khan Younis as director of the PRCS rehabilitation department, it was also necessary for me to travel across to PRCS headquarters on the West Bank at Ramallah, which is a centre for the government of the Palestinian Authority (PA). I needed to visit the PRCS rehabilitation centres in Nablus, Jericho, Ramallah and Hebron and work with the staff there to develop a unified policy for rehabilitation. The PRCS staff in the different centres were obviously dealing with difficult conditions, but they always entered enthusiastically into discussions about their work and plans. Although it was difficult to arrange for colleagues from the Gaza Strip to join these meetings, because of the permit situation, I was able to represent their work and to bring them information from the West Bank.

To get to the West Bank from the Gaza Strip, I had to go through the Erez crossing. Once the PA had been established, the structure of the crossing changed from a passage through occupied territory to a border crossing from territory partially controlled by the Palestinian Authority into Israel. It was no longer possible to join a share taxi in Gaza City and travel direct to Ramallah; the share taxi could only go as far as the PA military base. From there it was necessary to walk through to the Israeli station (somewhat incongruously named VIP) some hundred metres on. Here, one had to obtain a permit to enter Israel, then cross into an area where share taxis waited to take passengers to different towns of the West Bank or into Israel.

Palestinians had to cross at a different location from foreigners, which resembled a cattle-sorting area. In the early morning and again in the late afternoon, thousands who travelled each day from the Gaza Strip into Israel for work were herded through with much noise and confusion. It made for a very long working day, with people leaving home at 3–5 am and not returning until 7–8 pm. These workers had special passes to go through Erez crossing each day to provide cheap labour in Israeli construction and to fill general labour jobs. Without development of industry in the Gaza Strip, an economic dependency on Israel had emerged.

The Israeli VIP station was under military control, so all the personnel, both men and women, were heavily armed – a situation that made me feel very uncomfortable. When re-entering Gaza Strip following my work on the West Bank, there was always the additional tension of wondering how long it would take to get the permit, or if it might be denied. I only relaxed once my passport had been returned with the entry permit and I had completed the walk back to Palestinian territory.

Dealing with this crossing made me realise the significance of the arguments against the conditions set out in the documents of the Peace Process. It had been announced to the world that the Gaza Strip was now under the control of the Palestinian Authority, and President Yasser Arafat had established his headquarters in Gaza City. At the same time, however, Israel had complete control of the borders; Palestinians, including the President, required an Israeli permit to move in and out of the area; registration of Palestinian residency and authorisation of ID cards was controlled by Israel; and Israel required all merchandise and products to pass through its control at Karni crossing (Al-Mintar). Restrictions remained on how far out to sea fishermen were permitted to work, and the Israeli army patrolled the 'settler only' areas.

My puzzlement about the situation intensified each time I travelled to the West Bank and the taxi skirted parts of Jerusalem on the way to Ramallah. Everywhere there was evidence of construction taking place: the settlements were growing into cities with multi-storey buildings. Throughout the West Bank, the spread of Israeli settlements was evident, the neat white buildings with their red roofs stretched along the hilltops overlooking Palestinian towns and villages in the valleys below. I was told that the placement of settlements was significant in relation to control of water resources in the area, with a negative effect on many Palestinian farms and orchards. How could this be when there was supposed to be a Peace Process between Israel and the Palestinians, with the expectation of a viable, independent Palestinian State beside Israel made up of the pre-1967 green line areas of the West Bank, East Jerusalem and the Gaza Strip? I couldn't understand how there could be any continuity of area with all of this Israeli settlement development, which was obviously ongoing. There also seemed to be an ongoing program for the construction of additional roads to enable settlers to bypass Palestinian towns and villages – roads that were being built on farms and other land confiscated from Palestinian people. Israeli army patrols were ever present on the highways, and it was impossible for Palestinians to enter Jerusalem without a special permit.

We had all settled well into our new life in Khan Younis. It was quiet, the people were friendly, and although we were ever aware of the tensions and problems, we weren't directly involved with them. Our routine was generally uneventful.

I prepared breakfast and supper for Dalal and Badr each day, and we ate together. Women staff from the centre were rostered to clean, wash, cook and attend to chores in the residence. There were two male carers with Hamoudi at all times, and they kept a day book of the work and activities they did with him so as to ensure ongoing stability to his life. I spent some time with Hamoudi in the mornings, before going to work at the Al-Amal building or to Gaza City for meetings. Our special time of the day was in the evenings, an hour or so before Hamoudi went to bed. Dalal, Hamoudi, Badr and I, plus the men on duty, would sit and chat, play and share in a range of activities. Once Hamoudi was in bed, Dalal and Badr would leave with me to eat supper in the other flat, but I always returned to check on Hamoudi once his carers had changed him and prepared him for sleep. Once Dalal, Badr and I had finished supper, they went off to prepare for bed while I usually followed up work on the computer or corresponded via email with relatives and friends in different parts of the world.

Badr was now running a small stall in the rehabilitation centre where he sold sweets and potato chips to the children and staff. He enjoyed this task, and took it very seriously, but did need assistance in dealing with the money. On several occasions when I was with Badr in one of the stores in town, I was delighted to see him check out the range of sweets on display. 'Oh, look,' he'd call to me on discovering something new, 'the kids would like this. I'll buy some like this next time I am getting supplies for my shop.'

Dalal was enjoying university life, and with her group of friends around her, she had fewer stresses to deal with. More people were getting to know Hamoudi, and he enjoyed his outings and being included in activities and events that took place in the centre. Visitors to the centre always expressed how much they were impressed by these three young people: Dalal with her language proficiency and happy, wise manner; Badr's enthusiasm and friendliness; and Hamoudi's charm.

On several occasions I was very pleased to hear the reactions of visitors who saw how the men worked with Hamoudi. 'Where did you find men like that?' they'd ask. 'They are so skilled and caring; they really like Hamoudi and enjoy their work.' I felt proud of the men, and liked to see them receiving such compliments as they were still undervalued by some of the administration.

In November 1996, Al-Amal City was ready to accommodate the rehabilitation centre and the institute. By now there were approximately three hundred and fifty clients attending programs at the centre and more than twenty staff. Everyone was excited about the move into the new complex, but in a way I was sorry to be leaving the simple, more independent location in the garage areas.

The theatre, with over eight hundred seats in the stalls and balcony, was also complete and ready to host the official opening ceremony of Al-Amal City – Centre of Ability Development. The Palestinian President, Yasser Arafat, was to do the honours. The PRCS Seventh Congress, the first to be held in Palestine, was also to take place in the new building, immediately after the opening. This was a very exciting time: the official opening of the new complex, the first PRCS congress in Palestine, and the opportunity for the local people to meet their leader. It was beyond the imagination of most Palestinians that such an event could take place, and that they would have the opportunity to shake the hand of their President.

There was a feeling of anticipation as guests arrived, passing the reception line of young women dressed in traditional embroidered Palestinian dress (*toob*). A display of traditional embroidery was arranged in the theatre's ceiling, and the front row of chairs had been carefully crafted in the carpentry workshop by disabled young men and upholstered with the embroidery of young women attending workshops in the centre, the majority of whom were disabled. These young people were proud of what they had done and were delighted by the surprise and praise expressed by visitors. There was a feeling of pride and enthusiasm throughout the building, and a strong sense that this was a place where people with disability could contribute to the development of the community as a whole.

The theatre was packed to capacity by the time the ceremony was due to begin. Dalal, dressed in a *toob*, was proudly escorted across stage by Badr to play the Palestinian national anthem on her flute. Both were then warmly greeted by Yasser Arafat. I had the honour of presenting a small speech on PRCS's work in rehabilitation and the role of the centre in relation to the provision of opportunity for people with disability and their families.

The PRCS Congress opened with a film about the work of PRCS, which began with the Israeli invasion of Beirut in 1982. Suddenly the roar of war planes and exploding bombs filled the auditorium. Dalal was sitting with a group near the front of the theatre and I quickly moved towards them as I saw how distressed she was. Hysterical and shaking, she clung to me as I led her outside the theatre. Although clearly shaken by the noise of the planes and the bombing, Dalal regained her composure amazingly quickly. She expressed her surprise that she still had so much pent-up fear and that it could overwhelm her in such a way. Twenty minutes later, however, she was able to walk on stage and play flute.

As this was the first meeting of the PRCS Congress to take place inside Palestine, and within the first PRCS community centre to be built in Palestine, the entire proceedings were charged with happy excitement. People who had not been able to meet for years embraced one another. It seemed like a new beginning; the reawakening of hope.

One of the most emotional moments was when a small group entered the auditorium soon after proceedings had begun. Dr Fathi rushed from his seat to greet them warmly. Other officials moved towards them as well, bringing proceedings to a halt and generating a swell of conversations as people asked one another what was happening. Hand in hand, with Dr Fathi leading, the small group walked onto the stage. I recognised some of them but still didn't understand what was happening. Then Dr Fathi announced that these people were PRCS colleagues from Lebanon; that they had been trying to enter the Gaza Strip from Egypt for some days, and had just arrived. It had been a difficult journey, and some had not been permitted to enter at all. The response of the audience was a long and enthusiastic standing ovation. The arrival of this group seemed to signify that there would be a better future, *Inshallah*, when Palestinians, wherever they were, would be able to be together in Palestine.

Amongst the foreign visitors at the opening ceremony was Willem Vugveeten, a Dutch psychologist working in the fields of mental health and intellectual disability. Willem was a long-time friend of Dr Fathi's and a supporter of the Palestinian people. I was delighted to meet him and his colleagues, as I had heard a great deal about him over several years. He told me about an idea he had to organise a team of artists to come from the Netherlands to do some paintings to hang in the centre and to develop expressive and creative programs for the children.

A few months later Willem returned with a team sponsored by the Dutch HOPE Foundation (Holland Office of Personal Encouragement). The foundation had established programs for youth with intellectual disability and mental illness in the Netherlands, and was keen to support the development of an atelier – the Open Studio – in the PRCS centre. Ingrid Rollema, a well-known artist and sculptor, took on the role of project coordinator and so the activities of storytelling, expressive art, drama, puppetry, movement and music began to develop. Gradually the children's work and photos of their activities adorned the area and the Open Studio quickly acquired the appearance and atmosphere of a place for expression and creativity; a place that was fun. I enjoyed watching the faces of children who entered the Open Studio for the first time – their look of wonder as they discovered this place of sheer magic, a haven from the stress and destruction so common to their experience.

The staff were just as enthusiastic, and the Open Studio soon became a valued program for children in the rehabilitation centre and children coming after school to attend the Children's Club. The HOPE team continued to make regular visits, each time bringing different specialists to excite the children and to promote the staff's development.

In December 1996, we moved out of our flat and into two adjacent flats in a building a five-minute walk away. This gave us more space and a more comfortable living arrangement. The two boys were in one flat, with male staff on duty at all times, and Dalal and I shared the adjacent flat.

There had been changes in my personal family situation too. Clarice and Alan had decided to move to Australia as both their children, Geoff and Wibby, had settled there. Although I hadn't been to visit them in England since 1990, I felt they were close. Australia took them further away. I didn't know when I would get to see them again.

In Khan Younis, needs were great and services few, so there was an endless flow of people coming to the centre with their children to seek advice or a place in the programs. This wasn't surprising, as there were no other centres in the south of the Gaza Strip and there were so many people with disability. There seemed to be three main contributors to this higher incidence of disability: the very poor health services that existed under Israeli occupation; the trend for some people to marry close cousins; and the many injuries caused by the Israeli army during occupation, and particularly during the first Intifada.

The rehabilitation centre we were developing was based on the model we had followed in Cairo. We were open to children and adults, regardless of age and type of disability, but limited in accepting new clients because of space and staff numbers. Services and programs were provided for free. For those unable to enter programs, we tried to give at least some basic guidance, and in some cases we organised one group of children to come three days a week, then a different group to come the other three days, to be able to reach a greater number. Home visits were also organised for some of the severely disabled children, but we encouraged at least one monthly visit to the centre so they could interact with other children. An early stimulation program was established, with staff working with a small group of mothers and their infants or small children with disability. In addition there was a special kindergarten; a special-education school; training programs for severely and multi-disabled children and youth; and pre-vocational and vocational training programs. Physical education, music, art and crafts were an integral part of the programs, as were the therapies and psycho-social counselling. The adjacent PRCS Al-Amal Hospital provided some diagnostic and health services as needed.

Some of the staff – like many Palestinians – were skilled performers of the *Dabka*, the traditional line dance. They worked with some of the hearing-impaired children attending the centre to develop a special *Dabka* group: Al-Fersan (The Kinghood). The group performed at PRCS functions and at other functions in the community and soon became well known. It was wonderful to watch them perform. The boys and girls, all dressed in traditional dress, followed the teacher as he performed the steps and signalled in sign language when the steps or the formations were about to change. A group of singers accompanied the music, and the children captured the rhythm as they danced together. Many people watching them perform were amazed to learn that these dancers couldn't hear the music they were dancing to.

I was very pleased that we were able to incorporate such a wide range of services and programs into the work of the centre. It wasn't always easy, and we began with very basic equipment, but we always approached our commitments positively, according to the concept of 'doing what we can with what we have'. In many respects, development was more difficult than it had been in Cairo as we were no longer in a relatively stable situation, but the rehabilitation centre of Al-Amal City was making rapid progress nonetheless.

The Institute of Rehabilitation Studies was also working well – following the curriculum developed in Cairo – but we wanted to ensure graduates would be granted the professional accreditation they deserved. It became obvious that in order for the graduates to gain full recognition of their certificate, the curriculum needed to be restructured into a four-year degree program rather than the two levels of two-year programs we were currently running. I worked towards this goal with a committee from Al-Quds University for more than a year, and the title 'Institute' was changed to 'College'. The new program was put into practice by the PRCS College and was accredited by Al-Quds University. It was to be some years, however, before the College was fully accredited by the Ministry of Higher Education. Despite all the delays, it continued to make a marked contribution to developments in the field in the Gaza Strip, and graduating students had no difficulty finding employment.

We had our failures as well as our successes, of course. I always felt sad when a family came to me pleading for help and we were unable to fit their child into our already over-crowded programs. There were so many children and adults with many different problems. In some cases we lost trace of a family; in other cases, the family couldn't provide the follow-up activities needed; and sometimes we just weren't able to find the way through to achieve the outcomes we sought.

One young man, Salah, who was in his early thirties when he came to us, made remarkable progress over a couple of years thanks to the dedication and skill of the staff working with him. Salah was known in the town as a 'simple' man, always dirty and unkempt, who crawled around on his hands and knees begging for money. He was sometimes teased by children and shunned by people passing by. When I heard about him, I sent two of our social workers to find his home and family and to give an assessment about what we might be able to do to improve his life situation. They found that his inability to walk was related to his severe intellectual disability, not to physical disability. His lack of speech and other life skills were due partly to his intellectual disability and partly to lack of training. His elderly mother cared about him but was very limited in the help she could offer. His brother had rejected him and would only allow him into certain parts of the house. Salah began to attend the centre and, through the efforts of the staff and the cooperation of his mother, he learned to walk – a little unsteadily and needing some support – to say some words and increase his basic daily living skills. Most importantly, he was clean and his charming smile appeared readily and frequently.

It was very sad some years later to see Salah crawling along the side of the road again, ragged and dirty. Following the outbreak of the second Intifada, we lost contact with him. The social workers went to his home on several occasions, but there was nobody there and we were not able to get any information about him. I was glad to see him still alive, but it was a shock to realise he had regressed to where he had been when we first began to work with him. Salah was a reminder of our limitations. How could we truly reach people with severe disability and enable them to realise their potential? How could we ensure ongoing programs and services for children and adults with disabilities? The solution continues to elude me. At times, life seems made up of more failures than successes.

In addition to overseeing the developments taking place at Al-Amal City and the institute, it was necessary for me to keep in regular contact with the various branches of PRCS throughout the West Bank and visit the rehabilitation programs. I organised meetings of the directors of the different centres to bring people together as a team within one overall department of the PRCS.

During one of my early trips to the West Bank I had a very moving experience. I was in my hotel room when the telephone rang. It was the receptionist. 'There is a young woman in reception who has come to visit you and would like you to come downstairs to meet her,' he said.

'Who is she?' I asked.

The receptionist said the woman had instructed him not to tell me her name as she wished to give me a surprise.

When I entered the reception area, I couldn't believe my eyes. Before me was Abir, in her wheelchair, accompanied by one of her sisters and her own small son. As a child, Abir had been with us through so many difficulties in Beirut and had been left in my care when her family had to evacuate Lebanon following the 1982 Israeli invasion. I had heard some reports about her over the years, but had no real idea about where she was nor how she was. What a wonderful surprise to see her again now.

There were kisses and hugs and a lot of catching up about the years since we'd last met. Abir's family had entered Jericho with the return of Palestinians from 1993. She had heard from people she knew at the PRCS headquarters that I was in Ramallah and so had organised with her sister to drive across to make this surprise visit. It was wonderful to see her, to hear about her life, her marriage and her child. In return, she was keen to hear news of Hamoudi, Dalal and Badr. I was very touched that Abir had gone to so much trouble to make this special trip to see me.

THIRTEEN

THE PALESTINIAN HIGHER COUNCIL OF HEALTH (PCH) had developed links with the Israeli Economic Cooperation Foundation (ECF) and together the two bodies organised a wide range of exchange visits and shared seminars. As a consultant for the PA Higher Council of Health, I was involved in this interaction between Palestinian and Israeli health professionals. Initial meetings had an air of uncertainty and reserve, but as time progressed and more interaction took place, a more relaxed and trusting atmosphere developed. Some Israelis expressed their apprehension on their first visit to the PRCS centre in Khan Younis. 'At first, I didn't tell anyone where I was going,' one woman said to me. 'But then I did tell one friend. The reaction was, "Are you mad? Going into Gaza?"' Yet this woman expressed how pleased she was to be there and to be sharing in the developments that were taking place. Many Palestinians I contacted were keen to be involved, but some were unable to make visits to Israel, either because they didn't have an ID card yet or because their application for a permit was refused by the Israeli authorities. In spite of such reservations and difficulties, and due to on-going efforts, many exchanges were organised.

On 8 July 1997, a delegation of Palestinians from the West Bank and Gaza Strip visited the Child Development Institute at Soroka Hospital, Beersheva, together with ECF personnel. I sent twenty-seven

171

names from Gaza Strip to the PRCS headquarters for processing for permits; only eighteen people received permits, and of those only ten actually made the visit. Some of the permits hadn't been received by the end of the day before we were due to travel, and when asked if they were prepared to go to Erez with the group in the early morning in the hope of getting a last-minute approval most declined. They were well aware that they could be kept waiting for hours and then refused a permit to cross.

The whole process of applying for and receiving a pass to cross Erez was stressful for the Palestinian people. There was no evidence of the Israelis organising the 'safe passage' that was promised in the Oslo Accords and would, in theory, allow the free movement of Palestinians between the West Bank and the Gaza Strip. Until a permit was issued it was not possible to travel, no matter how important the reason – a situation the Palestinian people had learned to live with. When waiting for a permit, after being rejected or receiving no answer to an application, people would just shrug their shoulders and say, 'They are just playing with us. *Amal ae baa* (what can you do). *Al-hamdu lillaah.*' The whole process seemed to be one of deliberate humiliation, and many refused to take part in it at all.

Despite the difficulties getting to Beersheva, the visit was of great interest and the professional interaction was good, although we were disappointed that we weren't able to see more of the children they were working with at the institute. As I looked at the range of equipment and the attractive working space, I thought about our staff and how hard and well they were working with so much less. I wished more people knew about what they were doing and just how much they were in line with international trends, in spite of the limits of their situation.

At the end of the visit, our hosts requested the opportunity to make a return visit to Al-Amal City. We responded with enthusiasm, and two weeks later, the team from Beersheva, together with the ECF people, came to the Gaza Strip. The visitors were interested in taking the time to speak with staff and children when they entered the various education, therapy and activity areas within Al-Amal City. After lunch everyone discussed the visit and exchanged ideas. The Beersheva team expressed their interest in our baby and parent early stimulation program, especially the way we worked in small groups.

'Your baby program is great,' one of the visiting therapists said. 'We have been trying to do this work in groups for ages, but as yet we haven't succeeded.'

I was delighted by the feedback, and it was great for the staff to hear such a comment and to feel that we had things to offer our visitors in spite of our less sophisticated facilities.

During these visits there was always a warm and friendly atmosphere, although at times tempered by some feeling of reserve. Both groups were very interested in getting to know one another and learning about the work and activities of the other. Sometimes, however, the Palestinians felt they were being patronised by the Israelis and that their simpler facilities indicated lower standards of development. It seemed to me that this was a natural process that had to be worked through, and it was obvious that the people who were meeting more frequently were becoming very relaxed together and interacting as equal professionals.

The Israelis who made these professional visits into the Gaza Strip and West Bank became much more aware of what occupation meant to Palestinians, and often expressed their concern. Some were apologetic, saying that they hoped the exchange program would contribute to better understanding and progress towards real peace. When we held a seminar in late December at Al-Amal City and the Israeli delegation experienced delays in crossing through at Erez, they were surprised and annoyed. 'How can this be?' some of them exclaimed. 'How can there be such a situation? It is impossible to treat people in this way!'

Part of the Al-Amal City complex included a large sports hall. It wasn't yet complete, but I was keen to begin developing sports activities for people with disabilities, and also for women, who had much less opportunity in Gaza for involvement in sport than men did.

I was delighted to be able to get the dimensions for a swish table (table tennis for those with visual impairment) and a few bats and balls through the efforts of one of my Australian friends. I shared this information and some of the equipment with the school for blind in Gaza City, hoping to encourage involvement in sporting activities for people with visual impairment. Swish was a good game for Badr to play too: with his learning disability and divergent squint, he had great difficulty in dealing with the three-dimensional aspect of table tennis, but could manage the more structured play area of swish.

Around this time, I was approached by the United Nations Special Coordination Organization (UNSCO) about organising a visit by a group of Palestinian people with physical disabilities and a similar Israeli group to participate in a special camp program in Poland. Each group was to have five disabled athletes between the ages of eighteen and thirty years, the injuries sustained during the first Intifada for the Palestinians and war-related situations for the Israelis.

We selected five young male athletes, all wheelchair-users; four had been injured during the first Intifada and one as a result of a car accident. There was some disappointment with the Israeli group as they included participants much older than thirty years, and some who were disabled from polio. However, it was too late to make any rearrangements and the two groups prepared for the camp.

UNSCO commenced the process of obtaining permission from the Israeli authorities for the Palestinian group (seven of them, including two staff) to pass through Erez crossing in order to fly to Poland from Ben Gurion Airport. This took some weeks, and as the date for departure drew near we became anxious, wondering if our group would be able to travel. The bombshell came a week before the planned trip: permits denied for all seven! There was a great flurry of activity to try to rectify the problem, and the Israeli group said they wouldn't go if the Palestinian group wasn't permitted to travel. A couple of days before the departure date we were advised that six people could travel, but one remained refused – except we weren't given the name of the refused person until the day of travel. It was Kamal, the oldest of our group, who was the most proficient in English language and had been studying hard for some weeks to improve further. Despite a free plane ticket to Poland and a visa, he was left sitting in his wheelchair in Khan Younis.

For the rest of the group, the trip was a great success, and there was further interaction afterwards, including a weekend sports program in Israel. I accompanied our group on this occasion and was struck by the enormous disparity in facilities and expertise available to participants. At Al-Amal City, due to financial restrictions, we were only able to offer very basic sports activities, such as sitting volley-ball, table tennis and some athletic events. The Israelis offered a range of water and air sports, tandem bikes and well-equipped facilities that were way beyond our means.

The PCH and ECF organised another visit, this time to a day program for elderly people at a centre in northern Israel. This was of special interest to me, as I wanted to develop such day programs at Al-Amal City. The elderly people participating in the centre's activity programs were mostly Israeli Jews, however there were also a number of Arab Israelis. When some of our group spoke to them in Arabic and said they had come from Gaza, the atmosphere became electric. There were smiles, some tears, and an exchange of questions and answers. It was a wonderful moment as the elderly people asked about conditions in the Gaza Strip and where the families of these visitors had come from originally. 'Al-hamdu lillaah ala al-salama,' they said to their Palestinian visitors. 'Ahlan wa sahlan; ahlan wa sahlan' (Thanks be to God for your safe arrival; welcome, welcome).

During one of the visits by the HOPE team, Sake Elzinga, a photographer, said he planned to make an exhibit of photographs of Palestinian and Israeli children, each holding a favourite item. He took photos of Palestinian children while he was with us in Khan Younis, and then through the program between the PCH and ECF we visited some Israeli families with their children. It was a very pleasant visit and the families were pleased to receive us. It was a surprise to me to find families living in an urban *kibbutz* near Bet Shamesh. They told us about an interfaith school in the area, which their children attended, a school that was committed to providing an education based on tolerance and understanding.

I always felt a strange mix of emotions during the exchanges between Palestinians and Israelis. Both peoples spoke of being committed to building bridges and a future of tolerance and acceptance of one another. Justice and peace were made to sound so natural and so attainable. But then in the 'real world', where the rights of Palestinian people were denied and they experienced such difficulty in just moving around, the attainment of such goals became questionable. Like many around me, I kept asking why.

My own visa situation continued to be a problem as I was still only allowed to remain in Palestine for one month at a time. Although the PRCS had tried several times to obtain a long-term visa with a work permit for me, they hadn't been successful. Such permits could only be obtained through the Israeli authorities, and they seemed unwilling to respond to such requests from Palestinian organisations. Like hundreds of other people, Palestinians with passports from other countries and foreign nationals, I maintained my legal status by leaving the country some days ahead of the expiry date of the visa and then renewed it on my return. The maximum length of stay under this system was three months, but it was often for less, and re-entry could be denied. Each time I left, I worried that I might not be able to return. Dalal, Badr, Hamoudi and the staff at the centre shared this anxiety. Dalal would be eagerly awaiting my call on the day I was due to return. Once through with the new visa I would phone her: 'It's okay, I'm through!' Her response was always the same: 'How long did you get?' Then she'd get in touch with the PRCS administration to organise a car to meet me once I arrived in Palestinian territory.

In order to minimise the amount of time I had to spend away, I changed my approach. I would set out in the early morning to cross the Israeli and Egyptian borders, then immediately turn around and return the same day. When I turned around at the Egyptian border, officials would often run towards me thinking that I had lost my way. When I explained my purpose, they usually reacted with surprise and enjoyment and waved me on.

However in late 1998, when I was being questioned by the Israeli border control officers after submitting my passport to exit, I was told they would not permit me to re-enter on the same day. I explained that it was essential I return as quickly as possible as I lived with three young people who were disabled and needed my care, and that I supervised programs for other people with disabilities. Much to my relief, they eventually agreed that I could return on the same day this time, but warned me that if I arranged to go out and return on the same day in future, I would be barred from entering Palestine forever. When I returned that day to the Israeli border control building, the border control officers seemed to be waiting for me. They stamped my passport with the required visa, but the time given was for one week only. I felt so frustrated by this situation. Within a week, I would have to travel to Cairo and wait some days there before returning to the border, not knowing if I would be granted re-entry at all. I made the trip and was granted a re-entry permit, but it was an ongoing stressful situation that just seemed unnecessary and unreasonable.

During an international training workshop about children with cerebral palsy, there was great excitement when Dr Fathi announced that President Yasser Arafat would be coming to the centre and would like to meet the people participating in the workshop. Dr Fathi introduced each member of the group to him and Yasser Arafat shook hands with all and took time to ask about our work and the workshop. He expressed his appreciation for the contribution that the visitors were making to developments in the field of rehabilitation for the Palestinian people.

President Arafat was also there to see his older sister, Hajjah Inam, who was living in Al-Amal City's hotel. Hajjah was now in her eighties and her health was failing. A younger sister, Khadija, who lived in Gaza City, came each evening to be with her. Hajjah was always very interested in the welfare of Hamoudi, Dalal and Badr and was especially fond of Dalal, keenly following her progress in her education and music. We had established a pattern of regular visits to Hajjah – Dalal, Badr and I – which were enjoyed by all.

In December 1999, Hajjah Inam died. Her condition had deteriorated markedly during the last few months of her life, so it was no surprise to be advised one morning that she had passed away during the night. I went immediately to her room and was able to share in the initial condolences and preparations while family members and close friends arrived.

When a Palestinian person dies, there are traditionally three days of condolence. Men and women gather separately at such times; often a tent is erected across the street as the official place for men to attend, and women enter the house of the family of the deceased. In some homes it is necessary to remove shoes at the door and the women sit on cushions arranged around the walls of the room; in other cases, seating is on chairs in the lounge or another large room. Traditionally, a date and a *fingan* (small cup) of Arabic coffee are served to guests arriving at the condolence, and often recordings of the Quran are played. At lunchtime, a meal is offered to family and close friends. There is also a solemn remembrance by the family and close friends after forty days, and again on the first day of the next religious feast.

Dalal sat her final university exams in June 1999. In August came the news of her success at gaining a BA in English literature. This was a major achievement, the culmination of four years of hard work without the support for disabled students that is becoming more common in universities around the world. Dalal was over the moon. I felt very happy and proud of her, especially as it had been a tough period for her. We held a congratulatory party in the Al-Amal City hall, with *Dabka* dancing, singing and speeches.

After gaining her university degree Dalal began work at Al-Amal City as a translator – English and French from and to Arabic. This was a very important role as there were often foreign volunteers and visitors who required language assistance. We began researching computer technology that would further assist her work, but it would be some years before we were able to acquire such support.

Towards the end of 1999, Dalal was invited to travel to Norway in order to participate in a program with secondary school students. Iyat, a young woman working in the Gaza Community Mental Health Centre, was also asked to take part. The two women – Dalal, blind, but with perfect English language and some travel experience; Iyat sighted, but with no English language and making her first trip abroad – were able to assist one another during the journey. I accompanied them through the Erez checkpoint to Ben Gurion Airport in Israel and saw them into the departure area. I was able to assist them with the strict security and check-in process (everything was taken out of their bags, and even Dalal's flute case was taken away for further scrutiny) and then they were on their way.

It was a marvellous experience for Dalal to spend time in Norway with a guide and living with various families. She made several presentations to students about the work of the PRCS, and more specifically the work of the rehabilitation department. She also took lots of photographs, which may sound strange as she is blind, but Dalal likes to bring back pictures of where she's been and who she met to show me and her siblings.

I went to the airport to meet the travellers on their return: they were arriving late at night and I was worried about the Erez crossing. At the checkpoint, the soldier on duty ordered the girls to go back to the entrance for Palestinians rather than walking through the VIP section for foreigners. As it was very late and there was no movement through either crossing, I was very definite that the girls should be allowed to take this shorter route. Fortunately, the soldier eventually agreed. Dalal told me later that she was a little scared by my firm stance with the soldier. 'You are always so quiet and polite,' she said. 'How were you able to be so strong and angry? I was afraid that the soldier would hurt you.'

On Monday, 15 October 1999, Israel opened the 'safe passage' corridor between the West Bank and the Gaza Strip. '*Akherah!*' ('At last!') was the general comment all around. The establishment of a 'safe passage' was part of the Israeli–Palestinian agreements signed in Washington in 1995; however, it wasn't until early October 1999 that a detailed protocol concerning the passage was signed, which led to the opening of one of the two routes that were meant to be made available. Many Palestinians applied for the magnetic card that was needed to use the passage, and it was recorded that approximately four hundred people took the opportunity to travel through on the first day.

The Palestinians expected that this arrangement would lead to free interaction between the West Bank and the Gaza Strip, but the protocols were very restrictive. The route was open only during set hours, and in order to access it one had to travel south from Erez then travel north towards Jerusalem and Ramallah. The length of this journey made it impossible to use the route to attend a meeting in the other area, for example, and return the same day; one needed to factor in a day before and a day after. Although a 'safe passage' would undoubtedly be helpful in some situations, it seemed that it didn't bring the ease of travel that the Palestinians hoped for and needed.

At the PRCS's Eighth Congress, Dr Fathi, who had been a founding member of the organisation and its President for about thirty years, announced that he would not be standing for re-election. He had devoted his life to the Palestinian cause through the development of health and social services, and by contributing to the preservation of Palestinian culture. Under his leadership, the PRCS had gained international recognition, and had observer status at the International Federation of Red Cross and Red Crescent Societies.

Dr Fathi was awarded the position of Honorary President for life, and Mr Younis Al-Khatib, who had been Director General and worked closely with Dr Fathi for many years, was elected as the new President.

FOURTEEN

ON 14 DECEMBER 1998, US PRESIDENT BILL CLINTON and his wife, Hillary, visited the Occupied Palestinian Territories and Israel, accompanied by the then Secretary of State, Madeleine Albright. This created a great deal of interest and US flags were on sale for the occasion. We were advised that Hillary Clinton might visit Al-Amal City and I was given the task of organising a tour of the facilities.

The day arrived and we were all in place, waiting for information concerning the actual time of Mrs Clinton's arrival. All the televisions in the centre were tuned to coverage of the Clintons' visit, and we saw the delegation arrive at the recently opened Gaza International Airport, where they were welcomed by President Yasser Arafat. The group then climbed into a helicopter to fly to Gaza City for the formal ceremonies. We heard and saw the helicopters pass over Khan Younis on their way north to Gaza City. There was no way that we would receive a visit.

The Palestinian people, in general, were hopeful that this visit indicated the US president's willingness to work more closely with Palestinians, and would provide an opportunity for him to see what a vulnerable and disadvantaged situation they were in. Most expressed hope in the Peace Process, but this was inevitably tempered by doubt. I hoped that President Clinton would be able to see what was really

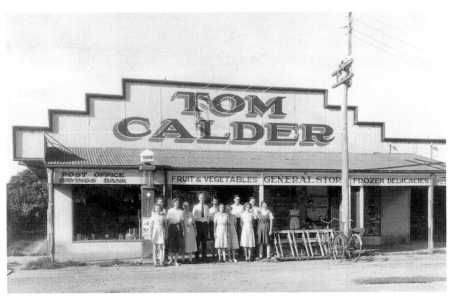

My father's shop in Mackay.

With my cousin Ruth McDonald (*left*) at the Mackay show.

With my parents and baby sister, Clarice, in 1940.

Clowning around at an education camp when I was a lecturer at Teacher's College in Brisbane, 1960. I'm in the middle.

Early 1981, when I first started working with Dalal (*left*) and Hamoudi in Beirut.

Dalal and Hamoudi.

With Hamoudi and Dalal in 1983.

Playing in the street beside Haifa Hospital, Beirut, with Dalal and Ahmed, early in 1982.

The view from my room at Haifa Hospital, looking across Burj Al-Barajneh refugee camp.

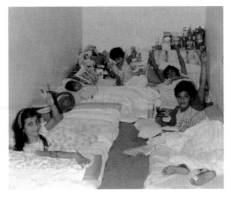

With five disabled children I lived under the staircase at College Protestant in Beirut during very heavy bombardment in 1982.

Hamoudi at the Palestinian Red
Crescent Society (PRCS) Ain Shams
Centre in Cairo, 1984.

Hamoudi attending the wedding of Nasr, one of
his carers. Dalal, myself and Badr are in front.

Badr, Dalal and Hamoudi during our time in Cairo, 1987.

Dr Fathi Arafat and Badr dancing *Dabka* in Cairo.

Dalal playing her flute at the opening of the PRCS congress at Al-Amal City in Khan Younis, 1996.

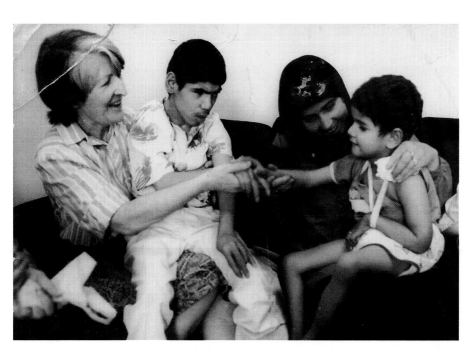

Hamoudi and Rusha learning to communicate in Cairo.

Meeting Yasser Arafat just after my speech at the opening of Al-Amal City in 1996 in the Gaza Strip.

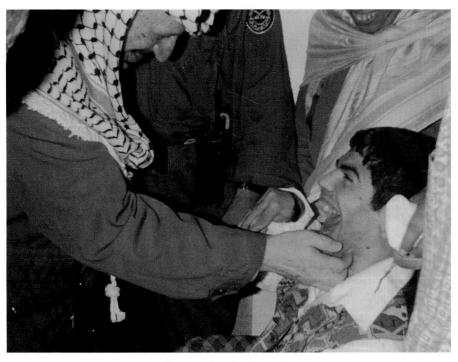

Yasser Arafat with Hamoudi.

(*Top left*) PRCS emergency medical staff under fire in Ramallah.

(*Above*) Qalandia checkpoint in the West Bank, 2002. (Tony Davies)

The view from our building of the Khan Younis refugee camp, the buildings and hothouses of the Israeli Gush Katif settlement and the sea in 2000. (Harry Cock)

An ICRC–PRCS convoy at the entrance of Al-Amal City, ready to take supplies to Al-Mawasi.

Children attending the Open Studio at Al-Amal City during one of the Dutch Hope Foundation's visits.

A family photo taken in 2003 with Badr, Dalal and Hamoudi (*seated*).

happening on the ground, the real obstacles to the progress towards peace.

The following year, in July 2000, the Camp David summit was heralded as an attempt by President Clinton to assist Presidents Ehud Barak and Yasser Arafat to work together to reach a permanent settlement of the Israeli–Palestinian conflict. The common feeling was that President Clinton was keen to accomplish this elusive peace agreement before the end of his second term in office. However, from the Palestinian perspective, the offer was not at all generous.

Already Palestinians were witnessing a marked increase in Israeli settlements, in spite of the Oslo Accords; more land confiscated and more military closures with their detrimental effect on the economy. The plan proposed by the Israelis at the Camp David summit would have resulted in Palestinian territory being divided into four separate cantons, surrounded and controlled by Israel. Movement between the areas would be extremely difficult and could be blocked completely at any time. Borders, air space and water resources were all to be controlled by Israel. Given such conditions, a viable independent State of Palestine would not be possible.

The PLO had recognised the State of Israel in the 1993 Oslo Accords and had maintained the position in relation to permanent settlement with full compliance with UN Resolutions 242 and 338. The status of Jerusalem, Israeli settlements in the Occupied Palestinian Territories and the right of return of Palestinian refugees, as contained in these resolutions, weren't included in the new plan. President Arafat could not sign off on such a plan: as he saw it – and, indeed, as the Palestinian people saw it – it denied the fundamental expectations of the Peace Process.

The negotiations failed, and both the US and Israel placed the blame fully on the shoulders of President Yasser Arafat, claiming that this had been the most generous offer given to the Palestinian people to date. However, the Palestinians viewed the situation completely differently, and were distressed by the way the media distorted the situation. Further, with the US supporting Israel in its pressure on the Palestinians to accept concessions that would never be accepted by the Palestinian people in general it was no longer seen to be a credible mediator.

Following the failure of the Camp David summit, the situation in the OPT deteriorated, and the level of frustration, disillusionment and disappointment amongst the Palestinian people increased.

In spite of the growing tension, the daily routine of programs at Al-Amal City continued. There was ongoing support from international groups, with volunteers coming to work side by side with our staff. The Dutch HOPE team continued with their regular visits, as did members of French, Japanese, British, Spanish, South American, Greek and Cypriot organisations. These people shared their knowledge and skills with our staff, and staff of the regular kindergarten and Al Amal Hospital but their presence also provided moral support for the staff as they felt there were people in the world who understood their problem. They provided a breath of hope when it seemed that no one cared.

Since the death of my mother in 1990, I had been trying to find time to make a visit to Australia. I had made annual trips to the UK to see Clarice and Mum, plus Clarice's family, but I hadn't been to Australia since 1983. Now I decided it was time to return. Had I been more politically astute regarding the rising tension in OPT, I would probably have postponed my travel plans.

Dalal, Hamoudi and Badr were used to my short periods away, and although this trip would be longer, they were happy that I would be visiting family and friends whom I hadn't seen for many years. Dalal and Badr assured me that they knew how to look after themselves, and that they would assist the men in caring for Hamoudi. Nevertheless, I organised for staff to keep an eye on them while I was away.

I was able to convince the PRCS administration to appoint Nagwa as director of the rehabilitation centre at Al-Amal City. Nagwa had been my deputy since we opened in 1995 and was managing the day-to-day running of the centre; she had the ability and qualifications to take the position and her leadership was recognised by the staff. In addition, I felt it was very important that recognition of leadership in the field was broader than a focus on me. I left for Australia confident that the centre was in good hands.

It is impossible to capture the excitement I felt as I set foot in Australia again after an absence of seventeen years. The trip was far beyond my expectations; thanks to the efforts of Clarice and Alan I was able to meet up with many relatives and friends. We drove up to Mackay, which gave me the opportunity to enjoy the beauty and smells of the Australian bush and the wonderful scenery.

When I returned to the Gaza Strip, I was much more aware of a general feeling of tension – possibly because I had been out of the environment for some weeks. The hope of the Peace Process seemed to have faded into oblivion. It was becoming increasingly obvious to Palestinians that their idea of an independent, viable Palestinian State was not shared by Israel. The Israeli interpretation of the process was to have a series of autonomous Palestinian areas, divided from one another by Israeli settlements and their bypass roads. Israel would retain control of borders, of vital underground water resources, the general economy and the movement of Palestinians between their designated areas. East Jerusalem was being cleared of Palestinian presence, and the right of return for Palestinian refugees from 1948 and 1967 was rejected outright.

Like many others, I had wondered about the feasibility of the Peace Process, but was hopeful that it was a genuine approach to justice and security for both peoples. This hope faded even further, however, when in early September 2000 Ariel Sharon – then leader of the opposition in the Knesset (the Israeli parliament) – announced a visit to the Temple Mount (Al-Haram al-Sharif) to examine archaeological sites. The City of Jerusalem is a highly emotive subject for both Israelis and Palestinians, and Palestinians were sure to interpret Sharon's action as yet another move to take over more of Jerusalem.

I was at the PRCS headquarters in Al-Bireh in the West Bank when I heard the news. Abed, the coordinator of the rehabilitation department there, came into the office looking very concerned. 'He has done it,' he said, 'he has gone in. You need to get back to Gaza immediately before it is closed. Who knows what will happen. Hurry and get your bags and I will drive you to the Gaza taxi rank.'

Ariel Sharon's act of marching on Al-Haram Al-Sharif accompanied by around a thousand Israeli police and soldiers was extremely provocative during this time. It was like putting a match to a keg of dynamite.

I collected my papers and hurried to pack my bag. I was almost breathless with tension as I quickly said farewell to colleagues and went down to the car with Abed. There was an air of shock and apprehension everywhere. I wondered if the taxi service back to Gaza would be running and began to worry about what to do if it had stopped because of the uncertainty of the situation. As we approached the side street in Ramallah where the taxi office was located I was relieved to see a car outside – the regular orange-coloured seven-seater vehicle. There were still a couple of seats vacant so I placed my bag in the boot and sat down to wait. Very soon the taxi was full and we set off.

Passing through Erez crossing went smoothly, and soon I was in a taxi travelling back to Khan Younis. I was relieved to arrive at the residence without any incident. Dalal and Badr came running to hug me, and the staff expressed their relief that I had returned. Hamoudi, as usual, was full of smiles.

The following day – Friday, 29 September 2000 – the second Intifada started: a tremendous outpouring of rage throughout the West Bank and Gaza Strip at the oppression of years of occupation. Tyres were burned in the streets; there were demonstrations; children and youth protested by attacking tanks, jeeps and military posts with stones. Hundreds of protesters were killed or maimed by tear gas and bullets. In the first two months of the Intifada, 264 Palestinians were killed and 9822 were wounded, many of them children.

On 30 September, Jamal al-Durrah and his son Mohammed were returning home from an errand when a violent clash broke out just south of Gaza City. They ran to take shelter by a wall at the side of the road to be safe from the Israeli fire in response to the protesting Palestinian youth. By chance, a French photo-journalist was at the scene and captured what took place: father and son crouched against the wall, the father waving a signal to the soldiers to stop their fire as he tried to protect his son. Both were hit several times. Jamal was severely wounded; his son Mohammed died. The film was quickly aired on television screens around the world. As I watched, I couldn't believe what I was seeing: a child being murdered. The scene was horrific – as was the feeling of helplessness at being unable to intervene. I felt afraid at what might lie ahead.

A PRCS ambulance driver, Bassam Balbeisi, was also killed in his attempt to rescue the boy and his father. Bassam, a key member of the emergency medical services (EMS) team based at the Khan Younis ambulance station, was liked and well respected by all who knew him. Other EMS personnel would experience denial of passage through checkpoints, detention, beatings, injury or death as the conflict continued.

In Palestine, the PRCS is the official organisation for emergency services and has a network of emergency stations throughout the West Bank and Gaza Strip. From the beginning of the Intifada, these services were struggling to cope with the numbers of people in need of help. At the same time, the PRCS had to maintain the range of health and social services within the hospitals, primary health care centres and rehabilitation centres, along with training. At times we were all afraid, but we tried to keep going and meet our many obligations.

It soon became evident – despite the international Geneva Convention directives related to the protection of citizens during periods of armed conflict and the respect for the role of the ICRC and its members – that the PRCS EMS personnel were suffering a great deal of abuse from the occupying forces. Thirty-five ambulances had been fired at and hit, forty paramedics and volunteers were injured, and one emergency medical technician had been killed. Ambulances had been prevented from reaching the wounded, and some patients were dragged out of an ambulance and beaten or arrested. The PRCS logged seventy-two specific incidents related to the prevention of ambulances reaching their destination; these were violations against the Geneva Convention and international law.

The PRCS management was extremely concerned about the vulnerability of their staff and volunteers working in the ambulance services and their psychological stress as well as any potential physical injury. I was involved in setting up a psycho-social support program for the EMS staff and their families in the Gaza Strip. Wives and children reported their fear each time they said farewell to their husband or father as he set off to work; they always wondered if he would return home. At times I wondered just how much we could help. We were trying to offer a supportive workplace, but there was no way to protect them from the violence they faced while trying to carry out their humanitarian work.

The US tried to bring Presidents Arafat and Barak together, but all attempts to return to peace talks failed. The violence seemed to be getting out of hand, with armed militants joining the stone-throwing protesters. Throughout this period, blockades and road closures seriously affected the movement of the Palestinian people and prevented essential supplies entering the OPT. Entire areas were closed off and towns and villages were placed under curfew. United Nations agencies warned of a looming humanitarian crisis if blockades weren't lifted.

There were several flashpoints in the Gaza Strip, located near army posts near Israeli settlements. Such places were the focus of the stone-throwers, and their actions were likely to result in gunfire and tear gas from the soldiers. Accompanying the shelling and shooting was the too frequent sound of ambulance sirens racing to help the wounded. Land adjacent to settlements and the roads used by settlers to travel into Israel soon became a vast stretch of desert as Israeli bulldozers razed everything in their path. One morning Hasen, one of the rehabilitation centre staff who lived in Gaza City and travelled by share taxi each morning to Khan Younis, came into work with his eyes almost popping out of his head. 'I can't believe it!' he said. 'They are clearing everything. I mean everything. Houses, shops, farms – everything in the path of the bulldozers. They have made a desert.'

This was frightening news, and it was heart-rending to see such needless destruction. I don't know how the people from the area managed. Some went to stay with relatives, some found temporary accommodation, and some depended on receiving a tent from the International Red Cross.

Just south of Kafar Darom settlement, which spread across the main north–south road of the Gaza Strip adjacent to Deir Al-Balah, there was a beautiful avenue of eucalyptus trees – perhaps a hundred of them in all. These were all cut down during the first week of the Intifada. Israeli army tanks established control of the settlers' roads from the Kafar Darom settlement and from the Gush Katif block, and occupied some of the Palestinian villas located in adjacent areas to use as their base. In some cases, families were permitted to remain but were confined to the ground floor, with all their comings and goings monitored by the soldiers. Although this made for a terrible living situation, these families were afraid to leave, learning from the events of 1948, when families left their homes and have never been permitted to return.

At the beginning of the Intifada, the Israeli army placed army units at crossroads, very soon extending this presence to a permanent checkpoint – Abu Houli – controlling the flow of Palestinian traffic on the main north–south road at the central section where there were road outlets from the settlements of Kafar Darom and Gush Katif. Eventually this section of road was completely closed to Palestinian traffic, which had to pass through the two stations of the checkpoint and then use a winding side road to go through Deir Al-Balah before returning to the main road. It used to take an hour to drive to Gaza; now it could take hours just to get through the checkpoint.

The avenue of eucalyptus trees was replaced by a high cement wall down the centre of the highway, providing a passageway for Palestinians for a restricted length of the area on one side, and Israeli settlers and army on the other. Eventually a road with a bridge crossing the old highway was built across the cleared land, providing the settlers and the army with a more direct route to and from the Gush Katif settlements along the coast into Israel.

Despite the difficulties, our programs continued, although I was no longer able to divide my time between the Gaza Strip and the West Bank. There were times when attendance at the Khan Younis centre was down because of heavy bombardment near where children were living, so it was safer if they didn't venture out. Dalal, Badr and Hamoudi were coping with the situation and we all followed our normal routine as best we could. Hamoudi's male staff were assiduous in finding a replacement if they were unable to get to their scheduled night duty because of the conditions around them.

In November, there were two Palestinian militant attacks against Israelis; and in December the Israeli army assassinated a leader of Hamas. December also saw the resignation of the Israeli Prime Minister, Ehud Barak, and his call for new elections.

At the end of 2000, George W. Bush was elected President of the United States of America. His refusal to meet with the Palestinian President, Yasser Arafat, created a stalemate. The Israelis were calling for the expulsion or death of President Arafat, and claimed there was no partner to talk to in the Peace Process. The Palestinians around me considered their position was being misrepresented once again, and that the sidelining of their leader was both an insult and a ploy to enable the Israeli government to settle more areas in the OPT. I couldn't understand the US President's refusal to talk with President Arafat. It seemed to me that the basic approach to resolving conflict was communication, and that if this had been followed, hundreds of lives would have been saved.

As we headed into 2001, the atmosphere in the Gaza Strip was highly charged. Israeli F-16 war planes, helicopters and tanks fired relentlessly on buildings and groups of people. Bulldozers were busy uprooting trees and demolishing buildings. Tear gas, thrown to disperse demonstrations or during incursions, seeped into surrounding houses. Our apartment was just a few hundred metres from a military installation and on several occasions the smell of gas penetrated into the flat and we had to run to close the windows. Once when I was walking home from the centre I smelled gas in the air and quickly ran the last hundred metres or so to get inside. The shelling, shooting and tear gas were becoming an established part of life. The pharmacist at the corner of our street told me that he'd set up a safe room inside his home for the family to escape from the tear gas and also in case of excessive shelling or shooting.

Most of the young men were excited about the confrontation. They were angry, their lives had been greatly affected by the occupation and the extensive military aggression, and often they had witnessed the death or humiliation of people close to them. Confronting the army seemed a way of joining the resistance, and they would throw stones at military checkpoints or at roving military jeeps or tanks. Parents and teachers fearful for the safety of their children attempted to discourage them, but to no avail. On one occasion on my way home, I saw a Palestinian police van crowded with dozens of children. 'What's going on?' I asked a colleague.

'The police go to the flashpoint areas, collect the children throwing stones and bring them back,' I was told. 'They are constantly trying to keep the children safe and to convince them not to expose themselves to danger.'

Life had become dominated by violence, destruction and disruption. On top of this was a high level of unemployment and rising rate of poverty. Many families were dependent on aid for even basic essentials. The PRCS, like other organisations in the OPT, relied hugely on donor assistance to enable programs and services to continue.

Frequently, the Palestinian Authority was advised by other countries that it must stop the violence. I wondered how the PA was supposed to confront militants when the Israeli air strikes had destroyed so many police stations; I often saw policemen sitting on plastic chairs under a tree or in front of a tent in the place where once had stood a police station. Further, there seemed to be far greater violence experienced *by* the Palestinian people, which didn't receive the same level of media attention.

Life became a three-dimensional exercise: on one dimension it was basic survival; on a second dimension it was about working to counter the effects of trauma on the people as a result of the ongoing destruction and disruption to life; and on a third it was about attempting to continue with issues of development and opportunity. The abnormal became the normal, with hope and perceptions of potential progress attempting to over-ride all setbacks.

On 25 January 2001, there was a particularly brutal incident involving PRCS paramedics at a checkpoint just north of Ramallah on the West Bank. The Israeli soldiers forced two paramedics out of their ambulance, stripped and searched them, then forced them to lie in the street. It was raining and windy and the temperature was 1 degree Celsius. The paramedics' ID cards and radios were confiscated; they were verbally abused, beaten and their heads were pushed into muddy pools of water. Finally, they were forced at gunpoint to roll down the hill while other soldiers looked on and cheered.

Because of the ambulance's loss of contact with the EMS station, another ambulance was sent out to find it. The two paramedics in the second ambulance received the same treatment when they reached the checkpoint. When one of the paramedics began to suffer chest pains due to shock and from hypothermia, the others had to plead with the soldiers to help him. When they were unable to stabilise him, they pleaded further to be allowed to transport him to the hospital. The second ambulance was not permitted to leave until an hour later.

In February 2001 Ariel Sharon defeated Barak in the Israeli election and was sworn in as Prime Minister of Israel in early March. This was a fearful omen for the Palestinians, who had experienced several attacks, massacres and other harsh measures under Sharon's direction over many years. Militant Palestinian groups responded to the harsh situation of occupation by carrying out a number of suicide bombings in Israel from mid-2001, which were condemned by the Palestinian Authority and the international community. The organisations involved claimed they were responding to the Israeli army's murder of Pales-tinians, and they would stop if the killing of Palestinians stopped. Their actions were counterproductive as the media presented them as 'terror attacks'; they paid little attention to the terror experienced by Palestinians on a daily basis. Reactions by the Palestinians were mixed. If the operation was against a military target, many felt it was justified. If against civilians, the reaction ranged from condem-nation to the comment, 'They kill our civilians.'

Personally, I found it impossible to imagine why and how someone could carry out a suicide bombing, and felt sad at the loss of life of both the victims and the bomber. In addition to being horrified by the act itself, I always feared the consequences. For sure there would be fierce reprisals, and immediately everyone around me would start worrying about what might happen in the OPT in the next few hours. I also worried about the negative stereotyping of Palestinians, which some of the media seemed eager to perpetuate. In comparison, the ongoing aggression against and killing of Palestinians received only passing news coverage, if any, and the occasional expression of regret. At the same time, if I looked at the sheer helplessness and desperation that many Palestinians experienced as they witnessed their rights violated, friends and relatives killed, wounded or imprisoned, their movement restricted and their homes demolished, I could see that such an act might seem the only way to contribute to the resistance against occupation. Many would criticise me for trying to understand the reasons behind the actions of a suicide bomber – some may even accuse me of approving of such actions even though I clearly condemn the act itself – yet it is accepted knowledge that the cause of an action needs to be understood in order to find the means to prevent the action. Unfortunately, this knowledge is rarely put into practice and so the cycle of violence continues.

The situation in Palestine deteriorated into an ongoing onslaught of Israeli incursions, helicopters and F-16 bombers; curfews, land clearances and detentions. It seemed that Israel was trying to stop the resistance of the Intifada with further oppression and at the same time acquire more land. The Palestinian militants responded with more suicide bombing operations. Too many people were killed, too many people were wounded – Palestinian and Israeli. In early March, the Palestinians called on the United Nations to send a security force for their protection, but this was opposed by Israel and the United States.

All around me, people existed in a state of fear. Every night there was constant shelling and shooting: tank fire from the Israeli army; rifle fire from Palestinian resistance groups. The night sky over the Khan Younis refugee camp, adjacent to where we lived, was often lit with flares. In several cases, these flares, when spent, landed on the asbestos roofs of the camp dwellings, burning those inside.

In February 2001, PRCS officials decided it would be advisable for Hamoudi, Dalal, Badr and myself to move to two flats across the road from the main Al-Amal City building, further from the conflict area. With the help of staff and a rented truck and a donkey cart, we moved all our possessions to the new location. The two flats were on different floors so it wasn't as convenient as our previous home, but we were much safer. We still needed to take care, however. At the end of the street, just a few hundred metres to the west, was a major Israeli military installation. On one occasion when there was heavy shelling, I went onto the balcony to see what was happening. To my amazement, a rocket passed right in front of me. This gave me a real fright and I decided not to go out there again when I heard shelling. The next morning, I went to the town centre to see where that electronically guided rocket had landed – a workshop on the ground floor in a side street. One of Dalal's friends who lived in a flat above the workshop told her how afraid she had been at the explosion and fire, and described how her furniture and other items in her flat had moved around. Many of my colleagues weren't surprised when I told them about the rocket; they'd seen many such guided missiles in the Rafah area and described how they hovered briefly when changing direction.

When shelling was heavy at night – which was often – we took mattresses into the back room to sleep together in the safest area. Once, a bullet struck the wall of Hamoudi's bedroom, which made me wonder about the lives of people closer to the flashpoints; their walls were riddled with bullet and shell holes.

In spite of the violence all around, and the difficulties of everyday life, we continued as best we could. Apart from weekly meetings in Gaza City I was in Khan Younis full-time, involved in the work of the college, the rehabilitation centre, children's club, sport activities, and the endless task of writing and monitoring projects. Unlike most of the other rehabilitation centes in the region, the PRCS continued to provide the services at Al-Amal City free of charge – even when the organisation itself was experiencing financial difficulties. These included parent and baby programs, kindergarten, special education school, vocational training and work placement, individual training programs for severely and multi-disabled children, and a home visit program. The kindergarten and the school had acquired accreditation with the PA Ministry of Education, so Education Department supervisors visited regularly, and the children received the books usually supplied to schools.

The several Israeli checkpoints scattered across the Gaza Strip had a huge impact on our ability to keep the complex running smoothly. Morning greetings changed from '*Sabah al kheer* (good morning)' to 'How is the checkpoint? What is the news?' Already people were becoming accustomed to the delays and closures of the Abu Houli checkpoint just north of Khan Younis. Each time I experienced delay at Abu Houli on my weekly visits to Gaza City, I wondered about the people who were dealing with this every day – some of them with small children.

On the West Bank there were hundreds of checkpoints blocking entry into major towns. Some looked like major border crossings, some were simple sheds placed at the side of the road, and some were mobile – that is, tanks or armoured cars could create a checkpoint at will for any reason. If it was necessary to pass through a checkpoint to get to work, school or university, to go to the doctor or to go shopping, what should be a short journey could become a day's outing, or even one that extended over several days as it was impossible to cross back through the checkpoint to get home.

The restriction on movement created by the checkpoints wasn't just a matter of inconvenience: ambulances were often prevented from assisting injured and sick people – people have died due to forced delay at a checkpoint; women have given birth; opportunities have been lost.

At Al-Amal City, staff who managed to arrive at work wondered if they would get home. Often they left early as news spread that Abu Houli would close very soon, but still had to wait many hours before getting through. Sometimes they arrived home well into the night. Sometimes they gave up on the wait and returned to Khan

Younis, or travelled back to Rafah to spend the night with relatives or friends.

Time spent waiting at checkpoints had a rhythm of its own. There were usually many false starts – people returning to cars and car engines starting up – then everything would stop again as it became obvious that the road wouldn't be opened. Sometimes the soldiers fired their guns over the heads of the waiting people. During the summer months, when the weather was very hot, it was even more stressful. Mothers sat in cars with small babies, frantically fanning the baby with a scarf or a piece of cardboard, trying to keep the child cool. Along the roadside, small stalls began to appear selling food, drinks and cigarettes. Young men walked through the crowds of cars and people with large hot teapots and plastic cups calling out 'shai, shai (tea, tea)'. When the road did open there was much confusion as the many cars and trucks tried to get into a position to filter through.

Like everyone else, I spent many hours waiting at the Abu Houli checkpoint, and often arrived too late for my appointments. When I needed to go to Gaza City, I began a routine of keeping a toothbrush and paste in my bag, nightwear and a charger for the mobile phone – at least these few items made any forced stop over in Gaza City somewhat easier.

Approaching Abu Houli on one occasion during the holy month of Ramadan, I could see that the checkpoint had been closed for some time. Already hundreds of cars, trucks and some buses were lined up – the queue stretching back towards the centre of the town of Deir Al-Balah. The share taxi I was in came to a stop at the end of the long line, with more soon pulling up behind it. The time was nearing sunset, approaching the hour when people broke their fast. Surely the soldiers know that the majority of the people are fasting, I thought. Surely they will open the road and allow the people to return home to be with their families and share the *Fitar* together.

How wrong was my assumption. The call for prayer could be heard from a distant mosque but the checkpoint remained firmly closed.

Then the most surprising thing happened. Taxi drivers and other people produced dates, which they handed around for people to eat (dates are a traditional commencement to the breaking of the fast). Drivers of trucks loaded with fruit shared their produce with people nearby, and others shared sandwiches. Although it wasn't the *Fitar*, everyone waiting at the checkpoint had something, be it ever so small, to break the fast.

FIFTEEN

IN MARCH 2001 WE HAD A VISIT from the four people of the Sham Al-Sheik Fact-Finding Committee – Suleyman Demirel, ninth President of the Republic of Turkey; Thorbjørn Jagland, Minister of Foreign Affairs of Norway; George J. Mitchell, former member of the US Senate; and Javier Solana, High Representative for the Common Foreign and Security Policy, European Union – who were gathering information about the tragic situation in the region and compiling recommendations to find solutions. Together with Dr Fathi and other senior PRCS personnel, I accompanied the group on a tour of the facilities, explaining the work being done in rehabilitation and training. I was very impressed by their caring and interested manner as they viewed our programs and listened to the information we were presenting. I also remember their surprise when we took them out on the top-floor balcony to show them the panoramic view over the sea, and across the red roofs and expansive areas of plastic-covered hothouses of the Gush Katif settlement block, which stretched from the border at Rafah to Deir Al-Balah to the north. The sight of this huge Israeli settlement, with its ongoing development, always elicited expressions of astonishment from foreign visitors, with comments like: 'But this is more than one-third of the coastal area, surely? I thought that the Palestinians were in charge of all of the Gaza Strip?'

The findings of the Sham el-Sheik Fact-Finding Committee, *The Mitchell Report*, were presented to George W. Bush in April and released in May 2001. Like many other reports, it stressed that specific actions were necessary by both parties and grouped them under three main headings: (1) End of violence; (2) Rebuild confidence; and (3) Resume negotiations. In summary, some of the major points that addressed both parties included the cessation of violence, the resumption of security cooperation, working together to implement confidence-building measures, and discouraging incitement to violence. Specific directives to the Palestinian Authority included taking action against the activities of terrorist groups; and to the Israelis, to freeze all settlement activity, including 'natural growth' of existing settlements, to ensure that the Israel Defense Forces (IDF) followed policies and procedures of use of non-lethal responses to unarmed demonstrators, and to lift closures and transfer all tax revenues owed to the Palestinian Authority.

On the ground, people tended to shrug off the endless talks and agreements that were taking place. 'Talk, talk, talk. For what?' The promised 'safe passage' between the OPT had opened for a short time only and then closed, and Israeli settlements were expanding at an increasing rate despite the fact that all such activity was to cease according to the Oslo Accords, and was illegal according to international law. Futher, the Israeli government had an active immigration policy to bring hundreds of Jewish immigrants, especially from Russia, to live in settlements on the West Bank.

The G8 summit of July 2001 called for international observers to monitor the ceasefire that had been declared between Israel and the Palestinians, but Israel objected to the call and so there was none of the international observers whose presence the Palestinians so desperately wanted. I could never understand the constant refusal by Israel to negotiate, or their refusal of an international presence in the region, especially in light of their declared concern for security.

Late morning on 8 May 2001, there was a sudden outbreak of heavy shelling by Israeli army tanks on the Khan Younis refugee camp. The Al-Amal complex is located at the edge of the camp and just a few hundred metres from the tanks. The noise was deafening, and as most of the children and staff lived in the refugee camps of Khan Younis or Rafah, they knew only too well the destruction and death related to such an onslaught. Immediately, the children started screaming and general panic set in. Fortunately, the staff very quickly contained the situation, quietly reassuring the children as they moved them into the inner areas of the main building.

Among those killed during this onslaught was a four-month-old infant, Iman Hegu, who, with her mother, had come from the mid-camp area to visit her grandmother who lived in a house across from the Israeli military position. The newly opened fruit and vegetable market opposite this front line of housing was destroyed during the shelling. The people, showing true resilience, returned to establish their stalls in the middle of the street, some hundred metres further away from the flashpoint and protected by several rows of buildings in the adjacent area.

In spite of the ongoing difficulties, we were able to run the integrated summer camp that PRCS organised each year. In Khan Younis, we ensured that both children with disability and children without were integrated into the program activities. One of the activities was learning sign language, which all the children enjoyed equally. It was delightful to see the non-disabled children eagerly including children with disabilities into their presentations on the final-day camp concert.

On 10 August 2001 the Israeli authorities occupied and closed Orient House – the offices of the PLO in East Jerusalem and a significant place for the Palestinians. It had gained importance during the first Intifada, when it had become a political centre, and later it was a key focus in the initiation of the Peace Process. Orient House was

---

the official political address for the Palestinians in East Jerusalem, despite the fact the Israeli government had placed great pressure on foreign governments not to meet Palestinian officials there. Diplomats from some countries ignored Israel's threats and met with Palestinian officials at Orient House, which continued its diplomatic activity, resisting changes that Israel was making to the landscape of Jerusalem and the difficulties being imposed on the Palestinian people. Now the Israeli army and police had entered Orient House and confiscated all computer equipment, files, data and statistics. As Orient House was the official body negotiating with Israel about the final status of Jerusalem, the loss of such confidential material was especially disturbing. The Israeli soldiers joyfully hoisted an Israeli flag over the building.

When I read the news and saw the photograph in the newspapers I was very worried and fully understood the anger and shock of the people around me. The closure of Orient House and the seizing of important material was a major move by the Israeli government towards its policy of reducing the Palestinian presence in Jerusalem. East Jerusalem is considered by Palestinians to be the capital of their future State of Palestine; a position strongly rejected by Israel, which claims sovereignty over all of Jerusalem and has worked to establish this claim with 'facts on the ground'. According to international law, however, East Jerusalem is occupied territory, with UN resolution 181 of 1947 describing it as an international city, separate from any national sovereignty. In relation to the current Peace Process, the final status of Jerusalem is still to be negotiated and any actions taken to alter its character during the interim period are illegal.

September 11, 2001. Like people all over the world, I watched with horror at the television pictures of the planes crashing into the World Trade Center in New York. This cannot be real, I thought. But it was real, and all around me people were equally shocked and saddened by the great loss of life.

On 12 September in Palestine, there was an increase in attacks, with Israeli army incursions into Jericho and fighting in Jenin, but world attention was elsewhere.

I was very concerned to see Israel quickly feeding the media with claims about the supposed links between Palestinian 'terrorists' and the terror attacks in the US. They were completely different situations and nothing to do with one another, but it seemed to be another propaganda ploy to denigrate the Palestinian people. Resistance to occupation is an internationally recognised right and is in no way related to arbitrary terror attacks. At the same time, demands were made of the Palestinian Authority 'to rein in terror' when the land was under occupation and people and places were being attacked daily by the occupier. The situation seemed impossible.

Between September and December 2001, the Israeli army used a very strange gas that caused hysteria in its victims. Many people were taken to the casualty departments of hospitals, as families had no idea how to manage the victims' cries of pain and distressed behaviour. On the first day such patients were brought into Al-Amal Hospital, the senior doctor in charge phoned me and asked me to send our psychologist, social workers and other staff to assist them with the patients, and also to assist the friends and family of each individual. This was a traumatic experience for the victim, and almost as stressful for the families. The hospital staff were puzzled by the phenomenon, but the Israeli army denied using a poisonous gas and claimed that the victims were just dramatising their situation. People treating the affected patients knew they were dealing with a real condition.

Another strange event at this time was the use by the Israeli army of a type of cluster shell, which, on impact, spewed out many small arrow-like projectiles. On one occasion I was in a share taxi going to the centre of the town, when a man got in at the end of our street, near to a flashpoint. 'Look at these!' he said, showing the contents of his hand. 'I have just picked them up from the ground here. They are like small arrows. I am sure that such a weapon cannot be legal.'

The numbers of people being killed and wounded continued to mount, and the general environment was one of stress and trauma for all. It was important to attempt to maintain some semblance of normal life, however, and so we continued our practice of doing something special on the birthdays of my three young people. Of course their real birthdates are unknown, so arbitrary dates have been assigned to them in September, October and November for Badr, Dalal and Hamoudi respectively. When they were still children in Cairo, we held big parties for them, and Dr Fathi, together with other senior PRCS personnel, always made a point of coming to see them on their special day. Now, though, we celebrated with a cake and cola in the evening, giving presents, singing together and having a happy time.

In late 2001, we obtained some funding from the Welfare Association in order to develop a sports and recreation program with physiotherapy and psycho-social support for youth who had been injured during the conflict. Some of the youth had suffered permanent disability, while others weren't left physically disabled after medical treatment but experienced post-traumatic stress symptoms. Many of the young people who joined our programs made a marked impression on me in the way they dealt with their changed situation.

Tarak, fifteen, now quadriplegic and a wheelchair-user, had been throwing stones at the Israeli army position at the western end of Khan Younis refugee camp when he was shot. Rami, eighteen, paraplegic and a wheelchair-user, was shot while working on farmland in the eastern area of Khan Younis governorate adjacent to the Israeli border. Mahmoud, seventeen, had been walking along the street near his home when he was wounded. He had metal clamps in his legs to correct multiple fractures and walked on crutches. The clamps would eventually be removed and it was expected that he would be able to walk freely, but it would take time. Osama, fourteen, hadn't been wounded but was traumatised by the conditions he was living in. His home was in the camp near the frontline with the Israeli army position, and he was surrounded by the constant noise of shelling, the associated fear, the house demolitions and seeing people wounded and killed. He was unable to sleep and unable to cope with his schoolwork. His disturbed behaviour was adding to his family's stress as well.

On 22 November 2001, five small children were walking along the pathway to their school when they stopped to look at an object on the ground. One of them picked up the object, which exploded, killing all five. It was a horrific incident and affected all of us deeply. Later that day some of the young people attending our program were very distressed. They had known some of the children who had died, and had gone to the area where the children were killed. They had found body parts, which, they told me, they had taken to the local hospital. I found it terribly disturbing that these youths had experienced such trauma on top of all of the other death and destruction around them. I wondered what their future would be like. How would I have turned out as an adult if I had faced such trauma daily, instead of my peaceful life in Queensland?

Christmas 2001 was much more subdued than previous years, due to the heavy presence of the Israeli army in Bethlehem. Many Palestinian Christians weren't permitted to travel to Bethlehem, and because of the conflict there were few foreign pilgrims. The Israeli authorities refused permission for President Yasser Arafat to travel to Bethlehem to attend midnight mass at the Church of the Nativity on Christmas Eve, as was his custom. Although Yasser Arafat was a Muslim, he was very supportive of and well respected by the Christian Palestinians, and liked to share with them at Christmas. I always enjoyed watching the midnight service from the Church of the Nativity on television, and was impressed at the respect shown this year to Yasser Arafat in his absence. The chair he would have occupied was left vacant, with the distinctive Palestinian *hatta* (black and white scarf) draped over it.

Dalal and Badr liked to do something special for me on Christmas Day. Sometimes we'd go to the restaurant in Al-Amal City for lunch, or they would buy a special sweet (*basboosa*) from a small stall near where we lived. Of course, a phone conversation with Clarice and Alan was a very special part of the day. We'd catch up on news, and exchange stories about what they'd done on Christmas Day and what we planned to do.

Despite the pleasure of Christmas, however, I couldn't stop thinking about what the New Year might bring. The increase in violence during 2001 had been terrifying, and I couldn't imagine how the situation could get any worse. But it did.

Early 2002 saw major Israeli incursions into several West Bank cities. There were night raids on houses, curfews, house demolitions, and endless closures or delays at the many checkpoints throughout the West Bank and Gaza Strip. The atmosphere in Khan Younis was one of expectation. 'We will be next,' was the general opinion. Palestinian people set up roadblocks using sandbags, barrels, old refrigerators – anything that could be piled across the streets to stop the army tanks.

The Gaza Strip had experienced incursions and night raids at different times during the 1950s, resulting in many dead and wounded in Gaza City, Al-Bureij camp and Khan Younis. When the local people told me about these raids, and how Ariel Sharon had been involved in many of them, I understood better their nervousness and the building of these roadblocks. I was also very concerned and angry about what was happening to the PRCS in Jenin, Ramallah and other areas on the West Bank: workers were facing a difficult time, receiving abuse and being prevented from carrying out their humanitarian mission.

The situation was very bad and I often felt afraid and uncertain about what to do, but daily life went on, whatever was happening around us. Like others during this conflict period, I took the precaution of getting staff to store some essential supplies in the flat, in case of an incursion and associated curfews. We discussed several ways of dealing with the situation in the event of such an emergency. Of particular concern was the need to maintain a supply of epilepsy medicines for Hamoudi and Badr, and also basic foods. We packed a suitcase of clothing for Hamoudi, along with disposable nappies, tissues, towels, etc. I was worried about how we would manage if all the men were called to leave the building. Hamoudi's carers would have to go, but I hoped that if any soldiers entered the flat they would realise the degree of Hamoudi's disability. However, I knew that in the event of such a situation Badr would have to go out with the men. How would he manage? Would he understand the soldiers' orders and respond appropriately? What if he were unable to take his epilepsy medicine? And what if all this happened at a time when I was away, renewing my visa? It was an extremely worrying period, and I thought a great deal about the many hundreds of families in the West Bank who had to deal regularly with such situations. Their fear and stress must have been enormous.

Some of the services of Al-Amal City were also affected by the situation. The kindergarten experienced some difficulties and its role in serving both staff and the community was reduced. The production workshops had difficulty getting materials, and then moving items to outside markets; and, of course, the economic restraints on the local population meant sales were limited. International professional teams that had visited to work with Al-Amal staff had stopped coming since the outbreak of the Intifada. The south of the Gaza Strip was no longer a desirable conference venue and so the hotel was empty for much of the time. It was only full when people were stranded by the closure of Abu Houli checkpoint and the Rafah border crossing to Egypt. On a couple of occasions, the hotel, the sports hall and the adjacent all-purpose hall were all crowded with people from Al-Mawasi who had been stranded in Khan Younis for more than a week due to the Israeli army closing the Tufah junction crossing back into the area.

Despite these difficulties, Al-Amal City continued to offer many important programs. Even though it wasn't functioning to its full capacity, the people working there gave their skills in a most remarkable way, even though many were experiencing extreme hardship themselves.

We also continued our professional training program at the PRCS College of Ability Development. The college is small, with approximately twenty to thirty students in each of the four years, and the majority of lecturers contribute to the program on a part-time basis. The program had been recognised by the Ministry of Higher Education, but the PRCS was working to obtain accreditation of the college itself and full accreditation of the program. In the meantime, the certificate awarded to our graduates was recognised, and several had gone on to obtain Masters degrees in related fields at local universities.

Since the beginning of the Intifada, the Dean of the PRCS College of Ability Development, Dr Bashir Sararj, who lived in Gaza City, had experienced a great deal of stress in driving to Khan Younis each day. Often he found the road closed. At other times he waited for hours to get through. Eventually, he could tolerate the situation no longer and stopped working at the college. To fill the vacuum, the PRCS set up a small committee to supervise the college, and asked me to take responsiblity for the academic programs. Some time later

I was appointed dean, a position I have continued to hold. I was pleased to have direct contact with the running of the college again, having introduced the underlying concepts back in our Cairo days and then worked with the Al-Quds University committee to restructure the curriculum according to university regulations. However, this did increase the demands on my time.

This was a worrying time for another reason too: Dr Fathi began to face serious health problems, having been diagnosed with cancer. This meant extended periods away in Jordan, and later France, as he underwent surgery and chemotherapy treatment. It was the beginning of a personal struggle for him, and we all felt great concern for him and anxiously waited for information about his progress.

In late March 2002, the Israeli army began Operation Defensive Shield in response, they claimed, to suicide bombings in Israel. Their stated goal was to move into Judea and Samaria (the West Bank) to arrest 'terrorists' and to 'dismantle the terrorist infrastructure'. Jenin camp was a key target, but incursions, raids and curfews also took place in Nablus, Ramallah and Bethlehem. There was massive destruction and loss of life throughout this period, which was classified as collective punishment – action prohibited under the Geneva Convention. The situation attracted international attention but although Palestinians cried out for an international presence, the Israeli government refused to allow international involvement. A UN mission sent to investigate the devastation in Jenin – claimed by some to be a massacre – was refused entry by the Israelis.

On 29 March the Israeli army began a major military attack throughout the West Bank with intensive bombardment of the Maqatta, the headquarters of President Yasser Arafat. Ariel Sharon had often voiced his wish to kill Arafat, and leading up to this onslaught the Israeli media had been calling for his death or expulsion. From this time until his death in late 2004, Yasser Arafat was a virtual prisoner in this battered compound. At the same time, the Church of the Nativity in Bethlehem, where some Palestinian militants had sought refuge, came under siege with sustained attacks. A lethal pattern was being played out. The Israeli army was carrying out incursions and assassinations, and bulldozing houses and farms. Palestinian militants responded with suicide bombings. Too many were being killed or injured. The Palestinian people felt increasingly that there was no relief; their call for an international presence fell on deaf ears.

I felt angry as I followed the news of the onslaught on Jenin camp and the towns on the West Bank and saw the impotence of the international community to intervene. I spoke on the telephone with some friends in Ramallah who had experienced night raids: soldiers had entered their building, forcing all of the occupants into one of the lower-floor apartments. Ramallah had been placed under curfew. They spoke of their fear during the curfew and their efforts to obtain food and other essential supplies.

The Rafah refugee camps adjacent to the border between the Gaza Strip and Egypt were in an extremely vulnerable position. The Israeli army had erected observation posts, border fencing and bulldozed out a no-man's land, which they continued to expand. From this position, the front rows of housing in the camp were marked for demolition. Shelling and shooting into the area was frequent.

On Sunday 7 April, the PRCS college students and staff were in a state of shock and grief. The day before, one of the students, Shadi Abu Gahli, was killed by Israel army gunfire while walking on the street close to his home in the Rafah camp. Two children and two other adults were also killed, and a number of people were injured. Some months later, one of his cousins, a graduate of the college, was to be killed in similar circumstances.

SIXTEEN

LIVING AS WE DID IN THE SOUTHERN PART OF THE GAZA STRIP, so much of our life was dictated by the Abu Houli checkpoint. On Wednesday, 29 May, I left my office at 8 am in a PRCS minibus to travel to Gaza City for a meeting. It took almost half an hour of queuing before our vehicle neared the checkpoint. There were about five cars ahead of us when frantic calls came over the loudspeaker for everyone to stop. We waited for some time, until a settler's car arrived from the north and turned into the Gush Katif settlement road. We were then let through.

The minibus set off back for Khan Younis around 5 pm. We were advised that the road had been closed since 2 pm, so we hoped it would soon open again. However, as we neared the area, we saw the line of cars, vans, trucks, taxis and buses spread back towards the town of Deir Al-Balah. The checkpoint was still closed and the length of time we might have to wait to cross was a complete unknown. Initially, I tried to do some work I had with me, but it was difficult to concentrate. Eventually I gave up and just sat waiting, overwhelmed by a strange feeling of timelessness. At about six-twenty rumours began to spread that the road might open at 6.30 pm. Many people returned to their cars, and started their engines to be ready. However, as six-thirty passed with no indication of any change, one by one the revving car engines fell silent again.

At this time of year the sun was hot during the day, but at night, the weather turned cool. Some people tried to sleep sitting in their cars; others lay on the road or the open area adjacent to the road. Some lit fires and sat huddled together for warmth, while others kept warm by walking around. I covered myself with some of my papers to keep warm and tried to sleep a little while sitting in the minibus. Often, I heard the cry of a baby or small child. During the night, the soldiers moved the beam of a searchlight across the open ground area and into the waiting cars and trucks.

There were about ten occasions during the night when word spread that the road would open, and again people ran to get into their cars and start their motors. Sometimes a car would decide to turn back, and there was a major reshuffle of vehicles to make room for the one wanting to turn around. During this period, we were able to move further forward in the queue.

The next day, the heat of the sun grew increasingly intense in the wide open area that the Israeli army had bulldozed. Some people found pieces of cardboard or paper to cover their heads or the heads of children with them. People sought shade beside large trucks. There were people selling food and drinks in the area, but the absence of toilet facilities necessitated caution regarding the intake of fluids. I wondered how the animals packed together in several of the waiting trucks would survive in such conditions.

By mid-morning, some cars from the south were allowed through. Because of the hundreds of vehicles waiting to go south, like ours, these cars had great difficulty in moving through the checkpoint and were directed along the open area beside the road. A couple of hours later some cars and trucks were allowed through. Now everyone was anticipating getting through and once again people ran to their cars or trucks and started their engines. However, only a few cars were allowed through, about thirty or forty, and they were stopped in between the two military check stations, just before the bridge over the road. They were kept in this position until evening. A tank covered the line of cars and moved towards them in a threatening manner if people got out to stand at the side of their vehicles. From time to time other military vehicles passed along the dirt stretch beside the waiting cars, completely covering them with a heavy cloud of dust. The sun was hot and coming direct from the west. There were no drinks or food available to these people.

The soldiers detained a number of the men in the cars and held them under gun control on the slope beside the bridge. I watched this area anxiously, wondering what would happen to the men. Later in the evening, a man I knew, Mohammed, walked up to our vehicle and told us how relieved he felt as his son had just phoned him to say that he had arrived home safely. His son had been in one of the cars that had been detained in the central area and Mohammed had been feeling very distressed as he'd feared for his safety. He said that his son told him that he had to remove some of his clothes, and that the soldiers wouldn't let him take his bag with him when he left. Mohammed explained that his son was a university student and that he stayed in Gaza City all week because of the blockade and returned home on Wednesday for the weekend. His bag contained his clothes and university books.

The number of waiting vehicles continued to increase. By now the number of cars and trucks must have been well over a thousand, and the number of people waiting into the several thousands. It was now Thursday, and many people were returning to their homes for the weekend.

In the late afternoon, a man walked along the cars near us seeking a nurse or doctor to give a woman a needed injection. There was an ambulance car not far away, so he was directed to go there. The PRCS had set up an emergency tent towards the middle of the line of cars in order to assist people in distress. The ICRC was also called in to help a woman in distress in the cars held for many hours in the area between the two military check stations.

About the same time, the group of men who had been detained on the slope up to the bridge were taken away. Anticipation grew that the road would open. However, a tank that had stopped in front of the line of cars waiting to get through backed into the electrical lightpost near the north military checkpoint and the waiting cars. There was absolute panic in the crowd as people ran to distance themselves from expected danger. Fortunately, although the post bent, the wires did not hit the ground; however, any hope of the road opening faded again. I began to worry about the battery on my mobile phone; if it ran down I would have no way of contacting Dalal, Badr and Hamoudi, or the PRCS administration.

A couple of hours later some jeeps and armoured cars came to inspect the damaged lightpost. People waiting by their cars were ordered to move back even though they weren't near the road. One of the jeeps then drove closer and about five soldiers got out and covered the crowd with their guns, shooting into the air to emphasise that people should move back. Some young men were called forward and made to lift their shirts up high to show their waists were clear. As one concerned person forced to wait at the checkpoint said to me, 'What are they doing? This behaviour feeds the terrorists.'

Around midnight, a tank approached groups of men sitting around small fires to keep warm, forcing them to move away. Not long after, there seemed to be an indication that the road might be opened. The road for the Palestinians was blocked by the fallen electrical lightpost, but the settlers' section on the other side of the cement wall was clear. After some time, a few cars and two cattle trucks were allowed through on this settlers' road; there were up to forty men hanging on to the sides of each cattle truck. It was forbidden to walk through Abu Houli, so it was common to see men hanging on to the side of trucks or scrambling to climb into the back of a utility van driving through. Very soon the trucks were returned and the men told to climb down. A tank drove into the crowd to force people to move further back. 'They like the cattle better than us!' I heard several people say. A woman with a small child was crying. She had been in the cabin of the truck, and the soldiers had ridiculed her and told her it was shameful for her to ride in the truck.

It was about 2 am before several armoured cars, a tank and trucks brought soldiers to replace the electrical lightpost. The tank was to cover the waiting crowd. The work finished, all of the equipment and personnel moved away. Another hour passed before an armoured jeep came back and its driver ordered more than a hundred men sitting in small groups around fires to move back. They all got up and moved, some more reluctant than others, except for one defiant young man who continued to sit by the fire. People called out to him to do as the soldiers ordered, worried that he would be hurt or killed. Eventually, the young man did get up, carrying the piece of cardboard he had been sitting on.

It was now almost four-thirty on Friday morning. Since late Thursday, the PRCS minibus I was in had moved closer to the blockade. There were only about ten cars ahead of us, so if the road opened, even for a short time, perhaps we would get through. The waiting time was especially stressful for many women, and some, when they saw the PRCS minibus, asked if they could sit inside for a while as it seemed a more protected place. As a result, several women and children occupied the back of the minibus, including one very tired pregnant woman and a small child who began to cry each time she woke up. Throughout, I hardly moved from my seat in the front of the vehicle.

Eventually we were able to pass through the north end of the checkpoint. Immediately behind us was a large truck stacked with empty crates to be filled with produce. Dozens of men jumped onto the side of the truck, hanging on precariously as it moved through. This truck was allowed through without any questioning or checking, yet many of the men were those who had attempted to go through earlier by clinging to the cattle truck and had been threatened at gunpoint and chased back by armoured jeeps and tanks.

We were now in the middle of the army-controlled area, with the main military check still to come. I always felt a mixture of hope and fear in this section of the checkpoint: hope because we were past the first post and on the way, but fear that we would be stopped before passing the second post. On this occasion we passed straight through, as did the cars and trucks immediately ahead of and behind us. It was sad to see a group of more than twenty young Palestinian men detained at the side of the road, though, huddled together under the guard of armed soldiers and several armoured cars and tanks. What would happen to those young men, I wondered.

I arrived home at 5 am on Friday, having left at 8 am on Wednesday to go to a meeting in Gaza City – a journey of less than one hour in normal circumstances. Instead, I had spent thirty-six hours, together with many other people, waiting to get through the checkpoint to return home. I didn't know if all of the traffic in line that Friday got through or not. I didn't know what the open–close pattern would be the next day. Nobody knew. Nobody ever knows.

On 6 June 2002, the Israeli army carried out another attack on the Ramallah (Maqatta) headquarters of President Arafat, destroying most of the structure that remained from previous attacks. As we listened to the news, we were fearful that this time the army would kill Abu Amar. They didn't kill him, but the constant bombardment and massive destruction all around him must have been extremely stressful.

Ten days later, Israel began to build the notorious security fence – known as the 'separation wall' or 'apartheid wall' by many – which they claimed was necessary for security reasons. The Palestinians saw it as a land grab, as the wall was to encroach beyond the green line. The wall was planned to be more than 600 kilometres long, and many sections were constructed from cement blocks up to 8 metres high, with 6-metre-wide vehicle barrier trenches alongside. It surrounded some towns and snaked through much of the Palestinian lands, and would lock Palestinians into separate areas, severely inter-fering with the livelihood and freedom of movement of hundreds of people. Despite countless demonstrations and the International Court of Justice ruling that it was illegal, the wall has continued to spread. East Jerusalem has become completely separated from the West Bank, and travel between north and south West Bank requires a wide and winding detour as the central road is blocked for use by Palestinians.

A difficult period occurred for Hamoudi in August 2002. He often suffers severe health problems related to his chronic chest condition, and at this time was admitted to Al-Amal City hospital with a high temperature and vomiting. Handling Hamoudi when he is very ill isn't an easy task. His body doesn't regulate temperature well and so responds to atmospheric temperature changes more than normal. When he has a high temperature, his extremities (feet, hands) are likely to be icy cold, while the rest of his body is oven hot. This creates difficulties in giving cold compresses so as to lower his temperature. Finding a vein suitable for an injection is also a problem, and once that's achieved care has to be taken that the needle does not come out because of his spasticity. Fortunately, the staff of the rehabilitation centre are both skilled and committed in managing Hamoudi's needs, and two of his carers remained with him at all times.

After a day or two it became obvious that his condition was worsening and that the situation had become very serious. There was indication of a partial collapse of the left lung and the doctors advised transferring him to the PRCS hospital in Gaza City where he would be seen by a chest specialist. Quickly we organised the items he'd require: X-ray charts, various test results, clothes and other possessions. Al-Amal staff organised the ambulance to transport us to Gaza City, and contact had been made with the hospital there to have all necessary arrangements in place for when we arrived. However, our most immediate concern was the Israeli checkpoint at Abu Houli. Would it be open or closed? If closed, how long would we need to wait?

We were kept waiting at the checkpoint for just over one hour – valuable time lost, but fortunately nowhere near as long as it might have been. The fact that there was a seriously ill patient in an ambulance made no difference to the soldiers manning the check-point.

A doctor at Al-Quds Hospital explained that Hamoudi had severe pneumonia with a build-up of mucus in the lung, which was life-threatening. He advised me that Hamoudi was in a very dangerous condition, and that the only thing that could be done at this point was to perform a thoracostomy in order to drain the mucus from the lung. He stressed that there was no guarantee Hamoudi would survive, but if the thoracostomy was not attempted, he would certainly die. There was no choice. I signed the consent form for the operation and prayed that all would be okay. The next few hours were very anxious and tense.

When Hamoudi was wheeled out of the operating theatre, the doctors told me that the surgery had been difficult but all had gone well. The relief I felt was short-lived as there was another concern: Hamoudi took much longer than usual to wake from the anaes-thetic. He was put under observation in intensive care, the drain in place, an infusion needle in his arm and oxygen mask at the ready. The two rehabilitation staff stayed with him and assisted the medical team as needed; in the meantime, I organised an ongoing schedule of carers to be on duty with Hamoudi, and arranged for Dalal and Badr to come to Gaza City. They were both very concerned about him and wanted to be near. We all stayed at the PRCS hotel next to the hospital.

Under the excellent care of the hospital staff and rehabilitation centre carers, Hamoudi began to respond and to move out of the danger period. The day he was able to produce his characteristic smile – be it ever so weak – was when we allowed ourselves to hope that he was on the path of recovery. During the first few days, however, it was impossible for me to relax and I spent most of my time with Hamoudi, even though the staff were caring well for him. I could see how intently they watched for problems and progress, and how careful they were when they needed to move him.

Maintaining the schedule of his care while he was in hospital was somewhat complicated because of the roadblock at Abu Houli. The majority of the male carers lived in Khan Younis or Rafah, south of the roadblock. On more than one occasion, the incoming staff would call from the checkpoint to say they had been waiting for more than an hour and there were no signs of the road opening. In such cases, someone living north of the checkpoint was called in until the men could get through, or those on duty would extend their shift. Eventually it was organised so that there were four men in Gaza City, two to be on duty with Hamoudi while the other two rested at the PRCS hotel, and vice versa.

While Hamoudi was in hospital, there was an Israeli bombing raid on Gaza City. It was late evening and Dalal, Badr and I had returned to our hotel room after having seen Hamoudi settle down to sleep. As the hotel was very near to one of the Palestinian Authority security buildings, once the bombing started we had to move to a safer place. I took Dalal and Badr with me to Hamoudi's room; I wanted to be near him during this dangerous time, and it was also safer. Besides, it meant we were all together, whatever happened. Badr was soon asleep on a chair, but Dalal, somewhat more anxious about the situation, remained awake. It was early morning before it was considered safe to return to the hotel.

By early September, it was obvious that Hamoudi was making good progress and it would soon be possible for him to return home. However, there was another issue to deal with. My three-month visa was due to expire on 8 September and I didn't want Hamoudi to return home while I was out of the country as I wanted to be there to monitor the care he would require at this stage of his recovery. I spoke to the doctors and they assured me that there wouldn't be any problem for Hamoudi to remain in hospital for some extra days beyond the discharge date, until I returned. I flew from Ben Gurion Airport to Amman, Jordan, on 8 September and returned on 9 September – fortunately without any problems this time. Dalal, Badr and the four carers from Khan Younis stayed at the PRCS hotel during my absence, and all was well.

Eventually the day came when Hamoudi could return home. It was 10 September, just on four weeks since he'd been rushed to the hospital in Gaza City. Thin and still weak, he was obviously happy to be going home. To add to the excitement, it was Badr's 'birthday' – the special day we had chosen to celebrate his life – and he was twenty-one. We still had to negotiate the Abu Houli checkpoint, but we had heard that it was 'not too bad'. In fact, we waited about ninety minutes, but without the same feeling of fear we had experienced when we were transporting Hamoudi to the hospital some weeks earlier, when he was in a life and death situation.

Hamoudi had a great welcome home. Staff in the residence had arranged everything exactly as they know he likes it, and as word got out that he was back other staff rushed over to greet him. Some of the neighbours came too, including Aly, the owner of the taxi who takes Hamoudi on his weekly outings and has become a friend. Hamoudi was very responsive to all the attention he was receiving. It was good to see his strong spirit shining as he told us through his sounds and body movement where he wanted to be fed his lunch, and his chuckles of joy when his request was understood and respected.

Hamoudi continued to gain weight and to become stronger and more alert. Even so, I couldn't rid myself of an underlying concern about his condition and found myself constantly checking on him and how the staff were working with him.

We were used to heavy shelling and shooting starting late at night or in the early morning, but one night in October 2002 the sound of tank fire was heavier than usual, and getting alarmingly close. We didn't know what was happening but it sounded serious. The male carers in the flat below took Hamoudi and Badr into an inside room, and in the flat above Dalal and I did the same. We tried to phone the Al-Amal building, but there was no answer.

The onslaught lasted many hours and the tanks came up the street, directly in front of the Al-Amal building, firing ahead but not advancing to enter the building. When I went to work in the morning I could see a great deal of damage at the entrance to the building. Such senseless destruction. Around seventy windows at the front had been smashed. The far wall of the cafeteria on the first floor was marked with huge shell holes. Where a shell had entered the corridor, it had travelled all the way through the door at the end. It was an unbelievable sight. The men who had been on duty during the night described how afraid they had been, and how they had sought for a safe place to wait out the attack. I realised why there hadn't been an answer to our phone call. I moved around inside, checking on the extent of the damage, and was shocked and saddened by what I saw. Was this a one-off incursion, or the beginning of something more intense?

Many children were amongst those killed or wounded during such incursions. The rehabilitation centre helped wounded children and their families in different ways. Sometimes staff visited a child in hospital to chat and play, or to work with them on school lessons. Other children attended the centre for physiotherapy, speech therapy, counselling, lessons or activities. For some children, this was an interim period offering support until they were able to return to school. Others continued in programs at the centre.

Mohammed, a ten year old, was walking with a crowd in a funeral procession to a cemetery to the south of Khan Younis, which is very close to one of the Israeli settlements. Witnesses said that soldiers suddenly began to fire shells into the crowd. Mohammed was shot in the chest and back, resulting in paraplegia. Because of complications regarding his injuries, he had been transferred to a hospital in another country with better facilities and expertise for the initial treatment that he needed. As in other, similar cases, the costs for his travel to and treatment in a foreign country were covered by Palestinian support groups or the government of the country concerned. On his return Mohammed required ongoing treatment, and both he and his family also needed a great deal of psychological support.

Haytham, nine, was shot in the leg when demonstrating with other children at the Tufah Junction in Khan Younis. He spent an extended period in Al-Amal hospital and received regular visits from the rehabilitation staff for school lessons and activities. On discharge, he attended the centre for schooling and therapy until he was able to return to his school, but was very upset at having lost a year of his regular schooling because of his injury. He was left with one leg shorter than the other and will need additional surgery when he is older.

Many children have lost an eye due to shelling. Some manage their new situation relatively well; others are severely affected and can no longer cope wth their schooling or interact with other children at play. One little three year old who came to the centre reacted by ceasing to talk.

Huda, an eleven-year-old girl, was severely wounded in early March 2003 while sitting in her classroom with her fellow pupils. Her school is located in the Khan Younis camp, near to an Israeli settlement. People at the scene reported that Israeli tanks suddenly moved towards the school. At the sound of the approaching tank-fire, the teacher shouted to the children to get down on the floor under their desks. Huda, like the other children, obeyed the command. However, one of the bullets that penetrated the classroom exploded, hitting her in the head. She was rendered blind. Both Huda and her family have been severely traumatised by her situation and need ongoing psychosocial support. Huda attended the centre for some months, learning some of the basic skills she needs to cope as a blind person.

On 16 March 2003, Rachel Corrie – a US citizen of Jewish faith – made a non-violent protest by standing in front of an Israeli bulldozer as it approached Palestinians homes to demolish them. The bulldozer rode over her, crushing her to death, then backed over her again. The Israeli army claimed the driver did not see her. Witnesses said this was not possible.

I didn't know Rachel, or any of the other young people protesting with her, but many of our staff who lived in the refugee camps knew these protesters and appreciated their efforts to protect the Palestinian people. There was a feeling of horror among us all at such a barbaric killing. Rachel's death was tragic and should never have happened. The Israeli denial of responsibility for her death was disturbing; especially in light of the constant call for Palestinians and supporters to use non-violent means of protest.

Less than a month later, on 11 April, Tom Hurndall, a British citizen, was shot in the head by a sniper as he attempted to shield children under fire on a road in Rafah. Tom remained in a coma until his death in January 2004, but it was not until much later that his family were able to get an Israeli court ruling that he had been unlawfully killed. On 3 May, a British photo-journalist was shot and killed while filming in Rafah at the Sal al-Din gate at the Egypt–Gaza Strip border. He was with another journalist and local people at the time, all of whom testified that the area was quiet with no firing prior to his being shot.

There seemed to be a campaign against foreigners entering the OPT. Those in the West Bank who attempted to cross into the Gaza Strip were often sent back, and for a period foreigners were required to sign a paper to say that if they were killed or injured by the Israeli army they themselves were fully responsible for the situation and the army would be free of blame. Some refused to sign such a paper and there was a considerable amount of international criticism until the procedure was eventually discontinued.

Although there was so much tragedy and distress all around, there were also some brighter aspects of life. Dalal, who earlier in the year had applied for a Ford Foundation Scholarship to study for a Masters degree, received notification that she had been selected as one of the recipients. This was very exciting for all of us. Dalal wanted to study social anthropology to acquire understanding and skills for working with people in the community. We chose Edinburgh University in Scotland, as it offered the best support available for disabled students and Dalal wanted to study in the UK. Another benefit was that Linda, the daughter of my late cousin George Moir, lived in Edinburgh with her family. They were delighted to know that Dalal would be studying in their city, where they could have close contact with her, and I was very happy to know there would be family near her during her period at the university.

Around this same time, several women and myself were presented by the Women's Department of the Khan Younis municipality with an award of appreciation for work in the community. This gave me a very special feeling of belonging, of being accepted as part of the local community. Such acceptance was important to me and I felt supported in my efforts to increase the effectiveness of the work I was involved in.

In April 2003, Dalal and other recipients of Ford Foundation scholarships – a group of ten young people – were required to attend an orientation workshop at a hotel in Gaza City for three days. The situation, in general, had been difficult for some time. There were ongoing incursions into cities, camps and villages in both the West Bank and Gaza Strip, with many Palestinians killed or wounded and hundreds of boys and men taken to Israeli prisons. Rafah was suffering nightly attacks. Many of our staff lived in the areas under fire and sometimes they weren't able to get to work. There were frequent delays and closures of the Abu Houli checkpoint just north of Khan Younis. I decided to travel to Gaza City with Dalal, and planned to stay with her at the hotel during the three days and follow up on work at PRCS Al-Nour City.

We were able to get through to Gaza City in time for the start of the workshop, but that evening the checkpoint was closed, and remained closed. When the workshop ended, we couldn't return to Khan Younis because the checkpoint was still closed. Dalal and I, and another scholarship recipient, Leila, who also is visually impaired and lives in Khan Younis, went to PRCS Al-Nour City to arrange to stay at the hotel there until the checkpoint opened.

When we arrived, we were told that Abu Houli checkpoint was open, but the road adjacent to Netzarim settlement, just south of Gaza City, was blocked. There wasn't a permanent checkpoint there, but at times the Israeli army blocked access to traffic by making large mounds of dirt across the road at the southern end and breaking up the asphalt with several shallow trenches to the north. Sometimes people were allowed to travel along the road on foot, until shooting over their heads signalled they should stop. People could then go down to the beach and walk around the headland, again until shooting signalled that this way was also closed.

We were told that at this time the Israelis were allowing people to go down to the beach to walk around the headland. It was then necessary to walk some hundreds of metres further south of the blockade and climb back up to the road to complete the journey south. It was getting late. Should we stay or should we try to get through? It was a gamble. We could be blocked on the journey at any point. It was said that Abu Houli was open now, but we didn't know if it would still be open by the time we arrived. Then again, if we didn't take the chance now, perhaps all areas would close again and we could be stranded in Gaza City for days. 'Let's try!' was our joint decision.

A PRCS car drove us to edge of the Netzarim settlement blockade from where we walked through the damaged fun park to clamber down the headland to the beach. This was tricky as I had to check that both Dalal and Leila were managing safely. A man with a horse cart, keen for business and observing our struggle, came up to us, took our bags and walked back across the sand to his cart. I followed with the two girls and assisted them to climb up on the cart. What a ride. The horse trotted along the edge of the water so we got splashed, and as the shoreline was sloping the girls kept slipping and felt very insecure. I managed to keep a hand on each one to assist their balance and reassure them. There were many other people on the beach, some walking and some riding in donkey or horse carts. It was heavy going along the sand, which was churned up due to the extensive traffic throughout the afternoon.

Once past the headland, we went another hundred metres along the beach then the horse pulled us up the slope to the road. By now it was dark, which was somewhat unnerving, but I hoped all would be well. We found a share taxi, but he would only take us to the beginning of Abu Houli checkpoint; he wouldn't go through. We really had no choice, so we climbed in and went to the checkpoint. It was still open, but there were very few cars, and those heading south were full. I was beginning to feel worried when at last we found a car that would take us. However, the driver said that once through the checkpoint he would only take us as far as Dowra Bene-Swila (Bene-Swila Circuit) at the main entrance into the town of Khan Younis. When he dropped us off, there were no other cars in the area so we had to start walking towards the town. After some distance, a taxi came by and, to our relief, agreed to take us the rest of the way home. What a journey!

The Palestinian people's euphoria and anticipation generated by the Oslo Accords had long dissipated. I could see just how tired they were becoming, and news reports seemed to reflect the general frustration and, at times, outrage, regarding the stalemate. There was no dialogue, violence continued with an ever-increasing number of *shahids* (martyrs), and the overall picture of the OPT was one of destruction and continuous restriction of movement. My colleagues talked of their struggle to support their families in the declining economic situation, and were very angry at the imprisonment of Abu Amar (President Yasser Arafat) and the destruction of his headquarters in Ramallah. They said they were being treated as less than human and then being told to 'stop the violence'. I too could not understand the way they were denigrated all around the world. It seemed ironic that President George W. Bush, who refused to meet with the Palestinian President and who supported all of the actions taken by the Israelis, should initiate the 'Road Map for Peace' on 30 April 2003.

The US, Russia, the European Union and the United Nations were given the responsibility of assisting the implementation of the Road Map for Peace and monitoring the progress being made by both involved parties. The goal of this Road Map was to begin a process towards establishing two States, Palestine and Israel, existing side by side in peace and security. There were three phases to the Road Map, with specific objectives at each stage. As with the Oslo Accords, difficult but key issues such as final borders, Jerusalem, refugees and settlements were to be left until the final phase. Again, Palestinians saw this delay as giving the Israelis opportunity to further develop settlements, roads and the wall to the extent that there was little land left to negotiate over. Further, they were horrified by President Bush's claim that the Israeli Prime Minister, Ariel Sharon, was 'a man of peace'. Sharon had a history of hard-line policies against the Palestinians: he had been involved in several of the past massacres of Palestinians and had championed the settlement movement in the OPT. His nickname was 'the bulldozer'.

Both the Israelis and Palestinians agreed to embark on this endeavour, however, and to follow the Road Map together with the assistance from the quartet. It was difficult to see where this would go when viewed from the ground. The core issues of the problem still existed and still had not been addressed.

SEVENTEEN

DURING 2003 I WAS INVITED to attend a meeting to discuss scholarships for students from the Gaza Strip to attend Bethlehem University on the West Bank. The main Palestinian universities – Beir Zeit near Ramallah; Bethlehem; Al-Quds near Jerusalem; and others – are all located on the West Bank and are internationally recognised; in addition to their high standards they offer a wider range of courses than the newer universities in the Gaza Strip. Bethlehem University had the only physiotherapy course, started during the time of the first Intifada, and in recent years had commenced an occupational therapy course, the only one in Palestine. There was a lack of occupational therapists in the Gaza Strip and no professional training program, so the scholarships were set up to help overcome this deficiency.

Everyone was aware of the difficulty for Palestinians to obtain permits from the Israeli army to move between the Gaza Strip and the West Bank, so the applicants knew that if they were successful in being selected for a scholarship and were also successful in gaining a permit to pass through Erez crossing to Bethlehem, they would have to be prepared to remain there for the four years of the course. If they attempted to return home for a holiday, they would be at risk of not being able to go back to continue their studies. Several students have suffered this fate in the past.

Ten scholarships were awarded, but despite many efforts by the university to obtain permits for the students, they were not granted. In May 2006, the university had a court hearing concerning the situation. A previous ruling from the court stated that two of the ten students were on their 'list' and would not be permitted to enter. Although there was nothing on the remaining eight, they also were not permitted entry; it seemed the judge considered that if they crossed to the West Bank they might become involved in militant activities.

The consequences of these students being refused permits to study at Bethlehem were great. In order to honour the scholarships that had been donated, the university had to run two courses in parallel, trying to find ways of providing the program in the Gaza Strip without the required personnel and resources.

I had further visa difficulties myself in 2003. At the end of May, I travelled to Egypt via the Rafah crossing in order to renew my Israeli visa. When I submitted my passport on my return on 3 June to the Israeli crossing, I was asked a number of questions and then told to sit in the area adjacent to that particular desk. After some time I was called back to the desk and advised that I would not be permitted to enter the Gaza Strip and that I must return to Egypt. The scenario I had feared each time I had to renew my visa had happened.

'I can't go back to Egypt,' I said to the officer. 'I am responsible for three young people who are disabled, apart from the work I do in assisting in the development of services for people with disability. I really do have to get back.'

At this point, I was fortunate. The officer I spoke to told me to return to where I had been sitting and he would see what he could do.

I spent the rest of the day being questioned by various officials – some security, some police, some army – and making phone calls to the PRCS and the ICRC. Eventually, at about 4 pm, just as the border complex was closing and employees were organising themselves to leave, I was advised that I could enter.

The area was strangely empty as I was escorted through to another area to process my visa. Before receiving my passport I was required to sign a paper. I feared it was the notorious paper I had heard about, giving up any rights to personal safety while in the OPT. However, when I read it, I saw that it contained items such as to promise not to interfere with the work of the Israeli army, to obey any instructions given me by the army, and to not enter declared military zones. I wasn't in any way involved in any of the prohibited activities and I signed the document. I asked the soldier if I could have a copy of the signed paper, which seemed to me to be a normal request.

'Why do you want a copy?' he asked, looking at me suspiciously.

'Because I have signed it,' I answered.

'I will check,' was the answer.

He went into another room, soon returning to inform me that such a thing was impossible. Oh well, I thought, and looked at my passport, which had now been returned to me. I was relieved to see the stamp stating that I was granted a three-month visa. However, on looking at the adjacent page I was shocked to see, in red ink, ENTRY DENIED written in capital letters, under writing in Hebrew that, I guessed, said the same thing. This stamp had not been cancelled and I wondered if it would cause me later problems.

Finally out of the building, I walked to the bus area and was relieved to see that the last bus of the day had been delayed on my behalf. Back home with the 'family', I thanked God that I had been able to return. The experience left me feeling very humble, as I recalled the many stories of people unable to leave or enter the OPT, of families separated for many years with no way of being reunited.

I spent some time with Hamoudi before he slept, then Dalal, Badr and I had supper and chatted together. For some days, the situation in Gaza had been very tense with sporadic shooting and shelling during the day, and a buildup in the evening, becoming intense late at night or early in the morning. Throughout supper, we were wondering what the night would bring. Did it seem safe for everyone to sleep in their beds, or should we bring mattresses into the back room so we could all sleep together in a safer place? We decided to stay in our beds, and Badr went downstairs to the flat he shared with Hamoudi and Hamoudi's carers. Dalal went to her room to work on her computer and listen to music before preparing for bed. For some reason, she left her room to come to my room and study at the back of the flat. She hadn't been with me long when we heard a loud explosion followed by the sound of something shattering. It was close by.

We both froze. Then, some moments after the explosion, I moved very cautiously towards the front door of the flat and Dalal's room. Dalal was frightened and I told her to stay where she was until I'd checked on the situation. I saw broken ceramic scattered across the floor and was puzzled. Then I realised that the shattering sound we'd heard was the washbasin on the wall near the flat's entrance. Amongst the broken pieces I saw the shattered metal of a large bullet. The magnitude of the scene hit me. This bullet had entered through Dalal's window, travelled through her room and smashed the wash-basin in the hallway. What if Dalal had still been in her room? The answer was too awful to contemplate.

I phoned the men in the lower flat to check that they were all right. They told me they'd moved the mattresses into the back of the flat. The main bedrooms were located in the front of the building, which was directly exposed to the edge of the camp where so much of the shelling and shooting took place. The back of the apartments was much safer as there was an apartment building directly behind our building, which sheltered us from any shelling from that direction.

Dalal moved into the back of our flat that night too, both of us taking care as we dragged the mattresses past the doorways of the front rooms. I was reminded of the story told to me and Dalal by our hairdresser. She lived very near the edge of the Israeli settlements and said there was always a large tank parked at the front of the house. This meant it was dangerous to be seen moving about in the house, so if they needed to get from one part to another they had to crawl so as to be under the level of the windows. It was some time before Dalal and I felt safe enough to sleep, and yet what we had just experienced was only a very small example of the constant fear and danger people nearer to the army positions lived with daily.

In August 2003, the Dutch HOPE team came to work with our staff on further training for the Open Studio. We always enjoyed these visits from Ingrid and the team of artists and other specialists who came with her. They have provided financial support and professional training for more than six years now, and have contributed a great deal to the magic of the Open Studio. Other foreign support groups who had sent volunteers to help with the development of the centre's programs and services had stopped coming since the beginning of the Intifada, but the HOPE team had continued to come once or twice a year. They were somewhat nervous at first, but, like the locals, they learned to deal with the difficulties and uncertainties. On this occasion, we greeted them on arrival as usual, and saw them settled into the Al-Amal City hotel. We had taken the precaution of arranging for a couple of the male staff involved in the Open Studio program to sleep in the hotel, to be on hand in the event of any problem. We told the HOPE team that if there was heavy shooting during the night, the men would take them across to the hospital where they would be safer.

Around midnight, an Israeli army incursion began. The tanks came in from the east, moving down the main north–south road into the centre of Khan Younis and into some of the side streets. The situation was very serious and we moved into the back rooms of our flats. I felt worried about what was happening and hoped that our visitors were okay. Soon I had a telephone call from Nihad, one of the men staying with them. 'Would you please phone Ingrid and explain to her that they must all leave their rooms and go with us across to the hospital?' he asked. I quickly phoned and explained that the situation was serious and that they really did have to leave with the staff; it seemed there had been some language problems interfering with their understanding of the situation.

I went across to the main building in the morning to check on our visitors. They were rather shaken, but were ready to go on with the program. We all had breakfast together, then I went with them to the Open Studio where we found the staff waiting for the program to start. The visitors were amazed. They thought that most of the people would be absent, or at least late. As awful as the situation was, the local people did not give in; if it was possible to get to work, they were present and fully involved in the tasks to hand.

Throughout 2003, attacks continued, with assassinations (the Israelis called them 'targeted killings'), and other aggressions. Palestinian militant groups reacted with suicide bombings – which resulted in further incursions, raids, home demolitions and the detention of many people, mostly young men. When the militants honoured the ceasefires, however, aggression against the Palestinians continued. For example, between 29 June and 12 August 2003, the various Palestinian militant groups maintained a ceasefire but throughout this period land confiscations continued and the Israelis published in their newspapers calls for bids for building in the settlements. Homes in the West Bank and Gaza Strip were raided and demolished, and an Israeli Knesset member threatened to force his way into the Al-Aqsa Mosque. On 11 August, about eight Palestinians were killed, including an eleven-year-old child. All of these events were largely ignored by the media. On 12 August there was a double suicide bombing in Jerusalem, which received extensive media coverage that condemned Palestinian terrorists and supported the heavy reprisals by the Israeli army as a right in terms of security.

In September 2003, the Israeli government announced once again that it was considering killing the Palestinian President, Yasser Arafat, as they claimed he was a liability to the Peace Process. How can such a situation occur in the twenty-first century, I wondered. It was some consolation to read a few days later that the UN Security Council had presented a resolution stressing that Arafat was not to be harmed in any way. Unfortunately, as is too often the case when attempts are made to censure Israeli aggression against the Palestinians, the US used its power of veto to defeat the resolution. Again I asked, why?

In September, it was time for Dalal to leave for Edinburgh. We had been busy for some months in preparing for this day, and it was a wonderful feeling to touch down in Scotland. Linda and her son Stuart were waiting at the airport to meet us and drive us to their home, where Linda's mother, Jessie, was waiting for us. She had travelled down from Elgin especially to see me again. This was very special for me as I was very fond of Jessie and my cousin George, her late husband, and had wonderful memories of the times I had stayed with them back in the early 1960s. I felt both emotional and pleased as I watched the way Jessie and Dalal got on, the two seeming to form a mutual bond of affection, overcoming the obvious barriers of the hearing impairment of one and visual impairment of the other.

Linda and Donald and family were very attentive and assisted us in setting up Dalal's new home. She had been assigned a ground-floor room in the graduate residence, one of two rooms equipped for disabled students, with an adjacent share kitchen. The university was helpful too and ensured Dalal had everything she needed to begin her studies. By the time I had to leave, everything seemed to be in place. I was grateful that Linda and her family were so close, and the support system at the university seemed good; I felt confident that all would be well. I must confess though, as the plane took off on its way to Cairo, I was gripped by a feeling of concern. What have I done? I asked myself. Dalal is totally blind and I have left her alone in a foreign country. My anxiety was unfounded: in addition to the support that was in place before I left, Dalal soon made many friends in Edinburgh.

Back home in Khan Younis, there was an obvious gap with Dalal away and all the staff talked about how much they missed her. I missed her a lot too, but was happy that she had this chance to study abroad. She talked to me often on the phone or sent email messages, and Badr and Hamoudi chatted to her on the phone sometimes as well. Initially, she had some problems getting enough of her reading material translated into Braille, which caused some difficulty in her first term. However, this was soon solved, and with Dalal's typically determined manner, she was able to catch up from the delay that had resulted.

The day after my arrival back in Khan Younis, there was another Israeli incursion into Rafah, with massive house demolitions. The four-storey building where the family of Fareal lived – a young woman responsible for the kindergarten in the PRCS rehabilitation centre – was destroyed. I went with several colleagues to visit her. We sat under a makeshift awning erected on the broken piles of cement that were the remnants of her home, and spoke with her and members of her family. They told us how afraid they had been as the tanks came in, and how they had moved some of their important possessions to their relatives' house away from the area where homes were being demolished. When they heard the advancing tanks they left the area to be with relatives. When they returned, it was to find the building completely destroyed. All that remained was a pile of broken bricks, with some broken pieces of furniture and belongings jutting through.

Even as they recalled the fear of the experience, and stepped around the broken remains of their home, Fareal and her family were calm and focused on coping with the situation. They even found, from 'somewhere', a cup of black Arabic tea for their visitors. Fareal's family were just a few of hundreds who have experienced the trauma of the loss of their home and belongings in the middle of the night. She continues to come to work and to fulfil her responsibilities with care and enthusiasm. The casual observer would have no idea of the trauma experienced by her and her family and the very temporary living conditions she has been subjected to.

Badr, about twenty-two now, had grown into a fine young man. He was very responsible about his work duties and caring about people. He loved everyone and wanted everyone to love him. Dalal and I called him 'friend of all the world', taking the expression from Rudyard Kipling's *Kim*, which Dalal studied at university. Whenever we walked down the street with Badr, he constantly received greetings from all we passed. Often I entered a share taxi or a shop downtown only to be asked, 'Where is Badr?'

His disability did present him with some problems apart from the physical difficulty of being left hemiplegic. His learning disability had prevented him learning to read and write well, and sometimes his social behaviour could be immature and he could become confused in complex situations. His epilepsy was mostly under control, but stress sometimes brought on a short episode of disorientation and confused behaviour. Badr had a general sense of the problems around him, but not a full understanding. I often spent time explaining the situation and emphasising the need to take care.

During the Intifada, the Israeli army made several incursions into Palestinian towns and villages. Usually, these incursions took place at night and males over the age of fourteen were called out of their homes to assemble in a specified area. Some were allowed to return to their homes but some were detained. I felt very apprehensive about how Badr would manage in such a situation. Would the soldiers realise that he was disabled and treat him accordingly?

On one occasion when I went to Gaza City for a meeting, I took Badr with me as he enjoyed catching up with folk he knew at PRCS Al-Nour City. As the share taxi returned south, heading towards the Abu Houli checkpoint, people became anxious about whether the road would be open or closed.

The road from the centre of town to the first bend was clear. On turning the bend, we saw the beginning of the line of cars, about halfway along the road to the next turn. This meant a considerable wait. Eventually we progressed around the second bend, and then the third. It seemed that the road had been closed for some time. Hundreds of cars were waiting, with many more hundreds of people.

Badr, always interested in an opportunity to stay in Gaza City, said, 'I think that we should go back to Gaza!' My response was, 'No, Badr, we have just arrived and hopefully it will open sometime. We really do have to get back to Khan Younis.'

Eventually the road opened and we passed the initial Israeli army lookout tower. As soon as we passed under the bridge, however, we found the road blocked by an army jeep. The presence of the jeep meant that our car would have to go into the search area. Oh no, now we are in trouble, I thought. Hopefully Badr will be okay. Please God, let everything be okay!

Within the walled-off area there were ten small towers, with a soldier in each one holding his rifle at the ready. As soon as our taxi stopped, soldiers came and told all of the men to take off their jackets and get out of the car.

I told Badr to take off his jacket, gave him his ID card and told him to do exactly as the soldiers asked. I watched him walk off to the wall area with the other men. This was the moment I had been dreading. He lifted up his clothes on command, like the other men, and showed his ID to the soldiers. He was then told to sit on the ground with the others. So far so good.

A soldier came to the car and told me to get out. I said to the soldier, 'Please take care of that young man – he is disabled.'

'I can see that,' he said. Then with a big grin he added, 'Is everything okay?'

Once my passport had been inspected, I was allowed to sit on the ground beside Badr and the others from the car. One of the young men was being given a rough time by the soldiers. They pushed him against the wall, his feet astride and hands high, and body-searched him. Suddenly a soldier placed his boot between the man's legs and pushed them further apart. It must have been painful and the man almost lost his balance, but he did manage to keep standing and to deal with the insult without any reaction.

We were kept in this situation for about an hour and a half; no one told us why. Eventually we were allowed to return to the car and drive on. As the car was about to move, the young soldier with the big smile came to the window and said to me again, 'Everything okay?' You surely must be kidding, I thought.

On some occasions international commentators have suggested that the Palestinian resistance should follow a non-violent pattern. What seems to be overlooked in such comments is that many Palestinians do advocate and follow non-violent resistance, and condemn acts of violence. The usual reaction of the Israeli army to the many non-violent demonstrations that have taken place over the years has been bullets, sound bombs, tear gas, beatings and detentions.

The International Solidarity Movement (ISM) has a commitment to non-violent resistance; many of its members have been detained, wounded or killed. The Israeli women's organisation Machsom (Check-point Watch) stations women at checkpoints on the West Bank who intervene if they see a soldier behaving badly towards a Palestinian, and report on the manner in which Palestinians are generally treated at checkpoints. Women in Black, a Jewish women's organisation that now has members of other faiths and from many countries, holds vigils and non-violent demonstrations against the excesses of the army in the OPT. Israeli organisations such as B'Tselem, Information Centre for Human Rights in the Occupied Territories and Physicians for Human Rights, also support Palestinian peace and rights endeavours.

The whole issue of violence, non-violence, terror, resistance and State terror seems to have merged into a grey area, confused and little understood. Who is the victim and who is the perpetrator is not always clear. The cycle of violence is impossible to capture in words. Often the whole population is subjected to collective punishment following the act of an individual or a group, or at times without any provocation at all. Ongoing harassment and humiliation is standard treatment of Palestinian people. In an International Labour Organisation (ILO) report, 'The Situation of Workers of the Occupied Territories, 2004', it was stated that in mid-2003, over 60 per cent of the West Bank and Gaza Strip population (excluding East Jerusalem) lived below the poverty line based on a calculation of $US3.60 per day per person.

In January 2004 it was again necessary for me to travel to Cairo to obtain a visa, and I decided to take Badr with me. While we were in Cairo, the Rafah border was often closed, and when it was open only a limited number of people were allowed through each day. Hundreds were sleeping at the border for days.

A few days later when we returned to the border, there were still hundreds of people waiting to cross, some lying on the cement floor asleep, others sitting up or walking around. There was barely space to move. Outside the departures building was a long line of suitcases, each one marking the place where its owner had stood the previous day – or, in some cases, days – waiting to get onto a bus that would take them across to the Israeli border checkpoint and eventually back to Gaza. There was a go-slow policy and only a few buses were allowed in per day.

By the afternoon we had managed to squeeze onto a bus. The women sat at least three to a seat, and the men stood in the corridor, crammed in to fit as many as possible. Part of the back of the bus was loaded with luggage – overflow from what was stacked in the special luggage area below. The atmosphere was suffocating. The bus reached the border gate, then stopped to wait until the Israelis gave the signal to go through. We remained like this for at least two hours. My mobile phone, which was in my pocket, rang but there was no way I could move my arm to reach it.

Eventually we were told that the bus had to return to the Egyptian border control area as the Israelis had closed their checkpoint for the day. This meant that we were in no-man's land: we had officially left Egypt but had still not entered Israel. Getting down from the bus, our little group discussed how we would manage for the night. It was still late afternoon, but we needed to stake out a place to sleep and organise ourselves in a suitable way. Badr and I had joined up with Mohammed and his mother, Mervit, who was returning from attending a graduate studies program at the Ain Shams University in Cairo, and Falula, a nursing student from Gaza who had been in Cairo for medical attention to an eye problem and to visit her father who was in the PRCS hospital there. We searched around the area to find pieces of cardboard to place on the cement where we would be trying to sleep. It was possible to buy tea or coffee, sandwiches and biscuits from a small stall in the building, but the toilet facilities in the area were grossly inadequate.

It was a miserable night, but we were very fortunate: we got through the border checkpoint the following afternoon. Some people spent many nights there waiting to get through.

On 2 February 2004, Ariel Sharon announced his plan to unilaterally remove the Israeli settlements in the Gaza Strip and four small outposts on the West Bank. This was a surprise coming from one of the main supporters of the settlement movement. The Palestinians, who had been calling for resumption of talks, were against any unilateral action on the part of the Israelis. Unilateral action meant the Israelis would do as they wished without any consideration of the implications for the Palestinians – a process of the powerful dictating to the weak. For the next year and half, this issue of 'disengagement' would dominate a great deal of debate and speculation.

Early in 2004, two high-profile Hamas leaders were assassinated by Israeli air strikes: Ahmed Yassin, the Hamas spiritual leader, in March; and his successor, Dr Abdel Azziz Al-Rantissi, in May. Both men had spent years in Israeli prisons and had been released. 'Why hadn't the Israelis kept them in prison rather than releasing them and then killing them in this way?' the people asked. Sheik Yassin, a wheelchair-user, was struck with a missile as he left early morning prayers at a mosque in Gaza. In the case of Dr Al-Rantissi, an F-16 jet fired missiles at the building where he lived, killing or wounding many other people, including women and children. There was international condemnation of Israel's use of the F-16 fighter plane to launch missiles in a heavily populated residential area. Angry demonstrations followed both assassinations.

On 13 May, following the killing of some Israeli soldiers by Palestinian militants in Gaza, the Israeli army launched an incursion on several areas of Rafah refugee camp. This was a worrying time for us as so many of our staff live in Rafah. We tried to keep contact with them by telephone, anxious for their safety during the heavy bombardment and the long curfews. There was no knowing how extensive the incursion would be nor how long it would last. With so many staff absent from work, it was hard for the rehabilitation centre to keep its programs going, but with extra effort by the remaining staff it was able to continue.

Forty Palestinians were killed during this nine-day incursion, and many others were wounded. Once the siege was over, I made a visit to the area with other PRCS staff. We went first to the PRCS ambulance base. In front of the base was an ambulance car that had been completely destroyed – run over by a tank. I was especially shocked to see this, even though I was aware of the Israeli army's many violations against the emergency medical services.

During this period, on 18 May, there was a small, unarmed demonstration in Rafah. An Israeli helicopter gunship fired on the protesters, killing at least twenty people, including three children, and wounding many others.

On 19 May the United Nations Security Council passed a resolution demanding that Israel cease the demolition of houses, and condemned the killing of civilians. The US ambassador to the UN abstained. The Palestinian people have come to expect that any UN resolution condemning their oppression will be vetoed by the US, or, as in this case, the US abstains.

EIGHTEEN

AS ALWAYS, IT WAS IMPORTANT TO KEEP LIFE IN BALANCE, and the work we were doing with children with disabilities at the centre and other children from the neighbourhood aimed at giving them the support and skills they needed to cope in such difficult times. Art, music and physical education were essential aspects of the weekly activities in both the rehabilitation centre and the children's club, especially during such stressful times.

In early May, a group from a US organisation, Fellowship of Reconciliation Interfaith Peace-Builders Program, made a surprise visit to Al-Amal City. They came on a Friday, which is the weekend holiday for the staff, so the administrator asked me to come across to meet them. I took them on a tour of the program areas and talked about the children and adults who were attending programs, expressing my disappointment that they weren't able to meet them in person. Later, I received a letter from the group's assistant program coordinator, Gretchen Merryman, in which she said how wonderful it was to see the artwork, classrooms and activities that were bringing 'joy and healing despite overwhelming obstacles'. She also noted that to visit the centre was 'like a breath of fresh air' and an inspiration, as they had just come from seeing the extensive destruction and devastation in Rafah.

Objections continued to mount to the construction of the wall on the West Bank, with international and Israeli groups joining with Palestinians to demonstrate against the confiscation of Palestinian land, the uprooting of olive groves, and the severe restrictions placed on an ever-increasing number of Palestinian people. Demonstrations were inevitably broken up with tear gas, gunshots, the forcible removal of people and some detentions.

On 9 July 2004 the International Court of Justice ruled that the wall was illegal and that its construction must halt. The building and its accompanying devastation has continued, as have the demonstrations and punishment of the protesters.

In mid-October 2004, an air of uncertainty permeated the region as news filtered through about the serious nature of Yasser Arafat's illness. Conflicting information was posted in the media and rumours were rife. The Palestinian people were concerned for him as a person and as their respected leader, and also about what would happen if he should die. The majority of Palestinians had known no other leader.

News coverage of him being airlifted out of his compound in Ramallah to be taken to a military hospital in Paris showed the frailty of the man. He was no longer the proud leader in his military fatigues and his characteristic *hatta*, but a tired old man dressed in a tracksuit and woollen cap. However, he still managed a wave and a smile for his people. The announcement of his death on 11 November wasn't unexpected, but the finality of death is always a shock. There was a heavy sense of loss throughout Palestine and a great outpouring of grief. Posters of Abu Amar were placed in all public places. Many people believed that he had been poisoned in some way, which heightened the emotional atmosphere. The refusal of Israel to allow Abu Amar to be buried in Jerusalem was felt keenly by the people; another reminder that all aspects of their lives were controlled by the occupier.

The coverage of Abu Amar's funeral was watched by everyone around me. The grandeur of the State funerals in both Paris and Cairo befitted his role as statesman and acknowledged his contribution in gaining international recognition of the Palestinian people and their situation under occupation. The frenzied burial ritual in the compound in Ramallah revealed the extent to which he was a man of the people. I cannot think of any other world leader, past or present, who has had or would have such a contrasting farewell. It was indicative of the complexity of the Palestinian situation and the lack of control they experience in all aspects of their lives.

Of course, people were also discussing the transition into a new era. How would it take place? What would happen?

I was in Ramallah for some days in December, carrying out some work for the rehabilitation department. I visited the tomb of Abu Amar to pay my respects and place a wreath in the names of Hamoudi, Dalal, Badr and myself. The tomb is mounted in the centre of a quiet glassed-in room in the upper section of the Maqatta; the top of the tomb and all of the area around was completely covered with wreaths and remembrances from many people, local and international.

For the people of the PRCS, there was also the concern of Dr Fathi's deteriorating health. He had struggled with cancer for several years and it was now obvious that he had lost the battle. In great pain and confined to his bed, Dr Fathi was not aware of the drama surrounding his brother's ill health and death. At the same time, given his own state of ill health, Abu Amar had not been aware of the terminal nature of his brother's illness.

I was in a meeting with representatives of PAZ, a Spanish organisation supporting the work of a number of the PRCS programs on the West Bank and Gaza Strip, when I received the news of Dr Fathi's death. Someone came to tell me that the PRCS President, Mr Younis Al-Khatib, wished to speak to me. I excused myself from the meeting and went to his office. I was very surprised to see other senior PRCS personnel there too. Very quietly Younis told me that he had received a phone call to say that Dr Fathi had passed away.

It was impossible to fully grasp the magnitude of losing Dr Fathi. In many respects he *was* the PRCS, always so supportive and caring of all the developments, a strong advocate of rights and justice for all people. Even at his busiest and most stressful times he always made a point of checking on the welfare and progress of Hamoudi, Dalal and Badr. He had been failing noticeably over the last year, and had been away much of the time; but he was still such a strong presence. Now he was gone, and his loss would be keenly felt. I knew that the work and activities would continue, but things would be different and I wondered just how this new era would emerge.

I couldn't continue with my meeting. I returned to the group and told them the news and they agreed to make another appointment later. I returned to Younis's office to sit with the people who had worked so closely with Dr Fathi over many years, sharing difficult situations but also happy times. It was a very sad time for us all. Dr Fathi was a founder of the PRCS and had been its president for thirty years; he and the organisation were seen as one.

Dr Fathi's funeral was to be held in Cairo, as his family lived there and wished his tomb to be accessible for them, and others, to visit. This would not be the case if he were buried in the Gaza Strip because of all the restrictions on entry.

While I was waiting at Abu Houli checkpoint the following day, on my way back to Khan Younis, I could see police all around. Would it be open? Apparently it was currently closed, but during the morning it had been opening and closing, so it seemed best to continue south in the hope of getting through. Someone important, perhaps even the President, must be passing through. Soon a voice from a police car ordered traffic to pull over to the side as the convoy was approaching. The sleek black cars came into sight and travelled quickly to the south. The people in the car with me were guessing as to who was in the cars and where they were going. When we finally arrived at the checkpoint, I noticed the convoy of black cars had been stopped by Israeli army jeeps, just below the first of the army watchtowers. They remained there for some time, then all the cars turned around and headed back towards Gaza City. Like everyone else, I peered through our windows to try to see who was being turned back. We learned that it was a Palestinian Authority convoy (including Dr Fathi's sister, Khadija) wanting to travel to Egypt to attend Dr Fathi's funeral. They weren't permitted to leave the Gaza Strip.

Although there was a condolence ceremony held at Al-Amal City, I decided to attend the official reception at Al-Nour City, and that Badr should come with me. Badr, dressed in his suit, was proud that he could express his condolence in this way. Dalal was still in Edinburgh, and felt very sad that she was unable to attend the ceremony for Dr Fathi's passing. He had been a 'father figure' for her, following her progress closely and always working to ensure the best possible care and opportunities for her, Hamoudi and Badr.

Dalal would complete her study program in December, and I made plans to travel across to assist her to finalise her stay in Edinburgh. I organised a plane ticket from Cairo on 15 December, but was unable to get to Cairo to join the flight. Palestinian militants carried out a major operation around this time, tunnelling under the main military base at the Abu Houli checkpoint and destroying part of it with explosives, killing a number of Israeli soldiers. The Gaza Strip was sealed off entirely and none of us could move. The Rafah crossing remained closed for about six weeks, the Abu Houli checkpoint for about five days. There was no way I could get to my flight.

As soon as Abu Houli opened, I went to Gaza City, travelled from there into Jordan by road, then flew to Cairo. I needed to return to Cairo with Dalal because, as a Palestinian resident of the

Gaza Strip, she could only enter via Rafah; she wasn't permitted to enter from Jordan. I eventually arrived in Edinburgh, and Linda and Dalal were waiting for me at the airport. They had begun to think that I never would arrive. It was great to see them both and I felt very proud of Dalal, who looked so confident and radiant. We spent Christmas with Linda and Donald and their family.

Arriving back in Cairo on 29 December, Dalal and I were met by PRCS staff and taken to the hotel at the Palestine Hospital. The Rafah border crossing was still closed so we were stranded in Cairo until it re-opened. It was a strange time: each day asking if the road was open, then using the enforced waiting period to visit friends. I tried to keep up with my work in Khan Younis via email. One benefit of the delay was the opportunity for me to have a much needed cataract operation. The PRCS arranged for me to see the specialist at the hospital clinic, who referred me to a surgeon. Dalal and I were delighted by the reaction when we entered the clinic: as Dalal is obviously blind, everyone assumed I was bringing her for attention.

We were still in Cairo on 26 January 2005: Australia Day. A couple of days before I started to receive phone calls from the Australian media asking for interviews. Apparently my name was listed to receive the award of Companion of the Order of Australia (AC) for my humanitarian work with the Palestinian people in the Middle East, international relations and professional training in education and rehabilitation. Friends from the International Cerebral Palsy Society had initiated the process of nomination; and other friends and people I knew in different walks of life had been asked to send comments about me and my work. I felt overwhelmed by the honour, but at the same time it seemed so far removed from the day-to-day difficulties we faced. I felt humbled when I thought of all I had hoped to do but had not managed, and of the many people I had worked with who struggled to provide important services in impossible conditions. I realised that the honour was not for me alone – it was also recognition of the Palestinian people and of people who are disabled. It was certainly a morale booster, a reinforcement to keep trying even when the situation seemed insurmountable. It also gave me a sense of connection between my life with the Palestinian people and my Australian identity.

The fact that I was stranded in Cairo had caused some confusion; the press had been trying to contact me in Khan Younis. Because of his English language skills, Badr was given the task of dealing with the phone calls and directing them to me in Cairo. He would then phone me himself, obviously pleased at being involved in relaying phone calls coming from abroad.

My friends and colleagues were delighted at the news, and the PRCS public relations department at Palestine Hospital organised a small congratulatory party. Several parents of children I had worked with at Ain Shams came to visit me, as did Mohammed Omar, severely disabled with cerebral palsy, who had attended the centre as a child. Now a young man with a baccalaureate degree in business management, Mohammed has his own shop. He has achieved a great deal, largely due to his own intelligence and persistence and the untiring support of his mother.

The world moved on from 2004 into 2005, but the Rafah border between Egypt and the Gaza Strip remained closed. Dalal and I were still stranded in Cairo. Our morning greeting became '*Akhbar aey?* (What is the news?)', meaning 'Is the border open?'

The complexity of the situation in Palestine remained the same too; even though 2005 heralded winds of change, early indicators did not give cause for optimism. The Israeli government was facing tensions related to its plan to unilaterally withdraw settlers and army from the Gaza Strip. Israeli tanks fired on seven children picking strawberries, killing them all. Five Israeli soldiers were killed by a bomb.

Mahmoud Abbas (Abu Mazen) won the election for President of the Palestinian Authority, replacing the late Yasser Arafat. In his inaugural address on 15 January, Abu Mazen called for support for the continuation of the ceasefire, implementation of the Road Map for Peace, and respect for the international ruling on the illegality of the wall. He called meetings of the different Palestinian factions in order to work towards unifying the people. On 24 January 2005, the Palestinian militant factions agreed to the ceasefire.

The US and Israel – both of which had so severely boycotted Yasser Arafat – gave indications that it would be possible for them to meet with Abu Mazen and restart negotiations. There was a feeling of hope that things might improve, but the hope was peppered with considerable scepticism, which I could understand. The people had seen too many occasions when the possibility of peace looked promising, only to be shattered by a more intensive occupation.

For the PRCS, the situation felt very bleak. The death of Dr Fathi was a huge loss. Although Younis Al-Khatib was still President, he was based in Ramallah on the West Bank and constantly faced the difficulty of obtaining an Israeli army permit to enter the Gaza Strip. Dr Fathi had been based in Gaza, so we'd had the benefit of strong leadership guiding developments and the maintaining of links with the PRCS headquarters. There were many good people in Gaza, but how a new leadership would emerge and develop was unclear. I was also concerned about whether the new structure would offer the same personal involvement Dr Fathi had given to the lives and wellbeing of Hamoudi, Dalal and Badr.

At last the long wait in Cairo came to an end – the border at Rafah was opened. On 30 January, Dalal and I arrived back in Khan Younis. The forced stay in Cairo had been very unsettling for Dalal: she felt suspended in a kind of limbo, eager to be home again after fifteen months away, but at the same time missing her friends and the student life in Edinburgh. She said it felt like being 'nowhere'. Dalal received a great welcome home, with what seemed like an endless stream of visitors bringing gifts of sweets in celebration. Badr and Hamoudi were both overjoyed to see her as they had missed her, a great deal.

Despite Dalal's joy at being home, there were many differences to deal with. Both Abu Amar and Dr Fathi had died while she was away and she felt their loss deeply. Initially she returned to her position of translator in the rehabilitation centre, with some involvement in the music programs for children, but she felt lost. She wanted work where she could use the knowledge she had gained through her studies and experience abroad. She was keen to learn more about social anthropology in order to be able to contribute more to developments in Palestine, and decided to try to find another scholarship within the next few years so as to be able to return to Edinburgh University to study for a PhD.

In February we were finally able to organise a PRCS conference on rehabilitation that we had been discussing for some years. Arrangements were made to hold the conference in one of the hotels in Ramallah on the West Bank, and we were surprised and very pleased to receive permits for a group of about ten of the staff from the centre at Khan Younis, including Dalal, to cross Erez to attend it. Given the difficulty for Palestinians to obtain a permit to pass through Erez, there is always a special atmosphere when Palestinians from the West Bank and the Gaza Strip have the opportunity to meet and share ideas.

After the conference, we visited a PRCS rehabilitation centre in Nablus, and also the residential centre for elderly people. The road to Nablus winds through rolling, stone-covered hills, offering some spectacular scenery; although the natural beauty is interrupted at times by the red roofs of settlements along some of the hilltops. To enter Nablus it is necessary to pass through the notorious Hawwara checkpoint, and as we approached there was obvious tension amongst our group. At the checkpoint we were required to get out of the car and the soldiers took our ID. Fortunately we were all permitted to pass, and it was with relief that we climbed back into the car to continue our journey. Once past the checkpoint, we could relax – and take the opportunity to eat some of the famous Nablus *kanafa* sweet.

The PRCS residential centre for the elderly, located high on one of the hills, was established in 1948 in order to accommodate some people who were stranded without family, having fled their homes inside what had become Israel and, as for all refugees at that time, were not permitted to return. Since then, the centre has also provided care for elderly people in the northern region of the West Bank.

To entertain the elderly people, a group of young men from Khan Younis used chairs and any other suitable object to hand as a *tabla* (Arabic drum) and beat out rhythms and sang popular Palestinian songs. The elderly people, shy at first, soon joined in with clapping or singing. Then one of the ladies stood up and sang a traditional Palestinian tale, much to the delight of all.

Whilst in the West Bank, Dalal and I were very keen to go to Jericho to visit Abir, who had held such a special place in our lives when we lived in Beirut. Although we were all now living in Palestine, it wasn't easy to visit one another because of the checkpoints, and I hadn't seen her for a couple of years. She and her husband, her young son and new baby, lived in a house in a refugee camp in Jericho, near the home of her parents and family.

We set out on the direct route to Jericho. This particular road is for the use of Israeli citizens only, but foreign passport holders and selected Palestinian health organisations also have permission to use it. We were travelling in a PRCS car and Dalal had her permit to be on the West Bank, so we thought we would be okay. What we didn't realise was that Dalal also needed to have a current PRCS employee ID card in order to travel on this 'exclusive' road. Having just returned from study abroad, she hadn't yet received her PRCS card, and no amount of argument with the soldiers at the checkpoint convinced them to allow us to pass.

'Use the other road,' they said, referring to the long, roundabout route that Palestinians are required to use, which would take some hours. There was no time to do this. We made some phone calls back to the PRCS headquarters, a stop at a photography studio, and then returned to the PRCS administration in the West Bank where Dalal was able to obtain her card. An hour or so later we were again on our way to Jericho, this time fully equipped with all the necessary paperwork. We passed the army checkpoint without difficulty.

It was great to catch up with Abir, to see her new baby, and to meet her mother again, whom we hadn't seen since our Beirut days. We spent a lot of time talking about the present, as well as recalling events during the period in Beirut. Although there were several checkpoints around the area of Jericho, and at times serious problems, there didn't seem to be the constant incursion and shelling that was being experienced in many other areas throughout the West Bank and Gaza Strip.

At the end of March I travelled via Rafah to Cairo in order to fly to Australia to participate in the Australia Day awards ceremony, which was scheduled to take place at Government House in Canberra on 8 April.

I stayed with Clarice and Alan in Brisbane, and, as always, they took very good care of me and made arrangements to enable me to catch up with as many relatives and friends as possible. It was wonderful to be able to see so many people, and although everyone was noticeably older (including myself), in many respects it felt as though I'd never been away. I also found myself marvelling at the beauty and calm of the country; it made me wish even more deeply that all the people of the world could experience such peace, freedom and quality of life.

Clarice and Alan attended the awards ceremony in Canberra with me, where I received the Companion of the Order of Australia (AC). It was very special to have them there. The ceremony itself was impressive, and so far removed from my everyday life in the Gaza Strip that it was almost overwhelming. I felt honoured at receiving the award, but felt that the honour extended beyond me to a recognition of the people I worked with and shared my life with. The Palestinian people are still denied so many basic human rights, and many of them work so hard to develop services for their communities without any recognition. It was such a sharp contrast to my own secure national identity, and the recognition given me for my efforts to contribute to a better world. I always feel puzzled by the unfairness of life and wonder if equality and acceptance will ever become cornerstones of existence across the world.

In Melbourne I was able to meet with some of the staff at the headquarters of the Australian Red Cross (ARC). It was interesting to hear about the work the ARC was doing, and also an opportunity to talk about the work of the PRCS. This type of exchange highlights for me the international bond that exists in the Movement of the Federation of Red Cross and Red Crescent Societies. I was also very privileged to meet the former Australian Prime Minister, Malcolm Fraser, who, unknown to me, had shown interest in my work in the Middle East and, through his contacts with Joan Mary Majali, an executive member of the International Cerebral Palsy Society, had supported their nomination for my award.

The time in Australia passed all too quickly. On 8 May it was International Day of Red Cross and Red Crescent – an occasion that focuses on the role of volunteers in the movement and reaffirms the organisations' ongoing commitment to their Agenda for Humanitarian Action. At the PRCS function held at Al-Nour City in Gaza City, I was honoured for twenty-five years of volunteer service to the

PRCS. I wondered where those years had gone, and reflected on the events I had been involved in over that time. I thought about the difficulties and tragedies that had occurred, and the fact that the Palestinian people were still struggling for recognition and a just peace. I also thought about the developments that had taken place within the rehabilitation department, and the many people I had worked with to achieve those developments. And I reflected on my life with Hamoudi, Dalal and Badr; their development from childhood into adulthood and the extent to which they had enriched my own life.

NINETEEN

THERE WERE ONGOING PROBLEMS both in the Gaza Strip and the West Bank. Every Friday there were non-violent demonstrations at Bi'lin village west of Ramallah by groups of Palestinians, Israelis and internationals. This village, like many others on the West Bank, was losing 60 per cent of its land because of the route of Israel's wall. The nearby ultra-orthodox Israeli settlement of Kiryat Sefer, a settlement built on land confiscated from adjacent villages, was to be extended onto this land lost to Bi'lin. Every Friday the peaceful demonstrators were dispersed roughly by the Israeli army with tear gas and plastic bullets.

There was some expression of international concern at this time about the Israeli wall, about the deteriorating situation for Palestinians in East Jerusalem, extrajudicial executions (assassinations) by the IDF, and home demolitions, together with other oppressive measures against Palestinians. On 26 May, Amnesty International classified the extrajudicial executions and home demolitions as war crimes and crimes against humanity. On 28 May, President Bush made a statement warning Israel that they should not take actions that would prejudice the final status negotiations on Jerusalem.

The team of artists and psychologists from the Dutch HOPE Foundation came to Khan Younis in June. This was to be the last of their regular visits to work with the staff and children in the Open

Studio as it was becoming increasingly difficult for them to enter the Gaza Strip and they worried about their safety. I was very sorry as their visits were stimulating for all, and their friendly, fun approach added a special component to the knowledge that was gained. Amongst the group of specialists who came with Ingrid on this final visit were two breakdancers. The children were fascinated by this activity, especially the boys from the children's club. For weeks after the team left, whenever I walked into the activity areas several of the boys would stand on their hands, do cartwheels or some of the other routines they had learned from the breakdancers. It was wonderful to see them having such fun.

The ceasefire of the Palestinian militants continued, although it looked to be in danger when six Palestinians were killed by the Israeli army in early June. In mid-June, Israel announced that it was planning to build a sea wall out from the coast at the border between Israel and the northern Gaza Strip. We all thought this a strange idea and wondered how it would be done.

Towards the end of July the situation continued to be generally tense, although relatively quiet. One day I was on my way home from giving my last lecture of the term to Masters students at Wafa Hospital, which is located at the very north of the Gaza Strip. As usual, I took a share taxi from near the hospital to the Al-Shajayah area at the eastern end of Gaza City, where I'd then catch a share taxi to Khan Younis. The Al-Shajayah area is a crowded residential area with a busy market sprawled along the footpaths. It has also been a target for Israeli planes on several occasions. I felt quite nervous as I left the taxi and began my walk through the adjacent shopping area to the Saha (Palestine Square), as there were police everywhere. As I travelled south in the taxi to Khan Younis, I was aware of more police on the road than usual. Later I heard that what I had seen was the beginning of a problem between the police and Hamas that had escalated during the night, and Israeli planes had carried out assassinations on selected people. There were frequent periods of intensive shelling and shooting in our area, and the noise of the *zanana* (pilotless spy planes) and fighter jets overhead. The situation wasn't good, but daily life went on as normally as possible, always with the hope that the hostilities would end.

Not long after this, some staff from Médecins Sans Frontières (MSF) came to the centre. They were concerned for the children living near the flashpoints along the western perimeter of Khan Younis refugee camp, which faced the Gush Katif settlements. These children were experiencing constant shelling and destruction and lived in fear. Many had lost family members and friends. The MSF team were interested in the work we were doing and our facilities, and were keen to discuss the possibility of referring children to activities at the centre and working together to give children the support they needed.

One of the MSF staff, Mohammed, told us of the problem they had experienced at Abu Houli checkpoint the day before. The checkpoint had been closed for some time and there was a long line of cars waiting. There had been shooting at and over the heads of the people a number of times – a common occurrence, especially if there was a long delay. Sometimes it was in response to people getting out of their cars and moving closer to the front of the waiting area. Mostly it seemed to happen for no apparent reason. On that day, a fourteen-year-old boy was killed. 'I have never seen anything like the situation yesterday,' Mohammed said.

He told us how the MSF car had previously been coordinated to go through the checkpoint, so they had moved up the waiting line expecting to be able to pass. However, they were stopped and, like all the other cars, just had to wait. Then the strangest thing began to happen. It seemed that some people who had been waiting for a long time in the heat had had enough.

'They just started to drive through the checkpoint in a reckless manner,' he said. 'The soldiers immediately began to shoot over the cars. One car came back, but others moved forward at speed in spite of the shooting. There was even one family who walked through – as if for them it was "the end" and they would not be intimidated any longer. It is forbidden to go through this checkpoint on foot, but the people obviously could not take any more of the situation and just didn't care. It was so awful to see this.'

Mohammed said he and the other MSF staff were fearful for the people, but they could not join the group in defiance of the military control. MSF is an international organisation and any defiance of military authority could have a damaging effect on their work. Eventually the situation quietened and they were able to pass through with the regular traffic flow.

'When I arrived home, I just sat and cried,' Mohammed said.

When Ariel Sharon had announced in 2004 his plan of unilateral disengagement of Israeli settlers and army from the Gaza Strip and four small settlements in the northern part of the West Bank, many in the Palestinian communities could not believe that this would in fact happen. Now it appeared that it would and the date was to be 12 August 2005.

The buildup to this date was a very strange period. Many of the settlers objected to the move and there were demonstrations in Israel. These settlers and their supporters adopted the colour orange as their symbol of protest, wearing orange clothing and attaching ribbons and banners to cars, roadside posts and their buildings. Sometimes there were groups of settlers protesting at the Abu Houli checkpoint, and the checkpoint would be closed for some time until the Israeli army had moved them away from the area.

We talked a lot about how great it would be when the settlers and army had left. We thought life would be safer as there would not be the constant shelling and shooting from the settlement areas; it would be possible to go to the beach; and, as there would be no Abu Houli or other checkpoints, it would be possible to move freely within the Gaza Strip. However, it was still unclear what the situation would really be like.

After the disengagement, the Israeli army would still control all the borders of the Gaza Strip – Rafah and Erez for people; Karni for goods – which would still restrict the movement of people and trade. There was no arrangement for ease of travel between the Gaza Strip and the West Bank – and any arrangement likely to be made would be under the control of the Israeli army. Israel would continue to collect and control tax monies of the Palestinian Authority, and the sea and air space would remain under the control of the Israeli army. Israel claimed the right to re-enter any areas of the Gaza Strip if they considered this to be necessary. The prison would remain a prison, with, perhaps, some greater internal comfort. The way the media presented the withdrawal was especially worrying: according to them, the unilateral withdrawal of the Israeli settlers and army was a major concession to the Palestinian people and the Gaza Strip was now free of occupation. Nothing could be further from the truth.

Many people felt that the hype about Israel's withdrawal from Gaza was a smokescreen to hide Israel's actions on the West Bank and Jerusalem. The construction of the wall – ruled as illegal by the International Court of Justice – continued at an increased pace. Farmers were cut off from their farms; people were cut off from education and health care services. The large settlements on the West Bank continued to expand and Israeli-only roads to snake across the West Bank. If Israel had kept to the agreements of the Oslo Accords of 1994, not even one brick would have been added to settlements.

The wall, the major house demolition program in East Jerusalem and the takeover of buildings in the Arab sector of the old city was basically aimed at driving the Palestinian population out of Jerusalem. The status of Jerusalem was scheduled to be discussed later within the Road Map plan and neither side had the right to alter the geo-political character of the city prior to such negotiation. However, Israel was making major changes so as to completely separate East Jerusalem from the West Bank and to divide the West Bank into small isolated areas with the Israeli army controlling movement between them. Each time I went across to the PRCS headquarters on the West Bank I was staggered to see the rapid progress of the wall, and the very many construction cranes protruding above the buildings in the settlements and areas adjacent to them.

Al-Mawasi – a Palestinian area dependent on farming and fishing – is located at the western edge of the Khan Younis refugee camp and surrounded by the Israeli settlements of Gush Katif. Although the Al-Mawasi people had not been evicted by the settlers, they were completely cut off; all their movements were restricted by an IDF checkpoint, which they weren't always permitted to cross.

Al-Mawasi had a population of approximately 7000 people. The fishermen were no longer permitted to fish. Some of the farmlands had been destroyed, and the crops that were ready for the market had to be taken through the checkpoint on foot. Sometimes the road was blocked for days at a time and people trying to get home were stranded and forced to seek shelter wherever they could.

The PRCS had a primary health centre at Al-Mawasi and I wanted to go into the area to follow up on work I had begun in locating people with disability, assessing their needs and trying to develop some type of programming service for them. With Dalal accompanying me as a translator, we set out with a convoy of two ICRC jeeps, a PRCS ambulance and a Ministry of Health mobile dental clinic in order to conduct a free medical service day.

When we got to the Tufah checkpoint that would allow us access to Al-Mawasi, we were confronted by overwhelming destruction. There was a wide expanse of churned-up ground and rubble from destroyed buildings, and the houses that were still standing were marked with shell holes. The view of the beach that I used to enjoy from this high vantage point was no longer visible because of a high cement wall that had been built by the Israelis.

I looked to the side of the road where there was a covered area; people sat here and waited until the soldiers gave them permission to cross the military area and enter Al-Mawasi – a wait that could vary from hours to days. The checkpoint opened twice a day: from 8 am to 1 pm and then 2.30 pm to 5 pm. Males from Al-Mawasi aged sixteen to thirty required special permission to pass through, as did females between sixteen and twenty-five. The IDF placed severe restrictions on these age groups as they claimed they were most likely to carry out resistance actions such as suicide bombings.

People had to walk through the checkpoint. There were women with small children in their arms, and old people struggling with various items. Products intended for market had to be unloaded and carried through crate by crate to reload at the other side, and all loads were searched by sniffer dogs.

The stretch of coastline along the Al-Mawasi area is a lovely natural beach and we had spent some happy times there in the past. Now, however, the main section had been fenced off and the buildings that hadn't been reduced to rubble had been taken over by settlers who objected to leaving the settlements; we could tell by the orange flags flying from them.

During this visit to Al-Mawasi, I carried out a general assessment of the people with disability (mostly children) in the area. I could see how much work was needed, but how to provide the services for these children and their families was beyond my imagination. One of the nurses at the clinic in the Swedish Village area volunteered to take me to the home of a family living nearby. As soon as I entered the house, I was served with a cold juice and warmly welcomed. A senior male of the family conducted the visit and gradually more and more women and children gathered around us – including four deaf children and one intellectually disabled boy. The children had been attending a centre for deaf children in Rafah, which was quite close to where they lived. However, since the Israeli army had closed the crossing into Rafah, they were now required to travel north to the Tufah checkpoint, cross into Khan Younis and from there find transport into the centre of town where there was a taxi rank for Rafah. All of this travel involved time and money, and there was also the danger of the Tufah junction being closed and the children being stranded in Khan Younis.

There was growing concern for the people of Al-Mawasi, and the PRCS, UNICEF and MSF tried to truck in emergency supplies in case there was a complete closure of the area. The people there were also in further danger from the influx of Israelis from the West Bank settlements, who had entered the area, against the ruling of their government, to join the resistance against the disengagement.

In August, I was able to go to Al-Mawasi again. It was a hot, humid day and as we waited to pass through the inspection area at the Tufah checkpoint I observed three young people playing together at the side of the road: a girl and two young men playing a children's clapping game, then stopping to chat and laugh. It was a perfect picture of youth relaxing and enjoying one another's company – except these were 'on duty' Israeli soldiers. A few hundred yards back, near the bombed-out entrance to the Khan Younis refugee camp, there was a small covered shelter where about a hundred people – men, women and children – sat waiting patiently for the call from a soldier to enter the inspection area. Many waited hours; some waited days. They were only trying to go home so why did they have to wait so long? The young soldiers happily playing together seemed oblivious to their suffering.

On top of all of the uncertainty and difficulties, a local problem developed. Employees from different organisations throughout the

Gaza Strip had been holding strikes in an attempt to improve their conditions, especially in relation to salary and associated rights. The economic situation in the Gaza Strip was extremely problematic. Over 60 per cent of the population was estimated to be living below the poverty line. This was mainly due to unemployment. For those who were employed, wages were often low. The employees of Al-Amal City staged a couple of short strikes during late July and early August. Then from Sunday, 7 August they staged a continuous strike, seeking increased salaries, retirement benefits and some other demands. The PRCS administration tried to address the issues and work towards solutions. At the same time, plans had been made for the PA Ministry of Internal Affairs to take over most of the Al-Amal City building, from where they would observe and supervise the situation as the Israeli settlers and army moved out of the Gush Katif settlements. This meant we had to close down the activity areas for the children's club and move the equipment to the kindergarten so programs could continue.

A further complication occurred on the evening of 7 August. It seemed there had been a conflict between the security department, which had detained a person, and the militant group associated with the person. Masked gunmen descended on Al-Amal City, and there was a confrontation between them and the striking staff who had been maintaining a presence in the building as part of their action. This was the first time something like this had happened and I wondered what it portended for the future. Fortunately, the situation was eventually resolved and the gunmen left, although we heard they created problems in other parts of the town.

Early the following Monday afternoon, two of the rehabilitation centre staff contacted me on my mobile phone to check where I was in the building. They told me that the same masked gunmen had taken three hostages, all foreigners, and were looking for more. They were attempting to put pressure on the security department to release the person who had been detained. The staff suggested that I should go home, and walked there with me to ensure I was safe. The hostage saga ended within a few hours and the people were freed. I did feel a bit uneasy afterwards, but I didn't let the situation affect my movements. Although, I did ask my colleagues about the general situation before walking into town on my own.

The strike actions and the hostage-taking reflected the instability of the country. Some of the people were supportive of these actions, saying that no one cared about the difficulties they faced and the extent to which their rights were neglected. They said the situation had reached a point beyond tolerance. Others were aware of the fact that such actions contributed further to the general disadvantage being experienced, and expressed concern that those involved in these actions, and their supporters, didn't understand this fact.

The endless publicity about the pull-out, planned destruction of the settlers' housing and the compensation to be given to the 'poor' settlers who had to leave their homes did not sit well with the Palestinian people. 'What were they doing here in the first place?' was a common reaction. 'Compensation for what?' was another. Too many people had suffered the relentless destruction of their homes, often in the middle of the night, with no thought of compensation, to feel sympathy for the settlers. Many of the older people I spoke to recalled events of 1948 and 1967 when they had to flee their homes in towns and villages where their families had lived for centuries, leaving everything behind.

During the period of the Israeli evacuation of the settlements of the Gaza Strip, there was the noise of explosives for days as the Israeli army destroyed the buildings they were leaving. There was great joy everywhere and Palestinian flags flew on buildings and cars. The nearby mosque called for prayers to give thanks for the pull-out. At midnight, as the last of the settlers and army left, hundreds of people from Rafah and Khan Younis streamed down to the beach – the place they had been denied access to for years. By morning, the numbers on the beach or touring the vacated settlement area had increased to thousands.

Dalal, Badr and I decided to join the crowds to 'have a look'. We phoned Aly who came with his taxi to take us on the tour. The experience was unbelievable. We went first to what had been the southern military post of the dreaded Abu Houli checkpoint. The feeling was 'Wow! No more Abu Houli!' From here we turned west along the road towards the beach, and drove south. At times we turned off the main road to view the now deserted Israeli settlements. The roads were crowded with cars lined up in both directions. Cars and donkey carts leaving the area were loaded high with pieces of scrap metal, timber and any other useful materials found amongst the rubble. Columns of black smoke wafted into the sky from piles of burning rubbish. The roads down to the beach were crowded with people walking to the sea. I described the scene to Dalal, with Aly adding details about the areas we passed.

The area that had been occupied by the settlers was extensive – stretching from Deir Al-Balah to the Egyptian border at Rafah. The roads and some gardens remained, along with the destroyed buildings. There were large areas of hothouses still standing, most having been sold to Palestinians to continue agricultural production. Generally, though, there was endless cleared land and destroyed buildings. The settlers had taken Palestinian land – farmlands or open uncultivated land – to build their settlements, but then destroyed areas adjacent to the settlements for 'security reasons'. As I surveyed this endless picture of destruction, my thoughts were, What was this all about? Why? For what? I had no answers. Hundreds of people had been killed, including too many children; thousands wounded.

The joy of the Palestinians at the removal of the Israeli army and settlers from the Gaza Strip was soon tempered by the reality of the situation. The occupation had not ended, although movement within the Gaza Strip was much easier. However, any movement of people or goods in and out of the Gaza Strip was completely under the control of the Israeli army. Air and sea were controlled by the Israeli army, the repair of both the airport and sea port forbidden. Water and electricity supplies were controlled by the Israelis. The international community congratulated Israel for ending its occupation, but it was a false picture. More and more land in the West Bank was being confiscated for settlement expansion, Israeli-only roads, and for the wall; harsher measures at checkpoints were preventing the people moving from town to town, or, in some cases, between home and services or farmlands.

Not long after the pullout, the Gaza Strip suffered days of sonic booms – military planes breaking the sound barrier. Wave after wave of explosive sound filled our flat, causing the building to shake, windows to break, pictures to fall from the walls and objects from the shelves. The roar of the jet itself followed the boom. At times there were several booms an hour during the day, the sound penetrating the whole body and often causing pain in the ears. This onslaught continued for some weeks, in spite of the outcry of the local people and international supporters. We began to leave our windows open at all times, to minimise the amount of broken glass.

During September there was a great deal of activity about the status of the border crossing at Rafah between the Gaza Strip and Egypt. The new arrangements were that the Egyptian army would monitor the strip of border, while the Palestinians managed the border crossing, with European Union monitors present and under camera supervision of the Israeli army. The Israeli army still had the authority to close the border at will. This arrangement – when the border is open – makes travel easier for Palestinians, but for foreigners, like myself, it is problematic, as we are required to pass through Israeli-controlled border posts and obtain an Israeli visa.

On 17 September, just after the Egyptian border agreements were finalised but before they had started operating, some Palestinians broke through the border fence. For some hours there was an uncontrolled passage of Palestinians from the Gaza Strip into Egypt and

Palestinians from Egypt going into the Gaza Strip. Some saw a relative or friend for the first time in years. Some of our staff took the chance to go through, and were very excited about the experience when they told us about it later. 'Just to be able to go to Egypt without a permit, without the humiliating treatment at the border, was like really being alive again,' they said.

The following day, President Bush stated that he supported Israel in its claim that major Israeli settlements in the OPT of the West Bank would remain within Israel in any permanent status arrangements. The Palestinians were shocked and angry. How could the US support this? If these large settlements remained, with their Israeli-only connecting roads, the West Bank would be cut into sections, making a viable Palestinian State impossible. President Bush's statement came just days after both Israel and the US had rejected the call of the Palestinian President, Mahmoud Abbas, to 'engage immediately' in final status negotiations. Again, I wondered why the rights of the Palestinian people continued to be ignored.

The fifth anniversary of the second Intifada fell on 29 September, and all Palestinian factions announced their commitment to continue their struggle against the occupation until the establishment of a free and independent Palestine. The struggle was costly, with reports of 4166 Palestinians killed and 45 538 wounded during the five-year period, and 1113 Israelis killed. There were 8600 Palestinian detainees in Israeli prisons; and the destruction of Palestinian property included the confiscation of over 2 million square metres of land, over a million uprooted trees, 7761 homes demolished and 93 842 homes damaged.

TWENTY

IN SEPTEMBER 2005, Badr was transferred from the rehabilitation department to work in the College. There had been changes to arrangements for his little shop in the rehabilitation centre that reduced his involvement, and as he was very reliable in carrying out odd jobs and delivering messages for the administration departments he was chosen to fill this vacancy in the College. Badr is a diligent worker and always willing to please. He also started playing sitting volleyball on Saturday and Tuesday evenings with a group of disabled young men at the Al-Amal City sports hall.

Dalal also experienced a change of employment around this time. She had received additional voice and Braille equipment to use with her computer, which greatly enhanced her work abilities, and she took up the position of head of the continuing education program at the College, as well as becoming involved with part of the lecturing program. She was very pleased with this new role, having felt the need to use and develop the knowledge and skills she had gained during her studies abroad. She and Badr walked together to the College each morning to begin their work day.

The political party Hamas, which had refused to participate in earlier elections, agreed to participate in the municipal elections in late

September. Hamas had a great deal of popular support because of its early base of providing social support to the people, assisting those in need and contributing to the strengthening of services. It also held a strong Islamic religious position and was committed to military resistance to the Israeli occupation. Hamas won a quarter of the seats in municipal councils, which was the first serious challenge to the Fatah party, which had always been the party in control and, until now, had been considered by many to be the only base for a Palestinian government.

In late November, Ariel Sharon spoke of unilaterally withdrawing Israeli settlers from some settlements on the West Bank. In order to carry out his plans, he left the Israeli right-wing Likud party to form a new centre party, Kadima. This party gained increasing support from the Israeli public. The concept of unilateral action was not supported by the Palestinian people, however, who pointed out that it was not possible to establish peace and build relationships unless there was dialogue and coordination between both sides. Again the Palestinians felt that their position was being neglected.

By the end of 2005, it was evident that the general situation in the OPT was deteriorating. I thought of how inaccurate the well-known saying 'It is so bad that it cannot get worse' could be. In Palestine, it continued to get worse. And worse.

Early in 2006, I was amazed to read of the Israeli government's advertisements for tenders for hundreds of new housing units in the West Bank settlements. Israel continues to defy the UN Resolutions, the Oslo Accords and more recently, the Road Map to Peace, all of which define the West Bank as part of the Palestinian State. Each time I visit the West Bank I feel depressed to see the large building cranes silhouetted against the sky, areas of adjacent land being cleared and new buildings being constructed. Israel's wall has invaded new areas, its ugliness blocking out the landscape beyond. The visual impact is minor compared with its greater assault on the lives of the people.

Israel continued to claim there was no Palestinian partner with whom it could negotiate and continued to follow a unilateral policy that couldn't possibly improve the situation. The US seemed to back all Israeli actions, regardless of how aggressive or oppressive they were. 'Security' was always the reason given for actions taken against the Palestinians, but no one seemed to consider the need for security for the Palestinians.

The ruling party of the Palestinian Authority, Fatah, was widely perceived to be corrupt and ineffective, which contributed to the situation of emerging lawlessness in the country. Armed confrontations, the taking of hostages and disregard for the authority of the police were causing a great deal of alarm.

Despite the surrounding tension, we still enjoyed the special celebration of New Year's Eve. It is a time for reflection on the year past and wondering about things to come. We had a quiet time in Khan Younis, without the late-night parties or elaborate fireworks displays usual in some countries, but there was an underlying excitement as people got together with family and friends, '*Kul aam wa intum bikheer* (good wishes to you all for all the year)'.

Hamoudi, Dalal, Badr and I, along with Hamoudi's two carers, had a happy time singing together, and Badr and the men performed *Dabka* dance steps. Later, after Hamoudi had gone to sleep, Dalal, Badr and I went to the upstairs flat for supper and watched the celebrations around the world on television. Badr went to bed before midnight, but Dalal and I waited for the countdown.

Just before midnight, we heard other noises – the ominous chopping sound of helicopters passing overhead. Later we heard that a Fatah party office had been bombed; perhaps an omen for the year to come.

On 1 January, three Palestinians were killed by Israeli tank fire in the buffer zone that the Israeli army had created at the north of the

Gaza Strip. On 2 January, three more people were killed, this time from targeted fire from a plane. There was always strong reaction amongst the community at large when people were killed; often a van with loudspeakers toured the streets to announce the new *shahids* (martyrs). If the *shahid* is local there is sometimes a procession to carry the body past places that were important to the person's life, before going to the mosque for prayers, then another procession to the cemetery for burial.

Meanwhile, political controversies were growing. The Israeli government announced that Palestinians living in occupied East Jerusalem would not be permitted to take part in the forthcoming Palestinian elections. Following some international pressure they conceded that they would allow limited access to voting for these Palestinians. Many Palestinians claimed that without people in East Jerusalem being able to exercise their right to vote, the elections should not go ahead.

The Israeli government also stated that if the Hamas party took part in the elections, they would prevent the elections from taking place. The US position was that if Hamas were elected into the Palestinian Authority, they would not work with the PA. Reactions by the Palestinians were strong. 'Who talks of democracy but tries to prevent a section of the population entering the election process?' 'What right do other countries have to determine who may or may not participate in our elections?'

Israel, the US and some other countries include Hamas on their lists of terrorist organisations. By contrast, local people saw Hamas as a well-organised charity, and the support it gave the needy was respected even by many Palestinians who didn't support its armed-struggle approach to resistance nor its fundamentalist approach to Islam.

Finally, Wednesday, 25 January was set as the day for elections. There were many parties standing, and a number of independent candidates, but the two main parties were Fatah and Hamas.

Fatah, a secular party, had dominated the Palestinian political scene since its foundation in 1959. Under the leadership of Yasser Arafat, Fatah had been the major party within the PLO since the latter organisation was established in 1964. Not linked to any particular ideology, Fatah attracted people from different religions and political beliefs. Because of its dominant position in the resistance and later political developments, many people thought of Fatah as a national movement rather than just a political party. During the buildup to these elections there was some internal conflict within the ruling Fatah party. The 'old guard', which had returned from Tunis with Yasser Arafat following the Oslo Accords, was being challenged by the 'young guard' – younger aspiring politicians who had grown up in the OPT.

Hamas was founded in 1987. Initially the party focused on social issues, and it was well known that during its early period Israel had supported Hamas in an attempt to weaken Fatah's control. The leader of Hamas was Sheik Ahmed Yassin. He was branded a terrorist by Israel and the US and was imprisoned by the Israelis for many years. When he was released, he was assassinated. His successor, Abdel Azziz Al-Rantissi, was also assassinated. These murders created great anger among all Palestinians, not only Hamas supporters.

The age-old rivalry between Fatah and Hamas was evident throughout their campaigns for the 2006 elections. Cars drove around with loudspeakers spilling out national and party songs interspersed by policy statements for the various candidates. There were posters everywhere, some showing photos of candidates together with photos of deceased leaders, such as Yasser Arafat, or a strange mix of posters of political candidates and those honouring 'martyrs' killed by the Israeli army.

On the first day of campaigning it was announced that both Hanan Ashrawi and Mustafa Barghouti, leading peace activists and politicians, had been prevented by the Israeli police from campaigning in East Jerusalem. The reason given was that Palestinians are forbidden to carry out any political activity there – a policy that has been severely imposed since the forced closure of Orient House in 2001.

The whole situation in Palestine and Israel became even more complex when the Israeli Prime Minister, Ariel Sharon, suffered a massive stroke and lapsed into a coma. His deputy, Ehud Olmert, was given full prime ministerial authority, and in March was voted in as head of the newly formed Kadima party.

In spite of the turmoil all around, the programs at Al-Amal City continued as usual. Children with disabilities at the school at the rehabilitation centre and the students of the College of Ability Development were involved in end of term examinations, as were pupils and students throughout the country. The staff were working on upgrading the after-school children's club and winter vacation was on the horizon. Planning was also under way to expand activities in sport and recreation for the community in general. However, both financial and administrative constraints presented difficulties.

The HOPE team provided funding for a winter day camp program for children with disabilities from the Al-Mawasi area, together with their siblings and friends. This work with the children from Al-Mawasi was possible now the Israeli settlers and army had left. One hundred and forty children attended the camp, about a quarter of them children with disability. After being confined to the Al-Mawasi area for so many years, and confronted with the aggression of the settlers and soldiers, these children were delighted by the camp's creative and play activities. It was a very special experience for the staff too, and hopefully the beginning of ongoing work with these children.

The last day of campaigning was filled with intense activity and noise. I happened to be in the centre of Khan Younis town in the afternoon and the tension and excitement were evident. There was a continuous flow of vans and cars with their flags and loudspeakers blaring out music and slogans at top volume. Suddenly a middle-aged man holding a large Palestinian flag stepped out onto the street near me and broke into a *Dabka* dance, much to the delight of the people nearby who gathered around him, clapping and cheering.

There was no campaigning on the day immediately before the election, and the sudden quiet seemed strange following the hype. I hoped that all those people, especially the youth, who were involved so intensely would be able to manage their emotions after the elections. There would be winners, but there would also be losers.

On the morning of election day I accompanied Dalal to the school where she was to vote. She was excited as it was the first time she would cast a vote. She still hadn't received her ID when the first presidential elections were held so was unable to take part. Badr had voted for the first time in the last presidential election as the ballot paper was straightforward, with just the list of presidential candidates, and he understood the issue fully. This time, however, he was very confused and decided not to vote.

There was a high turnout throughout the country, and except for some minor incidents the day went smoothly. The international observers declared the elections to be conducted well and fairly. The expectation was that Fatah would win the election and Hamas would come a close second, so it was a collective shock when results showed Hamas with a clear majority. It was said that not even Hamas itself expected, or wanted, to win outright. It seemed people had supported Hamas because of its undaunted resistance to the Israeli occupation, its extensive charity work, and because its leadership was perceived to be free of corruption. Despite the election process being praised as legal, well run and fair, Israel, the US and the European Union – all of which included Hamas on their lists of terror organisations – imposed a boycott on funds reaching the newly elected government.

In Palestine, some Fatah activists, angry about the Hamas victory, went onto the streets to demonstrate against their leadership, which they felt had failed them. I felt anxious about how the situation would evolve. Israel had initially given support to Hamas so as to weaken Fatah's control; then had directly attacked the Fatah authority and refused to deal with the President, Yasser Arafat, confining him to his bombed-out headquarters for a couple of years prior to his death. With Hamas now in power, the label 'terrorist organisation' made it an easy target for international sanctions and any other means to bring about its downfall.

Two days after the election, I was asked to go to Gaza City in the evening to attend a meeting with the President of the PRCS, Younis Al-Khatib. As I travelled from Khan Younis to Gaza City I was aware of tension in the atmosphere. Groups of people were walking along the roadside, obviously returning from demonstrations. During the meeting a demonstration passed by outside with a great deal of noise, gunfire and shouting.

It was about 9 pm when the minibus turned off the main road into Khan Younis on our way home. It was immediately obvious that something was going on. There were youths running in different directions. Our driver stopped and started to slowly back towards the main road. Then we heard shooting. The person beside me immediately dropped to crouch on the floor of the bus. I ducked down low as well, cautiously peeping up occasionally to see what was happening.

There was banging on the side door of the minibus and a crowd of excited men pulled it open and tried to get in. The confusion lessened and a wounded man was lifted into the bus by two other men, who demanded the driver take them to the military hospital, about a ten-minute drive to the east of the main north–south road of the Gaza Strip.

Having delivered the wounded man and his helpers to the hospital, our driver took alternative back routes to get us back to Al-Amal City without any further incident. To our surprise, everything was quiet there, and the people in the residence were unaware of the conflict taking place at the main entrance to the town.

From 15 January to late February, Karni crossing – the main terminal through which Israel permits the transport of goods – was closed, adding to the shortages. Television reports showed truckloads of bananas and other fruits dumped at the roadside, rotten from the long wait in the sun. Produce could not be exported, which meant that the farmers in the Gaza Strip lost their income and in some cases were forced to stop farming. The Associated Press reported that the Palestinian Authority lost US$7 million due to the closure. We all felt the effects: many items, such as milk, yoghurt, gas for cooking stoves, were no longer available in the shops. We organised an emergency carton of food and powdered milk for Hamoudi, Dalal and Badr, in addition to an extra supply of the epilepsy medicines needed for both Hamoudi and Badr.

Life is a curious mix of events and emotions, and January 2006 seemed to have the full range. Despite the political events, which would have a major impact on the future of the region, daily life continued. On 24 January I went with Dalal to Gaza City to attend the wedding of one of her friends. The couple made their ceremonial entrance down the centre of the hall, which was crowded with more than a hundred women well-wishers. (The men had had their event the day before, but male relatives and close friends were gathered outside the area for the women.) There was a podium at the front of the hall holding two decorated chairs surrounded by large flower arrangements, and as the couple made their way, they were accompanied by music and the high trill of joy, ululation (*zgrada*), by some of the women. Once the couple was seated, different women stepped up onto the podium to dance. Without the presence of males, many of the women who usually covered their hair removed their scarves and danced freely in the area in front of the bridal couple. This was followed by a dance with candles and the presentation of the *shabaka*, a jewel case containing the wedding rings and other gold jewellery.

A few days after the wedding, one of the staff came to offer me a chocolate – the traditional sharing of sweets to celebrate special events. Raad and Maha, two of our staff, had just become proud parents for the first time. The next day, Ismael, one of the staff who had been absent for many weeks due to illness, returned to work – another cause for celebration. The day after, I made a condolence visit with a group of staff to one of our colleagues whose father had died. On the same day, I went to see a PRCS colleague to offer my congratulations on her success at gaining a seat in the elections.

Towards the end of February I had the opportunity to attend a two-day symposium in Athens organised by Cerebral Palsy Greece in conjunction with the International Cerebral Palsy Society (ICPS). I was very excited as it was many years since I'd had the chance to attend an ICPS conference. I was also keen to meet with senior people at ICPS to express my appreciation for their support of me and my work with the PRCS.

The symposium – 'Education: a determining factor in the life of every human being' – was very interesting with a wide range of speakers addressing a variety of topics related to the theme. Central concepts were the need to observe and listen closely to children, recognise the learning pattern of individual children, respect the person who is disabled, and value the role of family and community in the educational process. I was pleased to be able to tell other conference delegates about the PRCS's commitment to all these principles.

On the way home, I visited the new PRCS headquarters building in Ramallah to catch up with several of my colleagues and to attend a two-day conference on special education organised by the Palestinian Authority Education Department. The PA Education Department had been working on an inclusive education program for about ten years and it was time for a review. Unfortunately, although Nagwa, the director of the rehabilitation centre at Al-Amal City, and her team had collated information about special education services of NGOs throughout the Gaza Strip (which had been forwarded to headquarters) none of them was permitted entry into the West Bank to attend the conference.

The conference was very good and there was lively discussion, with several people with disability speaking from the floor. The acceptance of people with disability and their rights was the dominant theme, and there were both questions and ideas on how best to realise this.

Halima, a young woman with physical disability, described her efforts, supported by her family, to complete her education; the mother of an intellectually disabled girl spoke about her struggle to get her daughter included in the education system. The father of a girl with Down's syndrome talked about how he had been in an Israeli prison when his daughter was born, and had felt a strong need to get out in order to give the baby and his family the support they would need in order to access the best possible means of enhancing the development of the child. He was released three months later, and told how he and his wife had sought advice and opportunity for their daughter.

It was a pleasant surprise to see a young woman from Bethlehem whom I'd known in Cairo back in the late 1980s. I had supervised Iptisam's proposal to study the pattern of children's play during the time of the first Intifada. She had noted that children no longer played the traditional games; instead, they played 'people and soldiers' – a game that quickly became reality if a jeep of soldiers arrived in the area. The children would turn from their play situation to throw stones at the jeep. Both parents and teachers were concerned about the situation and the possible danger to the children in so many ways. She had also told me at the time that she was fearful of working on her data at home in case Israeli soldiers entered the house, confiscated her work, and caused problems for her and her family. It was good to meet her again and to hear about the work she was doing at a cultural centre that she had founded herself.

The depth of information in the papers presented at the symposium, the range of questions and experiences put forward, was in sharp contrast to the country's general crisis situation. A number of the participants had come from the area of Nablus. Given the conditions in their area and the difficulties that they faced when travelling, it was remarkable to see them there. Within this last week, there had been several incursions of Israeli troops into the Balata refugee camp in Nablus, with many people killed and injured. There were also several targeted killings (assassinations) by the Israeli army in the Gaza Strip during this period.

One of my colleagues at PRCS headquarters, Namiti, told me how she'd been woken in the middle of the night by loud banging on the door of her flat. Her sister was asleep in her room, and Namiti had been in bed too. Apprehensive, she went and opened the door. She was confronted by a group of Israeli soldiers who immediately entered the flat. 'Stop, stop,' she said. 'My sister is asleep and you will frighten her. Please let me wake her and tell her.' The soldiers allowed this, then searched every room before leaving to search the other flats. 'It was 3 am by the time they finally left the building,' Namiti said. 'You know, I still feel unnerved by this experience.'

TWENTY-ONE

BY EARLY MARCH, there were further warnings from the international community about the desperate situation in the Gaza Strip due to the Karni crossing having been closed since 21 February. Again, tons of fruit, vegetables and other perishable goods were dumped at the roadside; again, we made sure we had back-up supplies of essential items in the residence.

As I looked over the day's busy schedule on Tuesday, 14 March, I had no idea that I was about to become personally caught up in political events. I had paperwork to attend to, email to check, and follow-up work with Sami, the administrator of the rehabilitation centre, concerning the children's club. Then there was a meeting with visiting lecturers, and discussion with some of the college staff concerning a problem with a couple of the students. Kamal, the director of the sports centre, wanted to see me too, to discuss getting more people involved in sports activities; I was particularly keen to encourage women in this area, as, in general, they have fewer opportunities to participate in sport and physical activity due to traditional attitudes about women playing sport. Kamal, a wheelchair-user, is especially involved in developing sport for people with disabilities, in addition to the regular sports programs.

During the morning, we heard that the Israeli army had stormed the PA prison in Jericho with tanks, helicopters and bulldozers to remove six Palestinian prisoners, held there under a special agreement between the PA, the Israeli government and the US and British governments. It seemed the Israelis had decided to take these six prisoners as they considered they might be released by the PA. Three Palestinian policemen were killed. Damage to the buildings was extensive; and prisoners and guards were stripped down to their underpants and marched out of the prison.

The Palestinian President, Mahmoud Abbas, returned promptly from Europe where he was due to give a key speech to the European Parliament about funding to the PA. 'What happened in Jericho was an unforgivable crime and an insult to the Palestinian people,' he said.

A general strike was called by all factions throughout the OPT in protest against the storming of the prison. This meant that all shops and services (except essential and emergency services) closed – a common method of registering a strong protest. Many people believed the attack had been coordinated between the international monitors and the Israeli army, although this was denied. Opinion on the street was that the whole operation was to boost the chance of success of the new Kadima party in the Israeli elections to be held on 28 March. Little credence was given to the Israeli statement that it was a matter of security. One young girl stated, 'It shows that Palestinians have control over nothing. We can't even stop Israel from taking our prisoners.' There was a very low level of morale all around; a feeling of being abandoned. There was little or no outcry from the international media against the storming of the prison.

Some of the militant groups reacted to the situation by destroying property of the British Council and the European Union, and in the Gaza Strip there was also a spate of hostage-taking. President Abbas strongly condemned these actions, pointing out that, 'These people are here to help us and we have the duty to respect and protect them.' However, he also condemned the act of the Israeli army in storming the prison, and the departure of the British and American monitors prior to the storming. This action broke the international agreement that had been signed by all of these parties.

Just after 2 pm, the Australian Embassy in Tel Aviv phoned to advise me about the problems in Gaza. I decided to complete some important work and then go home earlier than usual. Fifteen minutes later, the administrator of Al-Amal City phoned and said, 'You must leave work immediately and go to the residence. I have received a phone call from PRCS in Gaza and they say that the situation is bad in relation to foreigners. Also, they have taken a man from the ICRC office in Khan Younis.'

One of the PRCS administration staff came to my office and we walked together across the street to the residence. Dalal returned home just after 2.40 pm.

Soon after, the administrator at Al-Amal called again to say that a group of masked men carrying rifles had entered the College looking for me. He told me to go to one of our neighbours' houses. I didn't really know which neighbour to go to, so Dalal and I went down to Hamoudi and Badr's flat. I took a couple of books, my radio and mobile phone, expecting to stay there for an hour or two.

Very soon the flat was filled with PRCS staff, security personnel, policemen and neighbours. Apparently, the militants had gone into the College asking for me. Badr was in the administration office and told them he didn't know where I was. He moved towards the phone and one of the militants pulled the cord from the wall. 'Why did you do that?' was Badr's calm response.

After searching the College, the men broke down the door to my office then left to find the residence. Nihad, the staff leader of the residence committee, was walking back to the residence with Badr and realised they were being followed by a couple of the masked men so they continued past our building and on to the nearby mosque. The militants' van was parked at the entrance to our building, but the building owner and other neighbours gathered at the entrance and he told them that they weren't to enter, as to do so would be an act of aggression against them. The men left. I was very worried that the people who were protecting me could come into serious conflict with those looking for me.

The flat was crowded with people. Hamoudi, who usually has a rest in the afternoon, was on his bed but wide awake and wondering what was happening. Badr, a little shaken by his experience, returned. It was decided I should go to a safe place, and that Dalal should come with me rather than staying alone in our flat.

We were taken to the house of Dr Najat Al-Astal, President of the Khan Younis branch of the PRCS and a member of the PA Legislative Council. Once there, we tried to decide what to do. Everyone apologised for the situation in general and in relation to me in particular: 'This is very bad behaviour by some youth. They have been very angry about the storming of the Jericho prison and feel that the American and British monitors coordinated with the Israeli army to carry out the operation. They do not understand the broader picture and have reacted without thinking against anything or any person seen to be foreign. We are sorry for all, and especially sorry that they do not know who you are, sharing the hardships here with us and the extent of help you have given.'

I advised the Australian Embassy of my situation, and agreed to keep in regular contact with them concerning my movements. The PRCS President, Younis Al-Khatib, phoned from Ramallah to check on me and advised me to stay with the security and PRCS personnel. It was decided that I should go to the security headquarters in Gaza City for the time being, but that Dalal would stay in Khan Younis. It seemed that it may even be necessary for me to leave the Gaza Strip for a few days – but fortunately this did not happen. Then I realised that I had neither passport nor money with me.

'Never mind,' my escort said, 'we can go past the residence and you can get these and other things you need.'

However, a few minutes later a phone message came through that the militants had gone into the Al-Amal City building, ordered the staff out, and taken in the three foreign hostages they were holding – two French and one Korean. I gave my key to Maher, the administrator from the hospital, and advised him where to find my passport and money.

Maher stayed with me, together with security officers and representatives of some of the other groups. The convoy, which included a PRCS ambulance, sped us to Gaza City, passing a couple of roadblocks of burning tyres – a statement of the Palestinian people's anger. It was night by the time we arrived at the security centre at Saraia – a large complex with many buildings, cars and army personnel. I was taken to the officer in charge and there were discussions back and forth as to what to do. I felt as if I were in a movie rather than experiencing all this in real life; it was so remote from my usual routine.

It seemed there had been some misunderstanding and it wasn't possible for me to stay in the complex. The security personnel and police were trying to ensure any foreigners remained safe by taking them to a hotel in Gaza and then enabling them to pass through Erez crossing out of the Gaza Strip.

'No, no,' said Siliman, the son of Dr Najat who was among the group of people who had brought me to Gaza. 'It is best for her to go back to Khan Younis and stay at our house. She will be safe there and we know how to take good care of her.'

There were other suggestions, but it was generally thought it best that I return to Khan Younis. Once more we sped through the night, back the way we had come.

Later that night we were advised that the militants had released the hostages and had left the Al-Amal building. The hostages were okay and the problem was seen to be over. Maher went to the residence and returned with my passport and money.

Dalal and I spent the following day in Dr Najat's house. Dr Najat and her family made us feel welcome and looked after us very well. Dalal arranged for a car to take her back to the residence to check her email and to gather some of her things. She also got a change of clothes for me. Now I was ready for any event – after the crisis had passed!

By Thursday, the situation seemed quiet and it was decided that it would be safe for me to return to the flat. It was great to be home. Everyone had been very kind, but being surrounded by uncertainty and away from my base for a few days was like being in limbo. Badr came charging in to give Dalal and me a big hug. Hamoudi was on his bed for his afternoon rest, but sensed all the activity and began to laugh.

When I returned to work, the PRCS administration required one of the male staff to accompany me wherever I went. I didn't like this at all – being such an independent spirit – but I respected the PRCS's level of care for me. I was told that many people – some who knew me well and others who did not – were very angry about the hostage-taking in general, and in particular that I should face such a problem. They felt responsible for the actions of their young people.

On 22 March 2006 it was my birthday – a big one: seventy years. It seemed impossible to have reached such an age. I certainly have been blessed with good health. Dalal and Badr organised a cake and a small party, with Hamoudi and the two carers on duty. Phone calls from Clarice and Alan in Brisbane, Hadla in Jordan, and emails from cousins and friends in Australia brought many happy memories of past years.

Israeli war planes often flew over during this time, but with no sonic booms, low flying or bombing. It seemed to be just a reminder of their presence and what they could do. There was great uncertainty about the future with the newly elected Hamas organisation restructuring the PA, and people in Israel preparing for the government elections at the end of March.

With all the unrest, Dalal wondered whether she would be able to travel to the US in mid-April. The Taylor Institute in Chicago had invited a group of PRCS staff working in programs concerning psycho-social issues and with good English language skills. Dalal and one other person were selected from the Gaza Strip for the visit, together with five people from the West Bank. We sent all the necessary papers to apply for a US visa to the PRCS headquarters, from where the applications to the US consulate in East Jerusalem would be forwarded. Dalal was then advised to be on call as she would need to go to Jerusalem for an interview. It sounded so simple, but we all knew how difficult it was for a Palestinian to enter Jerusalem.

The next day we held a Mother's Day party for the children of the rehabilitation centre, the kindergarten and the children's club. On returning to her office, Dalal was advised that there had been a phone call from PRCS headquarters to say that permits to cross Erez had been granted and that she and Nadal, the other traveller, had an appointment at noon the following day at the US consulate. They were excited to be able to go to Jerusalem, but also doubtful as to whether they'd actually get there.

I accompanied them, and we passed through Erez with very little delay on Friday morning as it was the weekend; also, Erez was at that time closed to Palestinian workers going through to Israel so it was very quiet. Dalal and Nadal received their permits from the Israeli army office. The paper showed that they were allowed to enter Israel from 5 am on Thursday until 7 pm on Friday. It was only then, passing the final military check at the exit gate, that the young people felt they really were on their way to Jerusalem.

The beautiful, serene views along the sandy coastline of the Gaza Strip, into Israel and across the fertile plains with their variety of agriculture, the gentle hills and then the rocky mountainous terrain of Jerusalem all belied the ugliness and destructiveness of the ongoing occupation. With the coming of spring, there was the additional joy of an abundance of blossom – yellow mimosa, daisies, and white, pink and mauve wildflowers.

After their interview at the US consulate, Dalal and Nadal proudly showed me the new visas in their passports. We went to get a sandwich from the YMCA cafeteria next door, which brought back memories for me of being in Jerusalem in the late 1980s and early '90s. We still had some time before the permits ran out, so we walked down Nablus Road through the busy markets and across the main road to Damascus Gate at the wall to the old city. It was early on a Friday afternoon and the crowds were growing. At three, we decided it was best to start back to Erez, to be sure of getting back to Khan Younis before nightfall.

The new Hamas parliament received the vote of approval from the legislative council and was sworn in, despite the uncertainties of international reaction and threats to withdraw funds to the PA.

The Israeli elections resulted in greater power for the new centralist party, Kadima, with its policy of further unilateral actions of annexation and determining borders without any dialogue with the Palestinians. The Qalandia checkpoint was officially designated as an international border between Jerusalem and Ramallah, and the name changed to Atarot Crossing (an Israeli name). This effectively cut Palestinians off from East Jerusalem, their hoped for capital of a future Palestinian State. Restriction of movement through the Erez crossing limited interaction between Palestinians from the Gaza Strip and those of the West Bank; and Gazans who had previously worked in Israel were no longer able to do so. We were still suffering from shortages of essential products in the Gaza Strip because of the limited movement through Karni crossing, and I made sure we had a backup of food, medicines and disposable nappies.

Within all of this confusion, good things happened too. Clarice rang me to say that her daughter, Wibby, had just delivered a baby girl – to much joy and family excitement.

Thursday 30 March was Land Day (*Youm al-Ard*), a memorial day for Palestinians marking the deaths in 1976 of Palestinians in Nazareth making a peaceful protest against the Israeli government confiscation of Palestinian lands. Israeli troops fired on the protesters, killing six people, wounding more than ninety, and arrested over three hundred others. The Israelis declared all Arab villages and towns military zones and imposed curfews on some of them. Since that time, the commemoration has broadened into a demonstration against the continued occupation.

On the same day, I had to attend a meeting of the PRCS Gaza Strip committee in Gaza City, and Badr expressed his wish to come with me. Badr doesn't get to go out much as it's not really safe for him to venture alone beyond the Khan Younis town centre, and there aren't often people available to accompany him. He can get confused in places he doesn't know well, and there is also the possibility of him having an epileptic seizure. Going to Gaza City and seeing people he knows at Al-Nour City and the adjacent Al-Quds Hospital is a major treat for him, and he always changes into his good suit and wears a tie. On this occasion he was very lucky as there was a film showing at the cultural centre, adding to his pleasure in the outing.

The meeting I had to attend was significant for a number of reasons. The socio-economic crisis in the Gaza Strip had been building and the siege-like conditions since the disengagement of the settlers and Israeli army was creating great stress. With the withdrawal of international support from the newly elected Palestinian government, and the Israeli government withholding due taxes, the situation was becoming impossible. Where could PRCS find the money to pay salaries? People, including PRCS employees, were in a desperate situation because of lack of money and being 'jailed' in the Gaza Strip. I had great respect for the manner in which the PRCS staff handled their difficulties. At times they expressed their distress, and some had participated in strike actions, but they maintained their professionalism at work, contributing new ideas and striving to maintain standards.

During the meeting, attention was given to specific difficulties being faced in Khan Younis. It was decided to establish an Al-Amal City committee, and I was assigned the position of chairperson – which worried me somewhat as I didn't feel confident about my ability to add this responsibility to my already demanding schedule. But I felt strongly about the importance of Al-Amal City within the community and the extent to which we were falling short of our potential; perhaps I could set up an effective team approach to the work that needed to be done.

During the meeting we heard heavy shelling. The noise was disturbing and made me feel anxious, but it wasn't until the meeting ended at 10 pm that I was able to find out what was going on. It seemed that one of the Palestinian militant groups had carried out a suicide bombing at an Israeli settlement in the northern part of the West Bank. The bomber had been identified as coming from Hebron towards the south of the West Bank. In retaliation, Israeli war planes had heavily bombed the northern area of the Gaza Strip. I was keen to get back to Khan Younis in case the situation deteriorated and began to affect the southern Gaza Strip areas, and so Badr and I quickly left.

The bombing raised new concerns about Dalal's trip to Chicago. We had hoped that Dalal and Nadal could cross to Ramallah, so I could stay with Dalal until she linked up with the two other women in the group. This was not to be. The only possible route now was for Dalal and Nadal to cross the border at Rafah and then travel down to Cairo to catch a plane to Amsterdam, where they would meet up with the people from the West Bank. From there they could travel to Chicago. However, I was unable to pass through Rafah crossing because of the new arrangements; it was no longer possible to get an Israeli visa, required of foreigners, at that crossing. Nadal was quite prepared to guide Dalal and take care of her during the lengthy border processes and the long taxi ride across the Sinai Desert to Cairo. But there was a possibility that Nadal, like many Palestinian men wishing to go to Cairo airport, would be escorted directly to the airport by Egyptian officials. If this happened, how would Dalal manage? Dalal was also worried about how she would manage access to a toilet without a female companion. However, with her usual pragmatic approach to life, she said, 'I know I can manage. *Inshallah* (God willing) there will be no problem.'

As it happened, Nadal was able to travel normally to Cairo, and during the long wait at the Egyptian border control an old friend of Dalal's from university days saw her and came across to chat. She stayed with Dalal during the waiting period and was able to assist with her personal needs.

The trip was a great experience for Dalal, both professionally and personally. With her high proficiency in English language, her wide experience with the programs at the centre and her wise ways, she reportedly made a significant contribution to the program.

It was Wednesday, 24 May, and again I needed to travel out via Erez, to the Allenby Bridge near the Dead Sea, and into Jordan so I could renew my visa. On my way to Jordan I stopped off at the PRCS headquarters in Ramallah to follow up on some work. In the afternoon, I was sitting on the balcony of my room in the PRCS hotel when I heard gunfire and ambulance sirens. Later, vehicles with loudspeakers on the street below announced that four Palestinians had been killed and about thirty wounded. I went down to the office to find out what was happening.

'It is better not to go out just now,' I was told. 'The Israeli army had sent in some undercover men to detain a man they wanted. The local people spotted them as Israeli undercover soldiers and threw stones at them. The soldiers called in the army and army jeeps arrived at the scene. Four Palestinians have been killed and about thirty wounded. The centre of town is in an uproar. Just stay here in the building.'

I took their advice, remained inside all afternoon and evening, and the next day left for Amman, Jordan. I stayed in Amman for one day and caught up with an old friend from Beirut, Farida, who was the aunt of Lena Saleh. I first met Farida in 1981, when she and her family were so very kind to me during my time in Beirut, especially during the troubled times of the invasion and aftermath in 1982. Farida was by now well into her eighties. She had a lovely garden of flowers at the entrance to her flat, and her apartment walls were decorated with paintings of Palestinian women in traditional dress, a street scene of the old city of Jerusalem, and landscapes of the beautiful rolling hills of Palestine. There were cushion covers on the chairs and runners on the small tables, all rich with the colours and patterns of traditional Palestinian embroidery. Vases of Hebron glass and a large dish of Jerusalem pottery adorned a side shelf. Farida's family had lived in the village of Aboud for centuries and they still owned a large area of land there. She is a Palestinian Christian and had plaques with sayings of love and encouragement on the wall of her kitchen.

It was lovely to see Farida again and she was obviously happy to see me. However, her first comment following our greetings was, 'I am so sad. The situation in Palestine is very bad, and the world does not care. Look,' she went on, 'Ehud Olmert spoke to the US Congress yesterday and says he puts out a hand in peace to the Palestinians, and claims that the land is promised land. At the same time yesterday there was the incursion into Ramallah and people were killed and others wounded. The rate of settlement expansion has increased, the wall is taking more and more land – in fact, there are big problems concerning the wall in our village. And now there is conflict between groups of my own people. It is too much.' Her eyes filled with tears.

'Tell me about your village,' I asked.

Farida talked about Aboud, a beautiful village northwest of Ramallah with a population of around 2500 residents. She said it was a Christian village, with a large Muslim community. The two communities had lived in harmony and shared in community life for the last 400 years.

'Did you hear of the Israeli army blowing up St Barbara's Church in May 2002?' she asked me. 'This shrine was an ancient church and part of a religious site that dates back to somewhere between the fourth and sixth centuries CE. It was at the western edge of the village and the focus of many community activities including a special yearly festival. "They" said there were militants hiding there, but there was no evidence of this. There should have been an international outcry at this destruction of a religious site, apart from its importance as an archaeological area.'

At the time, I had seen some local reference to the destruction of this ancient shrine, but it was true that it hadn't seemed to receive any significant international coverage.

Farida continued: 'This wall that is being built is taking more and more land from the village, and will encircle the village on three sides. Hundreds of ancient olive "Roman" trees have been uprooted – some with trunks so thick that it took five men to encircle it with their arms. There is destruction in every direction and thousands of dunams (a dunam is 1000 square metres) of land will be outside the wall around the village. When the people from the village make peaceful demonstrations against the land destruction and the building of the wall, they are treated brutally by the Israeli army. Tear gas is thrown at the crowd and people are beaten. Sometimes people are detained. In addition, the rise of unemployment in the village has added to hardship; about a hundred or more who had worked in Israel are now cut off from working there.'

Farida also talked about two issues that have appeared in numerous documents addressing the situation on the West Bank. One is in relation to water supply – Aboud is a significant underground water resource; and the other is the Israeli harassment of the villagers by erecting numerous security blocks and checkpoints. This seriously curtailed the living activities of the inhabitants; often preventing them from reaching their work places, schools and hospitals.

I realised just how distressing it was for her to reflect on the difficult conditions in Aboud, and I didn't want to add further to her pain. However, I did ask when she had left Aboud.

'I was in Jaffa in 1948 at the time of the *Nakba* [the 'catastrophe' – the dispossession of the Palestinian people during the creation of the State of Israel],' she told me. 'I returned to my village, and after one year I was able to get a YWCA scholarship to study social work at a university in Beirut. After graduation I worked with UNRWA [United Nations Relief and Work Agency].'

Farida still has family and land in Aboud, but is unable to return there to live. She is but one of thousands who have suffered, and still suffer today, from the expansionist policy of the Israeli government. The Palestinian people continue to be dispersed and dispossessed.

Back in Khan Younis, everyone was trying to cope with the freezing of funds for the newly elected Hamas PA. Dalal, like some others working in the health and education sectors of the PRCS, is seconded from a Ministry of the PA. These employees hadn't received their salaries since February. Dalal and I went to the local post office to collect $US300 – an allowance being paid to employees who had a regular salary below 2500 NIS (New Israeli Shekel) per month (approximately $600).

Shortage of money, shortage of supplies and the continuing tension had an unsettling effect on some aspects of our work. Staff went on strike in protest at the lack of salaries and the administration's inability to deal with the situation. The difficulties began to undermine the efforts of those who continued to work in spite of the many problems they faced. I didn't like to think for even a minute of the consequences to the families and the community at large if any or all of the essential services were discontinued.

The role of the PRCS and the Israeli Magen David Adom (MDA) throughout the ongoing conflict was crucial, and although both societies had only observer status in the International Federation of the Red Cross and Red Crescent Societies (IFRCS), they had received support from the international movement for many years. In December 2005, the Memorandum of Understanding between the Palestine Red Crescent Society and the Magen David Adom was signed, admitting them to full membership. This established a direct link between the PRCS and MDA, and it was hoped PRCS would receive more support against attacks by the Israeli army. However, it was worrying to read reports after the signing of the memorandum that showed Israeli violations against PRCS medical teams had increased, the number of incidents rising from 71 in the five months before the conference to 138 after it.

TWENTY-TWO

IT WAS SOON SUMMER and the children were on school holidays. Children from the neighbourhood who had been coming to the after-school club were now keen to spend the whole day at the centre. I was especially pleased to see an increase in the number of girls attending as, in general, they have fewer opportunities than boys to be involved in activities outside the home.

With over three hundred children registered in the club, the organisation is quite complex; we divide them into groups and allocate them different days and times so as to enable access for as many as possible and allow us to provide interesting and manageable programs. The Open Studio is a core element; other activities include the library, toy library, computers, music, sport and drama. There are also special groups for choir and *Dabka*. The programs are run by volunteers together with staff from the rehabilitation centre, and they are a very enthusiastic team. I try to attend their weekly meetings and maintain the links with the funding organisations, but I am always sorry not to have the time to be directly involved in the activities with the children.

The situation in the Gaza Strip continued to be unsettled, and international organisations and foreign embassies advised foreigners not to enter the area. This was problematic for us as the direct contact with personnel from international organisations was important: it was refreshing and provided moral as well as material support.

Towards the end of June, the situation seemed to worsen. There were several assassinations, including civilian casualties, and incursions and home demolitions continued. There were Israeli war planes overhead and the constant presence of the *zanana*. Tanks were shelling the northern part of the Gaza Strip, and Palestinian militant groups sent Qassam rockets into southern Israel. The IDF was assembled on the border threatening to make an incursion into southern areas of the Gaza Strip.

Since the beginning of the year, the Prime Minister and other ministers and legislators from the Hamas party had been denied access through Erez crossing into the West Bank to participate in the meetings of the legislative council at the PA headquarters in Ramallah. All government business and official meetings had to be carried out by video conference or telephone.

Still, people clung to the hope that the situation would soon improve. Meetings were under way between the President, Mahmoud Abbas (Fatah) and the Prime Minister, Ismail Haniyeh (Hamas), with the view to forming a unity government. It would include technocrats and government members without affiliation with the major parties, resulting in a government that still included Hamas members but had sufficient others with whom Israel and the West would meet. With the government in a better position to govern, the people hoped that the lawlessness and many other problems would be overcome and the crippling economic boycott lifted.

On 25 June, a group of Palestinian militants tunnelled into an Israeli army base on the southeastern border between Israel and the Gaza Strip. Two soldiers were killed and one soldier, Corporal Gilad Shalit, nineteen years old, was captured. The group that carried out the raid was made up of members of three different militant groups and it seemed to be a breakaway action. They demanded the release of Palestinian women and children in Israeli prisons in exchange for the return of the soldier. When we heard of the capture we all held our breath, wondering what on earth would happen next.

Israel refused to enter into any negotiations and immediately launched their offensive, Operation Summer Rain. Within days a fierce bombing campaign was under way. All bridges in the Gaza Strip were bombed, as was the only power station. There were more assassinations and destructive incursions into the north, south and some eastern areas of the Gaza Strip. There was shelling of the coastal areas from ships; and the sonic booms returned – the first of these in the Khan Younis area coming unexpectedly, late at night, which was especially frightening.

The bombing of the power station didn't just cause an electricity problem; the resultant lack of power created problems with the water supply, sewage treatment plants and medical services. One of our college board members lived on the seventh floor of an apartment building in Gaza City, and as there was no electricity, there was no elevator and also no water for him to take a shower. His elderly neighbour wasn't able to leave her apartment at all, as she was unable to manage all the stairs.

The scheduling of electricity so that each region had some power for a short time each day provided some relief. In Rafah, the situation was made worse by the IDF shooting at the transmitter. There were some days without any electricity at all until the transmitter was repaired. Then the IDF shot at it again; the camp was without power until repairs were made, and the IDF struck a third time.

The loss of bridges was easier to overcome. As it was summer, the riverbed was mainly dry and so traffic was able to cross over a makeshift roadway alongside the destroyed bridge. I wondered how people would manage when the winter rains came and the river was flowing freely again.

Israeli warships patrolled the coast and intermittently shelled areas. An entire family, with the exception of one distraught girl, was killed while picnicking on the beach at the northern end of the Gaza Strip.

People became very wary of going to the beach, despite the excessive summer heat, or even of using the coast road. I'd hoped to take Hamoudi, Dalal and Badr to the beach this summer, as they hadn't been since the beginning of the Intifada in 2000, but this new danger erupted before we managed to get there.

The continued incursions in the north, south and some eastern areas resulted in many destroyed homes and farmlands and thousands of displaced persons. During one of the incursions into the Maghazi refugee camp in the central area of the Gaza Strip, my secretary was unable to leave her home because of the presence of Israeli tanks. I managed to speak to her on the phone and she said how frightening it was to have tanks right outside, and the family were praying that the tanks would not begin shelling the houses. She said it was impossible to do anything while the tanks were there, except wait for them to leave. Another colleague living in Maghazi told us how Israeli soldiers took over his relatives' house and used it as an observation base. The family's two sons and a nephew were taken by the soldiers into one of the tanks to act as human shields as the tank moved about in the area. When the tank reached the Israeli border, the young men were set down to find their way back home on foot.

Within days of the kidnapping of the Israeli soldier by the military wing of Hamas together with several small militant groups, the Israeli army, in an unprecedented action, detained many ministers and legislators of the Palestinian Authority. It seemed unbelievable that such action could take place.

During this period, the Israelis began a campaign of threatening or warning people via personal telephone calls or by leaflets dropped from a plane. A family would receive a call telling them to leave their house as it would be bombed within a specified period of time. In some cases, the house was destroyed; in other cases, not. Even if the threatened bombing didn't occur, the families were often fearful of returning home.

One day one of the women working in our residence arrived looking very tired. 'What is the matter, Katam?' I asked. 'Are you ill?'

'No,' she said, 'but I am so tired as I did not sleep all night. One of our neighbours received a phone call in the evening to move out of his house as it would be bombed. He and his family moved out but the planes did not come.' She said that she and her family were afraid, as their house was close to his and they could be in danger if his house was bombed.

Soon after, a residential building a few hundred metres from our flats was bombed. It was around two in the morning and I'd not long gone to bed. Suddenly I was woken by the deafening noise of an explosion and the shaking of our building, as if there was an earthquake. No one was killed – the families had been warned of the attack and had moved out – but a number of neighbours were injured. The adjacent mosque received some damage as well, and the large tank for sweet water located in an open area in front of the destroyed building was rendered unusable. There was always a crowd around this tank as it provided water for many people in the area. Tap water in Khan Younis is saline and undrinkable. Although many people have a filter in their home to make the water drinkable, many do not, and they depend on getting drinking water from such tanks. We used to depend on this tank ourselves, but fortunately, we had installed a filter at home just before the bombing. I doubted that it would be possible to repair the tank; and getting a replacement would be very difficult as the Karni crossing was mostly closed.

The other type of phone message people received was a warning not to listen to or cooperate with any extremists as they would only destroy the economy and security. The recorded voice said that the IDF did not want to close borders, but it was necessary because of security issues. Dalal received this call on her telephone several times – each time it came at about midnight, after she had gone to sleep, and made her very afraid.

The humanitarian crisis in the Gaza Strip escalated, in spite of warnings given to the international community by the United Nations and other international aid organisations. Six months had passed since government employees had received salaries and they were becoming desperate. Municipality workers responsible for the collection of garbage went on strike for some weeks, which resulted in mounds of garbage on the streets of Gaza, presenting a severe health hazard. Some of the health workers went on strike, which reduced the capacity of the health services. Children were due to return to school at the beginning of September, but teachers in the government schools called a strike because they hadn't received their salaries. On the West Bank, many children were unable to return to school because of the presence of the wall, while in other cases children were delayed at a checkpoint or unable to pass because the checkpoint was closed.

Much of the media seemed to give credence to the Israeli claim that they had left the Gaza Strip and so it was no longer under occupation. However, Israel was in complete control of most aspects of the lives of the people there. Human Rights Watch made note of this fact in various publications, claiming that the actions of the Israeli army created a severe negative effect on the health, education and humanitarian needs of the Palestinian people, which was contrary to their obligations as an occupying power.

From reports in the news, it seemed that the Egyptians were involved in negotiations for the release of the Israeli soldier, Gilad Shalit, in exchange for the release of approximately a thousand women and children prisoners in Israeli prisons. I hoped the exchange would be achieved, but there had been too much bloodshed, too many livelihoods destroyed in the interim.

True to the resilience of the Palestinian people, daily life proceeded as best it could. Money for transport to programs was always a problem for many, and the help the PRCS could give was very limited. Because of the financial freeze on the Gaza Strip, many organisations, especially those directly related to the PA, were unable to run their annual summer camps for children, but with support from the Norwegian Red Cross, the Netherlands Red Cross and HOPE Holland, the PRCS was able to run two-week camps in July in all of the centres throughout the West Bank and Gaza Strip. The focus of these camps, as usual, was on the integration of children with disability and children who are not disabled. The length of the camps had to be shortened, but it was very important that they were still able to function.

The sports program for young men with disability was discontinued for some weeks as people were afraid to go out in the evenings because of incursions and air strikes. By late August, however, the program was able to resume.

Towards the end of August, Badr planned to attend the pre-wedding party of one of his colleagues, Kafah, who lived near the eastern border with Israel, where there was frequent shelling and some incursions. Badr asked a friend who has a taxi to drive him there, but the friend replied, 'No way. I am not sure of the location and don't know the area well. If it were in the daytime, maybe. But in the evening, no way – it is too dangerous.' Badr was disappointed but he understood his friend's refusal. The next day he found that other friends had not attended the party either, for the same reason.

In addition to the overall crisis situation throughout the Gaza Strip, there was also growing lawlessness. With such poverty, the lack of any real authority, continued oppression and aggression from Israel, and too many guns, the situation was ripe for chaos. There was armed confrontation between opposing groups, family feuds, the taking of hostages, and militant groups firing their homemade rockets into Israel – all of which resulted in even more military bombardment. And so the cycle of violence continued with ever-increasing intensity. The majority of the people were tired and stressed. 'Enough!' was the common cry. 'Why can't there be international recognition of the reality of the Palestinian people's situation? Where is the justice and a fair intervention to stop this madness?'

Amidst the growing difficulties and pressures of work, I needed to once again travel out of the Gaza Strip to renew my visa. I was reluctant to go, but I had no choice. A few days before I was due to leave, I realised that I needed to get a visa to enter Jordan. To my surprise, when I went into Gaza City to the Jordanian Embassy to get the visa I found that the office had closed. I had two options: to go to Ramallah on my way to the Jordanian border; or to use the Jordan River border crossing in the north where I could purchase a visa on the way through. I hadn't used the far north crossing before, but it seemed to be the most suitable arrangement.

Although I arrived at Erez crossing before 8 am, it was a couple of hours before anyone waiting was able to start the walk through. When I emerged from the long tunnel I saw four or five buses taking people to visit family members who were prisoners in Israel. The families held a vigil every Monday in front of the ICRC offices in Gaza City, holding large framed photos of their imprisoned loved one, calling for their release.

As I moved to the waiting PRCS car an ICRC car entered the area with a man, a woman and five children inside. I didn't take much notice of the group, being somewhat lost in my thoughts, but then two of the children, little boys, came to our car and I realised they were blind. I was surprised to recognise the ICRC person with them – it was Natasha, who I had spoken to on the phone about my coordination to pass through Erez. She was taking the five children back to their boarding schools on the West Bank; they had spent the summer holidays in Gaza. Natasha was feeling very frustrated as even though it had been arranged in advance for them to go straight through, they were required to wait a long time. The two little boys were restless and not easy to manage. In addition, she had been advised that she wouldn't be able to walk through with the children for security reasons. She had arranged for two of the men who assisted with transporting luggage to help manage the children through the tunnel's turnstiles, electronic gates and X-ray machine. I said that I would like to help, but I was limited by whatever directions the voice from the wall shouted to me.

I had been ordered through the first large gate as the children were coming through the door, but had to go on. However, I was delayed considerably at the X-ray machine, where I had to take everything out of my pockets – money, passport, etc. – and run them through the machine individually. When I was told to pass a couple of Kleenex tissues through the machine, I thought things were getting particularly silly, but at least the delay meant that I was still in the area when the children came through and I was able to assist. They were delightful little children; one of the boys explained to me with great authority how he had received his permission papers that enabled him to travel.

I only stayed two days in Jordan, as I planned to visit the PRCS headquarters in Ramallah on Sunday. I completed the exit procedures from the Jordanian side of the Allenby Bridge crossing fairly early in the morning and was in the first bus to move into the Israeli border control area. The young soldier at the passport control counter was more than usually aggressive. When I described my work with the PRCS in response to her questioning, she snapped back at me in a disgusted tone, 'You mean you work with Palestinian children?'

Despite her attitude, and the wait of several hours, I wasn't expecting what followed. I was told that there was a new policy that required an organisation on the West Bank to apply for a permit before I could make an application for a visa. 'Nothing personal,' a senior officer told me. 'It just takes a week or ten days.'

The dreaded scenario had become a reality. Over the years, I'd held my breath each time I made a crossing, waiting to see if I would actually receive a visa and for how long, but to be denied entry still came as a shock. I phoned the PRCS headquarters, and contacts at the ICRC and the Australian embassy in Tel Aviv, to no avail. The border officials refused to speak to any of these peope via my mobile. After some time, and many phone calls, I understood that my contacts hadn't been aware of such a policy and weren't able to do anything to help. The security officer accompanied me to retrieve my bag, then escorted me to a bus that would take me back to the Jordan border control.

My passport was given to the bus driver, who was instructed to give it to the officer in the Jordanian border control area. I felt extremely upset and angry. The situation made no sense to me whatsoever.

There was nothing to do but wait it out in Jordan while the PRCS, ICRC and Australian Embassy tried to help me resolve the problem. Every day I called the PRCS headquarters with the same question: 'Any news?' And each day I got the same answer: 'No news.' Badr often left messages on my mobile: 'When are you coming? We miss you.' I tried to keep busy with work, following up with staff on a number of issues that needed my input, working on several proposals for funding, and dealing with regular correspondence concerning the college and other matters relevant to the rehabilitation centre.

The days dragged on to weeks and then to months. I soon became aware that my denied entry wasn't an isolated incident and that there were hundreds of people in the same situation. Since its occupation of the West Bank and Gaza Strip in 1967, Israel has maintained control of residency and visitor permits to the Occupied Palestinian Territories; and even after the removal of settlers and the army from the Gaza Strip in 2005, this control has continued. Soon after the occupation began, Israel carried out a census of the population and only those present at the time were registered as residents. Palestinians not physically present then lost their status as residents; and those with residency would lose it if they remained outside the OPT for more than six months. At the beginning of the Intifada in September 2000, Israel placed a complete freeze on the processing of requests for family unification, which was the only way for Palestinians who didn't have residency to gain it.

Many of the people unable to obtain residency were able to live with their families by going through the onerous process of leaving the country every three months (or less, depending on the length of their visa) so as to obtain another visa and return. A re-entry visa wasn't guaranteed, however, and from April 2006 the process of granting or denying permits became even more arbitrary. These restrictions didn't only apply to family unification; the denial of entry was being extended to include foreign nationals working with Palestinians in the OPT. Those being targeted included business people, teachers, researchers, community workers – anyone able to make an important contribution towards much-needed development.

During the period I was stranded in Jordan, I met people of several different nationalities, some of whom entered the OPT without a problem, some who were able to enter but received a visa for one week only, and others who received a three-month visa but with the additional stamp of 'last entry'. I began to wonder if I would ever be permitted to return to Khan Younis.

I was fortunate to have a number of very supportive friends living in Amman, but in many respects it was like living in a vacuum. The PRCS covered the cost of my accommodation, and Hadla kept in constant contact with me to check that I was all right. Close friends kept my spirits up, and rallied with others to supply me with warm clothing when summer turned to autumn and then to winter. I hadn't brought my laptop computer with me, which meant I had to make almost daily visits to an internet café to keep up with my work. I also worried about the extra strain I was placing on PRCS finances at such a difficult period.

I followed the news of the situation in the Gaza Strip with a great deal of concern. In October there were incursions into the southern border area of the Gaza Strip, followed by the incursion into Beit Hanoun in the north in November. Between 1 and 6 November there were at least forty-nine Palestinians killed, including seven children, two women and two PRCS paramedics who were assisting the wounded; and more than one hundred and fifty people injured. In one incident – which the Israeli army called 'a mistake' – tanks fired into private homes, killing nineteen people.

The severity of the onslaught on Beit Hanoun did elicit international condemnation, and resulted in an Arab-sponsored draft resolution in the UN Security Council calling for an end to violence, including the Israeli offensive into the Gaza Strip and the militant Palestinians firing rockets into Israel. The US vetoed the resolution, claiming it was unbalanced and biased, but it was later passed by the UN General Assembly. The UN General Assembly also called for a fact-finding mission to investigate the tank fire that killed people in their homes, but when the UN team, under the leadership of Archbishop Desmond Tutu, attempted to carry out their task, Israel refused to give them visas to enter the Gaza Strip.

On 27 September, exactly a month after I'd been turned back from the border, I was hit by a car coming out of a driveway as I walked along the footpath. My leg was fractured and I was required to wear a full-length leg cast for six weeks. This made life more complicated as I was no longer able to walk any distance and had to depend on taxis.

By early December, the shops and hotels were beginning to put up Christmas decorations. I was surprised to see the extent of the decorations, and to read that some of the hotels used their Christmas trees as a means of collecting money for charity. The Muslim pilgrimage, Al-Hajj, took place at this time too, followed by the Eid Al-Adha (Feast of Sacrifice) at the end of December. One of the restaurants I went to with friends had decorations for both Christmas and the Eid Al-Adha side by side.

Finally, a few days before Christmas, I was advised that I had a permit to enter the OPT. It had taken four months, but at last I was going home. I was excited, but still concerned about potential problems.

I arrived early at the Jordanian border so that I could take the first bus to the Israeli border control. After some waiting, I received a visa to enter. I took a taxi directly to Erez, arriving just after one o'clock in the afternoon. I submitted my passport and, after another wait, I was advised by the soldier at the desk that I couldn't enter the Gaza Strip as there was no coordination for me to pass through. I argued that there was coordination, and phoned the ICRC, the

PRCS and the Australian Embassy to advise them of my predicament. After many phone calls back and forth, it seemed there had been some mix-up. At five o'clock I decided to find a taxi and go to Ramallah as I was afraid to stay in the Erez area once it became dark.

I had been in touch with Dalal throughout the day and phoned her again when I arrived at the PRCS headquarters. She was due to visit on 26 December for a conference organised by the Mental Health Department, but said she didn't want to go if I would be returning home then. I thought it was important that Dalal shouldn't lose the opportunity she had to cross to the West Bank and to participate in the conference, so I decided to wait the extra few days, even if my coordination was finalised, and return with her and the group on 28 December.

We left Ramallah via the Qalandia checkpoint – the first time I had been there since the opening of the new, larger building. We were required to get out of the car and walk through the gates and turnstiles; the Palestinians had to show their ID cards and I had to show my passport. I had checked that all was well with my coordination at Erez earlier in the day, so I felt sure that I would get through this time, but I became worried when the soldier told me that there was no coordination. Fortunately, she soon found the information that confirmed my coordination and I was allowed to pass through with Dalal and the others.

Badr and Hamoudi were excited to see me and I felt so relieved to be with them all again. Staff on duty greeted me warmly; people came to see me or phoned. It was good to be back. Unfortunately, my situation was still unclear. I had received a three-month visa, but didn't know whether I could obtain a new visa without another extended stay outside the country.

I was pleased to see the rehabilitation centre was working well, and the children's club was as active as ever. Kamal told me about the goal ball team that had participated in competitions in Qatar following the Pan Arab Games, and of the invitation the PRCS Club had received to send the sitting volleyball team to a competition in Syria later in the year. The construction of parkland adjacent to our sports hall was also well under way. For many years we had wanted to develop this space into a community recreation area and now, with funding from a Spanish organisation, it was coming into being.

On the negative side, the Gaza Strip was still unstable, with the conflict between the Fatah and Hamas political rivals unresolved. The residence administrator, Asmat, told me that there was a shortage of disposable nappies, which we needed for Hamoudi, and so she'd spent a couple of hours going to every relevant shop looking for extra packs to ensure we had a backup supply.

The staff also warned me to be careful and not to go anywhere alone as there were still some militant groups who were threatening to take hostages. When I went to Gaza with Dalal and Badr, we were accompanied by Aly, who regularly drives Hamoudi on his outings. I noticed many groups of police and others, all with rifles, standing in clusters along the streets and it made me uneasy.

The situation seemed impossible, but life sometimes plays delightful tricks that give us the strength to withstand obstacles and hardship. On Wednesday, 17 January 2007, following the Al-Amal City weekly committee meeting, Nagwa invited me to go to the small theatre for a surprise. And surprise it was. More than one hundred employees had gathered there to welcome me back. They were mostly rehabilitation centre staff, but there were also people from other departments, and Dalal, Badr and Hamoudi of course. The program included a number of speeches, including one by Dalal, and I was presented with two pieces of embroidery – the work of some of the young women in the vocational training program. One was a framed picture; the other a tissue-holder with the neatly embroidered message (roughly translated): 'For Dr Jean – who is ongoing in her unlimited humanitarian work. We appreciate this. Your children, the rehabilitation centre.' I felt overwhelmed and it was hard to find words to express my thanks. Most of all I was so glad to witness the wonderful spirit and togetherness of the staff as they organised the function.

There was even more surprise when we all moved up to the restaurant, where I was confronted with tables set with attractively arranged cakes and soft drinks. I cut a special cake with a message written in icing in both English and Arabic: 'Dr Jean, welcome'. These were people who for decades had experienced displacement and oppression; some of them from families separated from one another by Israeli policy. What a homecoming!

THE ROAD AHEAD

'THERE IS MUCH TO BE DONE BUT THERE IS ALWAYS HOPE.'

I wonder about this statement of mine in relation to the path that my life has taken, to the situation I am in as I stand with the Palestinian people, and my work towards developing acceptance and opportunity for people with disabilities. In many respects the difficulties seem impossible to overcome, but at the same time I feel that it is important to remain constant in my endeavours, however small and insignificant they may be within the total picture.

As I write in early 2007, I wonder where the road ahead will lead me. I always have hope, but at the same time I fear for the future for Hamoudi, Dalal and Badr, and also for my colleagues. What path will emerge for the Palestinian people as they struggle for recognition and the establishment of a Palestinian state?

Hamoudi is in his mid-thirties – an age seldom reached by people with his severity of disability, even in life conditions free of the uncertainties and dangers he has faced. He is totally dependent, but experiences a full life because of the love and care around him. Will conditions in the future enable such care to continue?

Dalal, just a couple of years younger than Hamoudi, is so very concerned about her country. She wants to give more, to study further to strengthen her ability to contribute to developments, but she is

311

frustrated by the endless restrictions and unrest. She says that she has not lost hope, but that she is afraid of what the future may bring.

Badr, now in his mid-twenties, is able to deal independently with most aspects of his life, but he does need help at times. When stressed, he is likely to experience some minutes of disorientation or a psychomotor seizure. He often asks when he can travel with me again for a holiday, as in previous years when I left to renew my visa. But the days of taking Dalal or Badr with me for a holiday are past. I cannot travel through Rafah crossing with them as I need an Israeli visa. A Palestinian living in the Gaza Strip cannot go through Erez crossing and the Allenby Bridge border crossing into Jordan. We have to use different routes to travel out of and into the Gaza Strip. The ease with which I can be cut off from Hamoudi, Dalal and Badr, and the dangers they face, became clearly evident during 2006 when I was stranded in Jordan.

In the work situation, we are trying to reach as many people as possible to provide services and opportunity for people with disability and their families, and to enhance the lives of people in the community through provision of a wide range of activities. Many of our efforts suffer setbacks because of the stressful conditions, financial difficulties and limited coordination of departments in the centre. I am conscious of all the people we cannot reach, and of the constant attention required to maintain and develop standards. There is so much more that I wish we could accomplish, but I have to settle for doing what we can with what we have. I marvel at the steadfastness of many of the staff and worry that they don't receive the recognition they deserve. Others are tired from the situation around them and slack off in the workplace, and it isn't easy to find ways to increase their commitment when many are existing at a basic survival level.

In a BBC TV broadcast in September 2006, UN Aid Chief, Jan Eliasson, stated that Gaza was a 'ticking time bomb' and that the plight of the Palestinian people must not be forgotten. He noted that in his twenty-five years of visiting the Occupied Palestinian Territories he had never seen so much despair, bitterness and even hatred as during his recent visit. Other UN reports at the time indicated that there was a serious decline, with the poverty rate in Gaza reaching close to 80 per cent.

The stark reality of the destruction of the Palestinian economy is clearly demonstrated in the fate of Bethlehem, a city celebrated over the centuries for its spiritual and cultural heritage. I was reminded of this when I was stranded in Jordan and my friend Lena took me to meet her cousin, Widad Kawar. Widad, a Christian Palestinian originally from Bethlehem, has the most beautiful collection of Palestinian traditional dress and other cultural items that she has gathered over the years. The beautifully embroidered dresses, each with its own distinctive design and colours, came from villages throughout pre-1948 Palestine. Widad showed me a large map on the wall marking the four hundred or more villages that had been destroyed by the Zionist forces when they moved to create the State of Israel in 1948. It was obvious that she was fighting back tears as she spoke about the past. There were also more recent dress designs, showing the merging of older designs as women from the villages, now living closely together in refugee camps, share their techniques.

Widad gave me a small booklet that she had published for Christmas 2005, entitled 'Bethlehem – From Golden Threads to Cement Blocks', that showed something of Bethlehem's previous beauty through the colour and design of the exquisite *Malak* (royal) dress worn on special occasions by women of the town. Today, Bethlehem is being slowly strangled. Since 1967 more than 14 000 dunams of land have been confiscated to make room for nine Israeli settlements that surround Bethlehem. The separation wall encloses the town, cutting farmers in the adjacent Palestinian towns and villages off from their land. Entry into Bethlehem is through a checkpoint, with roadblocks and dirt mounds making any kind of movement difficult for the people. The sad fate of this very special area is cause for great concern. It used to be a vibrant place, with busloads of tourists coming to make pilgrimage and to absorb the magic of this town, but now the streets are empty, shops are closed and hotels are empty – and the world seems not to care. Widad summed up her feelings when she said, 'Will we ever be able to sing "O Little Town of Bethlehem" with feeling again?'

The boycott placed on the newly elected Hamas government of the Palestinian Authority from early 2006 was because the Hamas party refused to recognise the State of Israel and to renounce violence. But what of the Palestinians? Who asks for recognition of their right to exist? To live in peace in their homeland? To be safe?

I was interested to read of the controversy caused by the Israeli Minister of Education in late 2006 when she announced that she required the 'green line' to be shown on maps in school books. It would seem that prior to this Israeli children are taught that the OPT is but a part of greater Israel; and the extension of settlements and gradual annexation of East Jerusalem and large areas of the West Bank are working towards that reality.

With such expansion and annexation, the feasibility of an independent Palestinian State alongside the State of Israel would seem to be fading. Early founders of the State of Israel advocated the transfer of Palestinians out of the area – a policy that is openly advocated today by Avigdor Lieberman's Yisrael Beytenu party. In October 2006 Lieberman was appointed Deputy Prime Minister and Minister of Strategic Affairs in the coalition government of the Knesset. His appointment was controversial in Israel but received little attention outside. Many Palestinians believe that the aggressive actions of the Israeli army towards them, in addition to the land grabs on the West Bank and in East Jerusalem, are directed towards this purpose of transfer. My recent experience of being denied entry into the OPT alerted me to this more insidious means of population transfer. Thousands of Palestinians are prevented from returning to

Palestine. This means there are thousands of families living in the shadow of this policy.

Israel consistently states that the actions it takes are against 'terrorists' and to ensure the security of the State of Israel, but I wonder how actions such as the punishment of a total population, targeted assassinations, destroying housing and infrastructure, clearing land and depriving people of basic human needs bring security, much less peace. It is well known that violence breeds violence; that poverty causes violence and violence causes poverty. It is hard to understand why military power has become the tool used to try to restore stability and bring peace. Such an approach can only bring ongoing conflict and tragedy.

In such conflict situations atrocities are carried out by both sides, and reconciliation needs to face this fact. Trust has to be built, with both sides being accepted as equal and respected. In one respect it is simple: the recognition of equality, human rights for all peoples, and a concentration on the common or universal core of our humanity. But such an approach requires will.

The situation seems impossible but there is always hope. There are Jews in Israel and throughout the world who are deeply concerned about the suffering of the Palestinian people at the hands of Israel. They believe that redressing the situation is as important for the State of Israel and international Jewry as it is for the Palestinians. In recent years, many young Israeli soldiers have refused to serve in the OPT; these *refusniks* face imprisonment. In many cases, people who speak honestly about the past and the continued oppression of the Palestinian people are vilified; the subject seems closed to debate and the search for understanding. To break through this barrier is to recognise that both Israelis and Palestinians have the right to security, self-determination and a just peace.

During the recent tragic destruction of Lebanon, some world leaders acknowledged that there will be no peace in the Middle East until there is a solution to the Palestinian–Israeli problem. There must be a solution. There must be peace, as it is something that all of the people in the region hope for. However, peace must be based on equality, rights and acceptance; it cannot be something imposed by people with power on people without power who are expected to be subservient and silent. This would not be peace but apartheid.

When I was denied re-entry into the OPT in August 2006 I felt very angry, and worried about my three young people and my many work responsibilities. At the same time I was conscious that whatever inconvenience or hardship I experienced, it was infinitesimal compared with that experienced by the Palestinian people. They are resilient and they never lose hope.

Mr Younis Al-Khatib, President of the PRCS, demonstrated this hope within his statement for the society's 2001–02 report:

> *Yes, we will have peace in Palestine and Israel.*
> *Yes, our children will learn to live together and accept one another.*
> *This is not something we simply hope for, but something we work*
> *actively to achieve in our community.*

So, too, as I stand with the Palestinian people, I have resilience and I have hope; I pray and I hope for a culture of peace to emerge in place of the present culture of war.

SELECTED REFERENCES

A great deal has been written relevant to the Israeli–Palestinian issue over very many years. This selection of references is restricted to some of the more recent publications that have been read by the author and include the works of Palestinian, Israeli, and other authors.

Adams, M. & C.P. Mayhew, *Publish It Not: The Middle East Cover-up*, Longman, London, 1975

Ashrawi, H., *This Side of Peace: A Personal Account*, Simon & Schuster, New York, 1995

Avnery, Uri, 'The Great Experiment', http://www.gush-shalom.org,14 October 2006

Barenboim, D, 'In Memoriam: Edward Said (1936-2003)' in Barenboim, D. & E.W. Said, *Parallels and Paradoxes – Explorations in Music and Society*, Vintage Books, New York, 2004, pp. x–xi.

Baroud, R., *The Second Palestinian Intifada: A Chronicle of a People's Struggle*, Pluto Press, London, 2006

Bayoumi, M. & A. Ruben (eds.), *The Edward Said Reader*, Vintage Books, New York, 2000

B'Tselem, 'Israel's freeze policy on family unification in the Occupied Territories splits tens of thousands of Palestinian families', http://www.btselem.org/english/Press_Releases/20060815.asp, 15 August 2006

Butt, G., *Life at the Crossroads: A History of Gaza*, Rimal Publications, Nicosia, Cyprus, 1995

Carter, J., *Palestine Peace Not Apartheid*, Simon & Schuster, New York, 2006

Chomsky, N., *The Fateful Triangle – The United States, Israel and the Palestinians*, Pluto Press, London, 1999

Dajani, I.Z., *Palestine – its unknown history. A chronicle 2000 BC – 1948*, The American University, Cairo, 1990

Dimbleby, J., *The Palestinians*, Quartet Books, London, 1980

Doughty, D. & M. El Aydi, *Gaza: Legacy of Occupation – A Photographer's Journey*, Kumarian Press, Connecticut, USA, 1995

Dubrow, N. (ed.), *Suffer the Little Children under Israeli Occupation*, PRCS, Al-Bireh, Ramallah, 2004

El Khalidi, L., *The Art of Palestinian Embroidery*, Saqi Books, London, 1999

El-Saraj, E., 'The Psychosocial Causes for the Palestinian Factional War', http://www.miftah.org, 16 February 2007

Forced Migration Review, Issue 26, 'Palestinian Displacement: A Case Apart?', Refugee Studies Centre, Oxford, 2006

Fisk, R., 'Terrorists 1990/2001' in Pilger, J. [ed.], *Tell Me No Lies: Investigative Journalism and Its Triumphs*, Jonathan Cape, London, pp. 255–283

Grondahl, M., *In Hope and Despair: Life in the Palestinian Refugee Camps*, The American University Press, Cairo, 2003

Harms, G. with T. Ferry, *The Palestine Israel Conflict: A Basic Introduction*, Pluto Press, London, 2005

Hass, A., *Drinking the Sea at Gaza: Days and Nights in a Land under Seige*, Translated by Elana Wesley & Maxine Kaufman-Lacusta, Metropolitan Books, Henry Holt & Co, New York, 1999

——'Under Seige 1996' in Pilger, J. [ed.]. *Tell Me No Lies: Investigative Journalism and Its Triumphs*, Jonathan Cape, London, pp. 332–356.

——'The Slippery Slope of Expulsion', http://www.miftah.org, 6 September 2006

Jayyusi, S.K. & Z.I., Ansari, *My Jerusalem. Essays, Reminiscences, and Poems*, Olive Branch Press, Massachusetts, 2005

Kawar, W.K., *Bethlehem from Golden Threads to Cement Blocks*, Syntax, Amman, Jordan

Laird, E. & S. Nimr, *A Little Piece of Ground*, Macmillans Children, London, 2003

Massad, J.A., *The Persistence of the Palestinian Question. Essays on Zionism and the Palestinians*, Routledge, London, 2006

Médecins du Monde, *Gaza – Land Under Shadows*, Arab Bank, Cyprus, 2002

Menuhin, M., *The Decadence of Judaism in Our Time*, Exposition Press, New York, 1965

Merriman, R, 'Israel's Visa Freeze', *The Jordan Times*, 14 September 2006, p. 9

Middle East Quartet, 'A Performance-based roadmap to a permanent two-State solution to the Israeli-Palestinian Conflict', http://www.un.org/media/main/roadmap122002.html, 2003

Musallam, S.F., *The Struggle for Jerusalem. A Programme of Action for Peace*, Passia, Jerusalem, 1996

Nathan, S., *The Other Side of Israel. My Journey across the Jewish-Arab Divide*, HarperCollins, London, 2005

Nicolai, S., 'Education and Chronic Crisis in Palestine' in *Forced Migration*, Education Supplement, Refugee Studies Centre, Oxford, 2006, pp. 4–6

Pappe, I., *A History of Modern Palestine: One Land, Two Peoples*, Cambridge University Press, Cambridge, 2004

——*The Ethnic Cleansing of Palestine*, Oneworld, Oxford, 2006

Palestine Red Crescent Society, *Annual Report 2001–2*, PRCS, Al-Bireh, Ramallah, 2003

——*Humanitarian Duty*, Issue No. 4, PRCS, Al-Bireh, Ramallah, 2006

Qumsiyeh, M.B., *Sharing the Land of Canaan. Human Rights and the Israeli–Palestinian Struggle*, Pluto Press, London, 2004

Raheb, M., *I Am A Palestinian Christian*, Translated by Ruth G.L. Gritsch, Fortress Press, Minneapolis, 1995

Reinhart, T., *The Road Map to Nowhere: Israel/Palestine since 2003*, Verso, London, 2006

Right to Enter, 'Campaign for the Right of Entry/ Re-Entry to the Occupied Palestinian Territory (OPT)', http://www.righttoenter.ps, 19 October 2006

Rose, J., *The Myths of Zionism*, Pluto Press, London, 2004

Roy, S., *The Gaza Strip: The Political Economy of De-Development*, Institute for Palestine Studies, Washington D.C., 1995

Said, E.W., 'Covering Islam and Terrorism 1997/2002' in Pilger, J [ed.], *Tell Me No Lies: Investigative Journalism and its Triumphs*, Johathan Cape, London, 2004, pp. 583–601.

Smith, C.D., *Palestine and the Arab-Israeli Conflict*, 2nd edition, St. Martin's Press, New York, 1992

WEBSITES

Palestine Red Crescent Society
    http://www.palestinercs.org
International Committee of the Red Cross
    http://icrc.org
International Federation of Red Cross and Red Crescent Societies
    http://www.ifrc.org

There is an increasing number of websites dealing with the Israeli–Palestinian conflict. These vary a great deal in accuracy and quality. The following selection includes a number of websites of Palestinian, Israeli, and other sources.

http://www.amnesty.org
http://www.bbc.co.uk
http://www.btselem.org (Israeli)
http://www.caabu.org
http://www.counterpunch.org
http://www.electronicintifada.net (Palestinian)
http://www.genevaconventions.org
http://www.gush-shalom.org (Israeli)
http://www.haaretz.com (Israeli newspaper)
http://www.hdip.org (Palestinian)
http://www.machsomwatch.org (Israeli)
http://www.miftah.org (Palestinian)
http://palestinemonitor.org (Palestinian)
http://www.passia.org (Palestinian)
http://www.pchrgaza.ps (Palestinian)
http://www.phr.org.il (Israeli Physicians for Human Rights)
http://www.procon.org (Israeli)
http://www.reliefweb.int
http://www.un.org
http://www.un.org/unrwa

The following website includes detailed maps and links to other websites with maps: http://www.ochaopt.org

ACKNOWLEDGEMENTS

WHEN I REFLECT ON MY LIFE and view the threads which have woven together in unique and complex ways, the over-riding thread is the importance of other people in my life. It has been necessary to select out just some incidents and people in writing this book, and so I have omitted the names of many others who have affected me in different ways. Although not written into this story, these people are no less part of my story and I acknowledge my gratitude to each and every one.

The life I have led in the Middle East has been made possible by the acceptance of the Palestine Red Crescent Society (PRCS) of me as a volunteer in the field of rehabilitation of persons with disabilities. The more than twenty-five years I have spent with the PRCS have seen periods of sharing in hardship, development and friendship. I thank all of my colleagues and the families with whom I have worked for enabling me to share in their life experiences; with special acknowledgement of the support and encouragement given to me by the late PRCS President, Dr Fathi Arafat and the Public Relations Director, Hadla Ayoubi. Central to my life with the Palestinian people is my very special family, Hamoudi, Dalal and Badr. I treasure the way in which they have enriched my life.

My special appreciation for the ongoing interest and belief in my work to Joan Mary Majali, Anita Loring and other executive members of the International Cerebral Palsy Society.

Words are inadequate to express my appreciation for the love and encouragement given me by my parents, and the life role model they presented. My sister Clarice, together with her husband, Alan Barker, continue to give me love, support, and a home base. I value the continued involvement with my extended family, McDonald and Calder relatives, although scattered across the world.

I thank Hachette Livre Australia for giving me the opportunity to write this book, with special thanks for the encouragement and professional guidance of publisher Bernadette Foley and senior editor Deonie Fiford.

INDEX

Abbas, Mahmoud (Abu Mazen)
  249–50, 268, 282, 297
Aboud village 292–4
Abu Amar *see* Arafat, Yasser
Abu Houli checkpoint 189, 196,
  197, 208, 211–16, 217, 219,
  220, 224, 225, 226, 236,
  246–7, 258–9, 260, 266
Ahmed, Um 99–100
Ain Shams Centre 96, 99, 105,
  108, 110, 111, 113–14, 119,
  125–6, 127, 130, 135, 137,
  138, 249
  Mahmoud 115, 142–3, 144,
    145
  Mohammed 129
  Nasr 111
  Omar, Mohammed 249
  parents and friends group
    112–13
  training staff 100–1
Ain Shams University, Cairo
air raids 84, 192, 241
Akka Hospital 45, 46, 62, 71, 82,
  83, 84, 91, 104
Al-Amal City 152–3, 161–2,
  167–8, 172–3, 179, 182, 184,
  194–7, 206, 207–8, 243, 247,
  264, 274, 276, 283–4, 290
  Asmat 309
  Hasen 189
  hostages 285
  Ismael 278
  Katam 299–300
  Maher 285
  Nagwa 142, 145, 185, 279,
    309
  Nihad 232, 283
  opening 162–3
  Raad and Maha 278
  Sami 281
  sports activities 174–5, 308–9
Al-Amal City Hotel 232
Al-Amal Hospital 166, 203, 217,
  222
Al-Aqsa Mosque 233
Al-Astal, Dr Najat 136, 284
  Siliman (son) 285
Al-Azhar University, Gaza City
  138, 149–51
Al-Bireh PRCS headquarters 153
  Abed 186

Al-Bureij camp 206
al-Durrah, Jamal and Mohammed
  187
Al-Fersan (The Kinghood) *Dabka*
  group 167
Al-Ghad Al-Mushreq (A Better
  Tomorrow) 113, 137
Al-Hajj 156, 307
Al-Haram Al-Ibrahimi Mosque
  133
Al-Haram Al-Sharif (Dome of the
  Rock) 123, 124, 185
Al-Khatib, Younis 153, 181,
  245–6, 250, 276, 284, 316
Al-Maqassed Hospital 123, 128
Al-Mawasi 142, 208, 261–3, 274
Al-Nour wa Al-Amal School 109
Al-Quds Hospital 218, 289
al-Quds University 167, 209, 228
Al-Rantissi, Dr Abdel Azziz 241,
  273
Ali, Azza Mohammed 126
Allbright, Madeleine 182
Amal (Lebanese political
  organisation) 75
American University Hospital 83
Amnesty International 256
anti-semitism 29, 37–8
'apartheid wall' 216–17, 244,
  250, 256, 260–1
APEX scholarships 20
Arab American University
  Graduates Association
  (AAUG) 36–7
Arab League Council 28, 42
Arab Society for the Physically
  Handicapped (ASPH) 128
  founding members Akram and
    Yusif 128
Arabic language classes 98
Arafat, Dr Fathi 38, 43, 45, 51,
  53, 57, 65, 93, 95, 99, 101,
  104, 106, 111, 112, 120, 121,
  127, 132, 136, 139, 151–3,
  164, 178, 181, 199, 204, 209,
  245–6, 250, 251
Arafat, Yasser 28, 40, 57, 127,
  130, 132, 134, 135, 160, 162,
  163, 178, 182, 183, 188, 190,
  205–6, 209–10, 216, 227,
  233, 244–5, 249, 250, 251,
  273, 276

  Khadija (sister) 178, 247
Ashrawi, Dr Hanan 127, 273
  This Side of Peace 131
Athens 278
Australia Day awards ceremony
  253–4
Australian Association of Health,
  Physical Education and
  Recreation 22
Australian Council of Churches
  (ACC) 94
Australian Council of
  Rehabilitation of Disabled
  (ACROD) 26
Australian Embassies
  Beirut 81, 92, 101, 103
  Cairo 113
  Tel Aviv 283, 284, 304, 305,
    308
Australian Red Cross (ARC) 254
Ayoubi, Hadla 43, 45, 65, 78,
  100, 286, 306

Badr 50, 58, 64–5, 68, 82, 107,
  118–21, 125, 131, 134, 135,
  139, 144, 147–8, 153, 154–5,
  156, 158, 161–2, 163, 174,
  177, 178, 184, 186, 190, 194,
  204, 206, 207, 218–21,
  230–1, 236–8, 239–40, 247,
  249, 251, 266, 269, 271, 275,
  277, 283–4, 286, 289, 299,
  302, 308, 309, 311–12
  Kafah (colleague) 302
Baker, James 127
Balata refugee camp 280
Balbeisi, Bassam 187
Balfour Declaration 31
Barak, Yahud 183, 188, 190, 193
Barghouti, Mustafa 273
Barker, Alan 19, 34, 43, 44, 92,
  95, 120, 121, 134, 165, 185,
  206, 253–4, 286
Barker, Geoffrey 34, 165
Barker, Wibby 34, 165, 288
Bedouin 141
Beersheva 141, 171, 172
Begin, Menachem 32, 33, 35
Beir Zeit University 228
Beirut 4, 41, 42, 47, 55, 56, 63,
  67, 97, 104, 169, 252
  Farida (friend) 292–4

Beit Hanoun 306
Bernadotte, Count Folke 32
Bet Shamesh 176
Bethlehem 151, 205, 209, 210, 229, 279, 313–14
Bethlehem University 228
Bi'lin village 256
Bliss symbols 117
boarding school 10–11, 12
bombing raids 55, 60, 63, 67–8, 219, 298, 300
Bowen Hills 20–1
Bowring, Mary 72, 75, 76–7, 79, 81
Braille 109, 150, 235, 269
Brisbane 12, 24, 39, 57, 253
British Council 282
B'Tselem 238
Burj Al-Barajneh refugee camp 42, 45, 51, 61, 68, 73, 82
  Hanan 52
Bush, George W. 190, 200, 227, 256, 268

Cairo 16, 93, 95, 96–9, 112, 114, 131, 134, 138, 147, 158, 166, 234, 239, 245, 246, 247, 248, 250, 253, 279, 290
  Ain Shams Centre see Ain Shams Centre
  work with PRCS 96–9
Calder, Alexander Thomas (brother) 6
Calder, Clarice (sister) 6, 7, 8, 16, 19, 34, 43, 44, 79, 92, 95, 109, 120, 121, 134, 165, 184, 185, 206, 253–4, 286, 288
Calder, Tom (father) 5–10, 19–20, 27
Camp David Accords 35–6
Camp David summit 183, 184
Canada refugee camp, Egypt 112, 114
Canberra 94, 253
car bombs 86
Carter, Jimmy 35
ceasefires 233, 250, 257
cerebral palsy 3, 4, 23, 38, 47, 52, 107, 117, 126, 145, 249
Cerebral Palsy Greece 278
Chatila refugee camp 45, 72, 77, 79, 82, 94
checkpoints 42, 142, 153, 187, 189, 196–7, 211–16, 239–40, 251–2, 258–9, 261–2
Chicago 286, 290
Child Development Institute, Beersheva 171–3
childhood 6–11
children in Beirut
  Abir 58, 59, 64, 65, 67, 70, 71, 76, 169–70, 252, 253
  Ahmed 58, 64, 67, 71
  Ali 68, 71
  Amira 62
  Badr see Badr

Dalal see Dalal
Hamoudi see Hamoudi
Khadija 84–6, 92
Nour 58, 59, 62, 63, 64, 67–8, 71, 77
Ream 58, 59
children in Cairo
  Khaled 117–18, 126, 139
  Rusha 115–17, 126, 139
  Salah 126
  Yasser 114–15
children in Khan Younis
  Halima 145
  Ibraheim 146
  Mahmoud 145
children injured in conflict
  Haytham 222
  Huda 222
  Mahmoud 204
  Mohammed 221–3
  Osama 205
  Tarak 204
children with difficulties 13, 14–15, 18
children with disabilities 23–6, 46, 108–9, 111, 145
  Christine 26
Christian Maronite Party see Falange
Church of the Nativity 205–6, 210
Clinton, Bill 130, 182, 183
Clinton, Hillary 182
cluster shells 203–4
College Protestant 64, 66, 67, 68
Companion of the Order of Australia (AC) 248–9, 253–4
Corrie, Rachel 222–3
Council for the Advancement of Arab-British Understanding (CAABU) 39, 40
curfews 122, 193, 207

Dabka 166, 275, 296
Dajani, Hana 100
Dalal 47–50, 52–4, 57–9, 60–1, 64–5, 67, 71, 74–5, 78, 79, 81, 82, 87, 92–3, 95, 97, 99, 102, 104–7, 109, 112, 118, 120–1, 125–7, 131, 134, 135, 137, 139, 144, 149–51, 153–6, 157–8, 161–2, 163, 165, 177, 178, 179–80, 184, 186, 190, 194, 204, 206, 218–21, 224–5, 230–1, 234–5, 247–51, 252–3, 261, 266, 269, 271, 275, 277, 283–8, 290–1, 294, 299, 308, 309, 311–12
  Ford Foundation Scholarship 223–4
De Smidt family 48, 60, 77
decision to work in Middle East 1–4
Deir Al-Balah 189, 197, 199, 211, 266

Deir Yassin 32
demonstration 33–4
  detention in Beirut 87–91
disabilities, people with 3, 20–2
  deinstitutionalisation 34
  needs of 35, 111
disengagement of Israeli settlements 259–60, 264, 265–6, 270, 289
dispersion of Palestinian people 2–3, 40, 96, 294
dispossession (Nakba) 2–3, 142, 294
Dutch HOPE Foundation (Holland Office of Personal Encouragement) 165, 176, 184, 232, 256, 274, 301
Dybwad, Dr Rosemary 24
Dybwad, Professor Gunnar 24

East Jerusalem 122, 131, 135, 160, 185, 201, 202, 217, 239, 256, 260, 261, 272, 273, 287, 288, 314
Edinburgh 224, 234, 248, 250
education 7–8, 9, 10–11
  Bachelor of Arts 15
  Diploma in Physical Education 13, 15
  Masters program 23, 25
Egypt 16–17, 36, 70, 96, 141, 143, 158, 164, 208, 210, 229, 249, 267–8
Eid Al-Adha (Feast of Sacrifice) 307
Eid Al-Fitar 155
Eliasson, Jan 312
Elzinga, Sake 176
epilepsy 55, 63, 107, 116, 154, 236, 277
Erez crossing 122, 159, 173, 174, 179, 186, 228, 251, 260, 285, 287, 288, 291, 297, 303, 307
European Committee on Palestinian Human Rights 39
European Union 267, 282
expulsion from Lebanon 92, 107

Fait, Professor Hollis 24, 25
Falange 37, 41, 69, 79
Fatah party 40, 270, 271, 272, 273, 275, 309
Fellowship of Reconciliation Interfaith Peace-Builders Program 243
Finland 118
Ford Foundation Scholarship recipients
  Dalal 224–6
  Leila 225–6
France 31, 42, 120, 209
Fraser, Malcolm 254
freelance consultancy 25
Frien Secondary Modern School 18

Gahli, Shadi Abu 210
gas 203
Gaza City 151, 159, 160, 161, 174, 178, 182, 187, 189, 195, 196, 197, 206, 208, 211, 216, 217, 219, 224, 236, 247, 254, 257, 276, 277, 284, 285, 289, 298, 303
Gaza Community Mental Health Centre
Iyat 179
Gaza Hospital 68, 76, 82
Gaza Strip 114, 115, 122, 128, 130, 134–5, 136, 138, 140–2, 147, 151, 152, 153, 154, 156, 157, 159, 160, 164, 166, 167, 171, 172, 175, 180, 185, 187, 188, 189, 190, 191, 206, 207, 210, 224, 228, 229, 233, 239, 240, 245, 247, 249, 251, 256, 257, 259, 260, 264, 265, 266, 267–8, 272, 276, 277, 278, 280, 281, 284, 287, 288, 289, 290, 296, 297, 298, 299, 300, 301, 302, 305, 306, 312
G8 summit 200
Gemayel, Bashir 71
Geneva Convention directives 187–8, 209
Georges, Senator George 53, 81
Gilbran, Bishop Gabriel 95
Gindi, Aida 129, 130
Goldstein, Baruch 133
'green line' 69, 160, 314
Gulf War 126
Gush Katif settlement 142, 153, 189, 190, 199, 211, 258, 261, 264
gymnastics, pause 22

Haganah 31, 32
Haifa Rehabilitation Hospital 46, 51, 57, 58, 61, 64, 68, 73, 82, 83
Hamas 190, 241, 257, 269–70, 272, 273, 275, 286, 288, 294, 297, 299, 309, 314
Hamoudi 47–51, 52, 53, 54–5, 57–9, 61–5, 67, 71, 74–5, 78–9, 81–3, 87, 92–3, 95, 97, 99, 102, 104–8, 111, 115, 120, 125–6, 134–5, 139, 142–4, 147–8, 153, 156, 158, 161–2, 177, 178, 184, 186, 190, 194, 204, 207, 217–20, 221, 230–1, 247, 250, 271, 277, 283–4, 286, 299, 308, 309, 311
Haniyeh, Ismail 297
hawea 157
Hawwara checkpoint 251–2
Hayden, Bill 93, 113
Hebron 133, 159, 290
Hegu, Iman 201
Heritage House 132
Holocaust 30

hostages 264–5
house demolitions 256, 260, 297
Fareal and family 235–6
human movement, study of 15
Human Movement Studies, Department of 20, 25, 39
human rights 2
Human Rights Watch 301
humanitarianism 3
Hurndall, Tom 223
Husseini, Feisal 127, 131

Inam, Hajjah 132, 178
inequality 1
Information Centre for Human Rights in the Occupied Territories 238
Institute of Rehabilitation Studies 114, 125, 132
development in Khan Younis 136, 167
International Cerebral Palsy Society (ICPS) 129, 248, 254, 278
International College of the American University of Beirut 68, 69, 70
International Committee of the Red Cross (ICRC) 74, 76, 78, 81, 82, 103, 188, 213, 229, 261, 283, 303, 304, 305, 307
International Court of Justice 217, 244, 260
International Day of Red Cross and Red Crescent 254
International Federation of Red Cross and Red Crescent Societies (IFRC) 3, 40, 131, 181, 254, 295
International Labour Organisation (ILO) report 239
International Red Cross 103, 189
International Solidarity Movement (ISM) 238
interrogation 89–90
Intifada, first 112, 113, 123, 126, 137, 140, 142, 154, 174, 201, 228, 279
Intifada, second 168, 186–91, 194, 207, 236, 268, 299, 305
intolerance 1
Iran 42
Iraq 31, 126
Irgun 32, 41
Irish Embassy, Beirut 92
Ismaeil, Doctor 143, 144
Israel 42, 128, 130, 141, 250, 261, 297
unilateral policies 270–1
Israel, creation of state of 30–2, 40, 313
Israel Defense Forces (IDF) 200, 256, 261, 297, 298, 300
Israeli-Arab war 1967 135, 140, 141
Israeli army 72, 74, 77, 122, 128,

133, 141, 160, 189, 190, 194, 203, 204, 205, 209, 210, 216, 223, 225, 230, 232, 233, 236, 237, 238, 241, 257, 260, 263, 266, 271, 281, 282, 297, 299, 301, 314
Israeli Economic Cooperation Foundation (ECF) 171, 172–3, 175
Israeli elections 288
Israeli invasion of Lebanon 69, 163
Israeli-Palestinian peace conference, Madrid 127
Israeli settlements 124, 142, 160–1, 183, 199, 200, 221, 222, 231, 240, 256, 259–60, 261, 263, 265–7, 268, 270, 313, 314

Jabalya refugee camp 142
Jagland, Thorbjørn 199
Jamal, Dr 115, 144
Jawad, Dr 123, 124
Jenin 203, 206, 209
Jericho 131, 159, 169, 203, 252, 253, 281
Jerusalem 2, 32, 41, 130, 138, 151, 160, 181, 183, 186, 202, 228, 233, 244, 256, 260, 287, 288
Jordan 33, 39, 42, 141, 146, 209, 220, 247, 291, 292, 303, 304, 306, 312
Judea 209
Jumblat, Walid 82, 86
justice 3, 110–11

Kadima party 270, 274, 282, 288
Kafar Darom settlement 189, 190
Karni crossing 277, 281, 288, 300
Kawar, Widad 313–14
Kelvin Grove Teachers College 21
Khan Younis 136, 138, 142, 144, 147, 149, 151, 158, 161, 166, 171, 182, 186, 189, 190, 194, 195, 201, 204, 206, 208, 211, 220, 221, 222, 225, 232, 235, 237, 246, 248, 249, 250, 252, 256, 257, 258, 261, 263, 265, 271, 274, 276, 283, 284, 285, 288, 289, 290, 294, 298, 300, 306
emergency medical services (EMS) 187–8, 192, 241
Salah 168–9
setting up rehabilitation centre 138, 144, 151–2
King David Hotel 41
Kiryat Sefer 256

Laban Institute 18
Land Day (Youm al-Ard) 289
League of Nations 31

Learn to Play - Play to Learn
25–6
Lebanese Red Cross 64
Lebanon 3, 28, 31, 36, 37, 38,
40, 41, 43, 47, 56, 57, 93,
112, 141, 164, 169, 315
civil war 42, 69
Israeli invasion 1982 52
Leilat Al-Qadr (The Night of
Power) 155
Libya 127
Lieberman, Avigdor 314
Likud party 154, 270
London 16, 17, 18, 92, 93, 120
Loughborough University 18

McDonald, Winifred (mother)
5–10, 19–20, 27, 43–4, 79,
92, 95, 109, 113, 120–1,
184
Machsom (Checkpoint Watch)
238
Mackay 16, 95, 185
McKenna, Jackie 90, 92
Magen David Adom (MDA) 295
Maghazi refugee camp 299
Majali, Joan Mary 254
Mansfield Training Centre 25
Maqatta 209–10, 216, 245
Maronite Christian Party see
Falange
Mayflower Hotel 78, 79
Mecca 156
media 93, 94, 248
Medical Aid for Palestinians
(MAP) 120
Médicins Sans Frontières (MSF)
263
Mohammed 258–9
Medina Al-Amal (Hope City) –
Centre of Ability
Development see Al-Amal City
Meir, Golda 36
Melbourne 94, 254
Menuhin, Moshe 30
The Decadence of Judaism in
our Time 29
Merryman, Gretchen 243
Mid-East Council of Churches
78
Mitchell, George J. 199
Mitchell Report, The 200
Mitchelton Infant School 13
Leslie 13–14
Moir, George and Jessie 17, 224,
234
Moir, Linda 224, 234, 248
Mount of Olives 123
Mubarak, Susan 129

Nablus 159, 209, 251–2, 280
Naples 16
Naqba 33
Naserah Children's Hospital 45,
46–7, 58, 72
evacuation 74–5

Nasser, President 16
National Command of the
Uprising 112
National Rehabilitation Plan 129
Nazareth 289
Netanyahu, Benjamin 154
Netherlands Red Cross 301
Netzarim settlement 225
New York 33, 202
Newmarket Primary School 13
Newton Ferrers 44, 121
1967 Israeli-Arab war 135, 140,
141
Nobel Peace Prize 132
Nolan, Perry 81, 91–2
non-violent resistance 238–9, 256
normalisation 23
Norway 110, 114, 179, 199
Norwegian Embassy, Beirut 75
Norwegian Groups for Palestine
110, 117
Norwegian Red Cross 301

Occupied Palestinian Territories
(OPT) 112, 113, 121, 122–5,
128–9, 132, 138, 139, 140–2,
183, 184, 188, 200, 223, 226,
227, 230, 238, 268, 270, 282,
305, 306, 307, 313, 314, 315,
316
Odeh, Namiti 46, 105, 106, 280
Olmert, Ehud 274, 292
Open Studio 165, 232–3, 256–7,
296
Operation Defensive Shield 209
Operation Summer Rain 298
oppression 33
Oriana 16
Orient House 201–2, 274
Oslo Accords 130, 131, 132,
134, 172, 183, 200, 226, 227,
260, 270, 273
osteomylitis 116
Ottoman Empire 30, 31
Oxfam 115
Oxfam UK 78

Palestine, history of 30–2
Palestine Central Council 40
Palestine Hospital, Cairo 96, 107,
127, 248, 249
Palestine Liberation Organisation
(PLO) 28, 29, 36, 39, 40, 42,
70, 72, 79, 126, 183, 201,
273
evacuation from Beirut 70, 96
executive committee 40
Palestine National Council
(PNC) 40
Palestine Red Crescent Society
(PRCS) 3, 4, 38, 40, 42, 43,
45, 47, 50, 53, 63, 64, 68, 78,
79, 82, 86, 92, 93, 95, 96,
100, 102, 103, 120, 127, 129,
131, 135, 136, 137, 142, 144,
147, 153, 156, 158, 176,

187–8, 192, 194, 195, 201,
204, 213, 229, 245, 248, 250,
254, 261, 263, 264, 283, 286,
289, 294, 301, 304, 305, 306,
308
Al-Nour City 224, 225, 236,
247, 254, 289
College of Ability
Development 208–9, 274,
283
Congresses 162–4, 181
rehabilitation conference 251
rehabilitation policies 159
Palestinian Authority (PA) 130,
135, 151, 158, 160, 192, 203,
247, 249, 260, 271, 272, 277,
297, 299, 314
Ministry of Education 196,
278–9
prison 281–2
Palestinian Autonomous Region
135
Palestinian elections 272–6
Palestinian Higher Council of
Health (PCH) 171, 175
Palestinian Ministry of Health
129, 136
Palestinian partition 32
Palestinian people
attitude to 2
dispersion 2–3, 40, 294
dispossession 2–3, 294
image of 2
negative stereotyping 3, 193
treatment of 239
Palestinian resistance 238
Palestinian Women's Union 34
Palestinians, The 3, 37, 38
'Palestinians Have Rights Too'
campaign 38
Paris 120, 244, 245
pause gymnastics 22
PAZ 245
Peace Process 130, 160, 182, 185,
190, 201, 233
Pennsylvania State University 28,
29–39
Hideko 29
Naheel 29
'people and soldiers' 124–5,
279–80
Peres, Shimon 130
Perkins machine 109
permits 3, 157, 160, 171–7, 228,
229, 252, 304
petit mal seizures 55
physical education 14–15
Physicians for Human Rights 238
Physiotherapy and Occupational
Therapy department 20
Poland 174

Qalandia checkpoint 288, 308
Queensland 6, 8, 10, 12, 140
Queensland Education

Department, Physical Education Branch John 14–15
Queensland Sub Normal Children's Welfare Association (QSNCWA) school 20, 21
Queensland Teachers College 12–13
Physical Education Department 15–16
Queensland University 13, 20

Rabin, Prime Minister Yitzhak 130, 154
Rafah crossing 138, 142, 143, 151, 156, 195, 197, 199, 208, 210, 223, 229, 235, 239, 241, 242, 243, 248, 249, 250, 253, 260, 263, 265, 266, 267, 290, 312
Fareal 235–6
Ramadan 154–6, 197
Ramallah 131, 151, 158, 159, 160, 170, 181, 186, 192, 206, 209, 210, 216, 227, 244, 245, 250, 251, 256, 278, 284, 288, 290, 291, 297, 303, 304, 308
Red Cross 19
Reddaway, John 39, 40
Redgrave, Vanessa 37
refugee camps 42, 45, 51, 61, 68, 69, 72, 73, 76, 77, 79, 82, 94, 140–1, 142, 280, 299, 313
massacre 81, 94, 98
refusniks 315
'Road Map for Peace' 227, 250, 261, 270
Rollema, Ingrid 165, 232, 257
Royal National Institute for the Blind 150

Sabra refugee camp 45, 68, 72, 76, 79, 82, 94
Sadat, President Anwar 35, 36
'safe passage' 180–1
Said, Professor Edward 130
Samaria 209
Samir, Um 73–4
Saraia 285
Sararj, Dr Bashir 206
Save the Children UK 78, 101, 102, 103
scholarships for Palestinian students 228–9
Schonell Educational Research Centre 39
Scotland 5, 16, 17, 35, 234
Sea of Galilee 128
'separation wall' 216–17, 244, 250, 256, 260–1
September 11, 2001 202
Shafi, Dr Haider Abu 127
shahids 272

Shalit, Corporal Gilad 297, 301
Sham Al-Sheikh Fact-Finding Committee 199, 200
Shamir, Yitzhak 32
Sharon, Ariel 185–6, 193, 206, 209, 227, 240, 259, 270, 274
shelling 73, 194, 201, 210, 220–1, 230–1, 258, 260, 298
Shiijah camp 45, 84
Shiites 41
siege, Beirut 69
sign language 17, 35, 201
Sinai, the 135, 143
Singapore 94
snipers 72, 223
Solana, Javier 199
sonic booms 267
Soroka Hospital, Beersheva 171
South Mackay 6, 7, 9, 10
special education conference 278–9
Halima 279
Iptisam 279–80
Special Olympics 23
special physical education 24
spina bifida 146
sports activities 174–5
Kamal 175, 281, 308
Mohammed 146
Stern 32, 41
strikes 264–5, 282, 294, 301
student teaching 11–12
students
Iptisam 124, 279–80
study of human movement 15
Sudan 70
Suez Canal 16, 125
suicide bombings 193–4, 209, 210, 233, 290
Sweden 110
Sydney 39, 93, 94
Sykes-Picot Agreement 31
Syria 31, 42, 70, 82, 93, 128, 141

Tal Al-Za'tar 3, 29, 37, 47
Taylor Institute, Chicago 286
Nadal 287–8, 290–1
teacher-training program 11
teaching 13–18
terrorism 29, 40, 41, 203, 315
terrorist organisation 40, 272, 275
Thompson, Geoff 94
travel 16–18
Triumph Hotel 63
Tufah checkpoint 261–3
Tunis 96, 273
Tunisia 70
Turkey 30, 199
Tutu, Archbishop Desmond 307

UK 114

Umrah 156
unemployment 264
UNESCO theatre, Paris
UNICEF 130, 263
United Nations 28, 32, 130, 134, 183, 202, 227, 234, 242, 270, 300, 306, 307
United Nations Relief and Works Agency (UNRWA) 58
United Nations Special Coordination Organization (UNSCO) 174
United States 23–4, 203, 250, 272, 287, 307
State Department Human Rights Report 33
University of Connecticut 24

violence, cycle of 238–9, 302, 307
visas 157, 176–7, 219, 229–30, 239, 287, 291, 302, 304–7, 312
Vugveeten, Willem 164–5

Wafa Hospital 257
Walid, Um 78
war planes 71, 79, 85–6, 163, 191, 241, 286, 290, 297
Warwick 10
water supply problems 293
weddings 277–8
Welfare Association 204
West Bank 121, 122, 123, 128, 130, 134–5, 140, 151, 157, 159, 160, 169, 171, 172, 180, 186, 187, 190, 192, 196, 206, 209, 210, 217, 224, 228, 229, 233, 239, 240, 244, 245, 251, 252, 256, 259, 260, 261, 267, 268, 270, 279, 287, 288, 290, 293, 297, 301, 302, 303, 305, 308, 314
Wilson, David 81, 82
Women in Black 238
work permit detention 87–91
World Health Organization 40
World Trade Center 202
World War I 30, 31
World War II 8–9, 30, 32
World Zionist Organization office 34
Wright, Doug 92

Yassin, Sheikh Ahmed 241, 273
Yemen 31, 70
Yisrael Beytenu party 314
YMCA 124, 288
Yousria, Dr 129

zanana 258, 297
Zionism 29, 30